HOME. SWEET HOME.

# Sabbath Readings
## for the
## Home Circle

Reprinted by:

## ANGELA'S BOOK SHELF

9746 N. MASON ROAD
WHEELER, MICHIGAN 48662
(Mail order only)

To order by mail send $7.95 plus $1.25 for first book and 35¢ for each additional book.

This book is not available from publisher. To order contact local dealer. Price $9.50 after Aug. 1, '92.

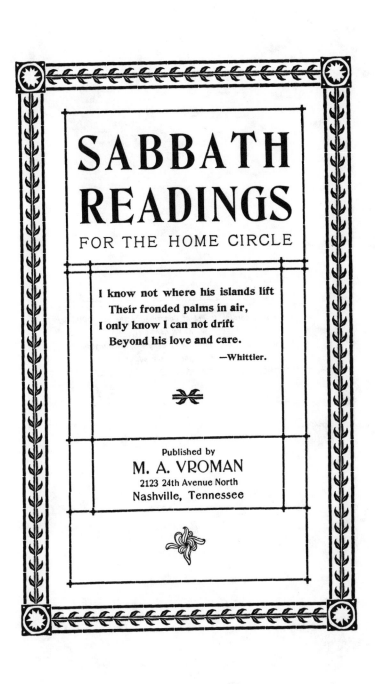

# SABBATH READINGS

## FOR THE HOME CIRCLE

I know not where his islands lift
    Their fronded palms in air,
I only know I can not drift
    Beyond his love and care.

—Whittler.

Published by

## M. A. VROMAN

2123 24th Avenue North
Nashville, Tennessee

# PREFACE.

THE compiler of this volume has been gathering a large amount of moral and religious reading, from which selections have been made, admitting only those which may be read with propriety on the Sabbath.

This volume will be found to contain the best lessons for the family circle, such as will inculcate principles of obedience to parents, kindness and affection to brothers and sisters and youthful associates, benevolence to the poor, and the requirements of the gospel. These virtuous principles are illustrated by instances of conformity to them, or departure from them, in such a manner as to lead to their love and practice.

Great care has been taken in compiling this volume to avoid introducing into it anything of a sectarian or denominational character that might hinder its free circulation among any denomination, or class of society, where there is a demand for moral and religious literature. The illustrations were made especially for this book, and are the result of much careful study.

The family circle can be instructed and impressed by high-toned moral and religious lessons in no better way during a leisure hour of the Sabbath, when not engaged in the solemn worship of God, than to listen to one of their number who shall read from this precious volume. May the blessing of God attend it to every home circle that shall give it a welcome, is the prayer of the

PUBLISHER.

# NOTE TO THE PUBLIC.

To all who are really interested in the reading and circulation of good literature, of an interesting nature, and at the same time of *high moral tone*, this work is dedicated. As its name implies, it is truly a book for "The Home Circle." The stories and poems it contains cover nearly all phases of life's experience. Each one presents lessons which can but tend to make the reader better and nobler.

We believe all who read this book, will heartily accord with us in our desire to see it placed in every home in the land, and will do their part toward this good end.

The first edition of "Sabbath Readings" was published about two years ago, and it now enters upon its *third edition*, with the demand rapidly increasing.

Many have joined us in canvassing for it, and it has proved to be not only a noble work and a service to the people, but it brings good financial returns. Many students have worked their way through school by using their vacations in this work.

The publisher's *name and address* is on the title page, and he will see that *all orders* are promptly and carefully filled, and all letters of inquiry cheerfully answered.

Believing that the "Sabbath Readings" will be appreciated by all lovers of the true and beautiful, and that the book will make for itself not only a place, but a warm welcome, in thousands of homes during the coming year, it is cheerfully and prayerfully sent on its mission by

THE PUBLISHER.

# TABLE OF CONTENTS.

## POEMS.

# LIST OF ILLUSTRATIONS.

## THE SABBATH.

SABBATHS, like way-marks, cheer the pilgrim's path,
His progress mark, and keep his rest in view.
In life's bleak winter, they are pleasant days,
Short foretaste of the long, long spring to come.
To every new-born soul, each hallowed morn
Seems like the first, when everything was new.
Time seems an angel come afresh from heaven,
His pinions shedding fragrance as he flies,
And his bright hour-glass running sands of gold.
                                        —*Carlos Wilcox.*

# The INDIAN'S REVENGE

THE beautiful precept, "Do unto others as you would that they should do unto you," is drawn from our Lord's sermon on the mount, and should be observed by all professing Christians. But unless we are truly his children, we can never observe this great command as we ought.

History records the fact that the Roman emperor Severus was so much struck with the moral beauty and purity of this sentiment, that he ordered the "Golden Rule," to be inscribed upon the public buildings erected by him. Many facts may be stated, by which untutored heathen and savage tribes in their conduct have put to shame many of those calling themselves Christians, who have indeed the form of godliness, but by their words and actions deny the power of it. One such fact we here relate.

Many years ago, on the outskirts of one of our distant new settlements, was a small but neat and pretty cottage, or homestead, which belonged to an industrious young farmer. He had, when quite a lad, left his native England, and sought a home and fortune among his American breth-

ren.   It was a sweet and quiet place; the cottage was built
upon a gently rising ground, which sloped toward a spark-
ling rivulet, that turned a large sawmill situated a little
lower down the stream.   The garden was well stocked with
fruit-trees and vegetables, among which the magnificent
pumpkins were already conspicuous, though as yet they
were wanting in the golden hue which adorns them in
autumn.   On the hillside was an orchard, facing the south,
filled with peach and cherry-trees, the latter now richly
laden with their crimson fruit.   In that direction also extended the larger portion of the farm, now in a high state
of cultivation, bearing heavy crops of grass, and Indian corn
just coming into ear.   On the north and east, the cottage
was sheltered by extensive pine woods, beyond which were
fine hunting-grounds, where the settlers, when their har-
vests were housed, frequently resorted in large numbers to
lay in a stock of dried venison for winter use.

At that time the understanding between the whites and
the Indians, was not good; and they were then far more
numerous than they are at the present time, and more
feared.   It was not often, however, that they came into the
neighborhood of the cottage which has been described,
though on one or two occasions a few Minateree Indians
had been seen on the outskirts of the pine forests, but had
committed no outrages, as that tribe was friendly with the
white men.

It was a lovely evening in June.   The sun had set,
though the heavens still glowed with those exquisite and
radiant tints which the writer, when a child, used to imagine were vouchsafed to mortals to show them something

while yet on earth, of the glories of the New Jerusalem. The moon shed her silvery light all around, distinctly revealing every feature of the beautiful scene which has been described, and showed the tall, muscular figure of William Sullivan, who was seated upon the door-steps, busily employed in preparing his scythes for the coming hay season. He was a good-looking young fellow, with a sunburnt, open countenance ; but though kind-hearted in the main, he was filled with prejudices, acquired when in England, against Americans in general, and the North American Indians in particular. As a boy he had been carefully instructed by his mother, and had received more education than was common in those days ; but of the sweet precepts of the gospel he was as practically ignorant as if he had never heard them, and in all respects was so thoroughly an Englishman, that he looked with contempt on all who could not boast of belonging to his own favored country. The Indians he especially despised and detested as heathenish creatures, forgetful of the fact that he who has been blessed with opportunities and privileges, and yet has abused them, is in as bad a case, and more guilty in the sight of God, than these ignorant children of the wilds.

So intent was he upon his work, that he heeded not the approach of a tall Indian, accoutred for a hunting excursion, until the words :—

"Will you give an unfortunate hunter some supper, and a lodging for the night?" in a tone of supplication, met his ear.

The young farmer raised his head ; a look of contempt curling the corners of his mouth, and an angry gleam darting from his eyes, as he replied in a tone as uncourteous as his words :—

"Heathen Indian dog, you shall have nothing here; begone !"

The Indian turned away; then again facing young Sullivan, he said in a pleading voice :—

"But I am very hungry, for it is very long since I have eaten; give only a crust of bread and a bone to strengthen me for the remainder of my journey."

"Get you gone, heathen hound," said the farmer; "I have nothing for you."

A struggle seemed to rend the breast of the Indian hunter, as though pride and want were contending for the mastery; but the latter prevailed, and in a faint voice he said :—

"Give me but a cup of cold water, for I am very faint."

This appeal was no more successful than the others. With abuse he was told to drink of the river which flowed some distance off. This was all that he could obtain from one who called himself a Christian, but who allowed prejudice and obstinacy to steel his heart—which to one of his own nation would have opened at once—to the sufferings of his redskinned brother.

With a proud yet mournful air the Indian turned away, and slowly proceeded in the direction of the little river. The weak steps of the native showed plainly that his need was urgent; indeed he must have been reduced to the last extremity, ere the haughty Indian would have asked again and again for that which had been once refused.

Happily his supplicating appeal was heard by the farmer's wife. Rare indeed is it that the heart of woman is steeled to the cry of suffering humanity; even in the savage wilds of central Africa, the enterprising and unfortunate Mungo Park was over and over again rescued from almost certain death by the kind and generous care of those females whose husbands and brothers thirsted for his blood.

The farmer's wife, Mary Sullivan, heard the whole as she sat hushing her infant to rest; and from the open casement she watched the poor Indian until she saw his form sink, apparently exhausted, to the ground, at no great distance from her dwelling. Perceiving that her husband had finished his work, and was slowly bending his steps toward the stables with downcast eyes—for it must be confessed he did not feel very comfortable—she left the house, and was soon at the poor Indian's side, with a pitcher of milk in her hand, and a napkin, in which was a plentiful meal of bread and roasted kid, with a little parched corn as well.

"Will my red brother drink some milk?" said Mary, bending over the fallen Indian; and as he arose to comply with her invitation, she untied the napkin and bade him eat and be refreshed.

When he had finished, the Indian knelt at her feet, his eyes beamed with gratitude, then in his soft tone, he said: "Carcoochee protect the white dove from the pounces of the eagle; for her sake the unfledged young shall be safe in its nest, and her red brother will not seek to be revenged."

Drawing a bunch of heron's feathers from his bosom, he selected the longest, and giving it to Mary Sullivan, said: "When the white dove's mate flies over the Indian's hunting-grounds, bid him wear this on his head."

He then turned away; and gliding into the woods, was soon lost to view.

The summer passed away; harvest had come and gone; the wheat and maize, or Indian corn, was safely stored in the yard; the golden pumpkins were gathered into their winter quarters, and the forests glowed with the rich and varied tints of autumn. Preparations now began to be made for a hunting excursion, and William Sullivan was included in the number who were going to try their fortune on the hunting-grounds beyond the river and the pine forests. He was bold, active, and expert in the use of his rifle and woodman's hatchet, and hitherto had always hailed the approach of this season with peculiar enjoyment, and no fears respecting the not unusual attacks of the Indians, who frequently waylaid such parties in other and not very distant places, had troubled him.

But now, as the time of their departure drew near, strange misgivings relative to his safety filled his mind, and his imagination was haunted by the form of the Indian whom in the preceding summer he had so harshly treated. On the eve of the day on which they were to start, he made known his anxiety to his gentle wife, confessing at the same time that his conscience had never ceased to reproach him for his unkind behavior. He added, that since then all that he had learned in his youth from his mother upon our duty to our neighbors had been continually in his mind; thus increasing the burden of self-reproach, by reminding him that his conduct was displeasing in the sight of God, as well as cruel toward a suffering brother. Mary Sullivan heard her husband in silence. When he had done, she laid her hand in his, looking up into his face with a smile, which was yet not quite free from anxiety, and then she told him what she had done when the Indian fell down exhausted upon the ground, confessing at the same time that she had kept this to herself, fearing his displeasure, after hearing him refuse any aid. Going to a closet, she took out the beautiful heron's feather, repeating at the same time the parting words of the Indian, and arguing from them that her husband might go without fear.

"Nay," said Sullivan, "these Indians never forgive an injury."

"Neither do they ever forget a kindness," added Mary. "I will sew this feather in your hunting-cap, and then trust you, my own dear husband, to God's keeping; but though I know he could take care of you without it, yet I remember my dear father used to say that we were never to neglect the use of all lawful means for our safety. His maxim was, 'Trust like a child, but like a man;' for we must help ourselves if we hope to succeed, and not expect miracles to be wrought on our behalf, while we quietly fold our arms and do nothing." "Dear William," she added, after a pause, "now that my father is dead and gone, I think much more of what he used to say than when he was with me; and I fear that we are altogether wrong in the way we are going on, and I feel that if we were treated as we deserve, God would forget us, and leave us to ourselves, because we have so forgotten him."

The tears were in Mary's eyes as she spoke; she was the only daughter of a pious English sailor, and in early girl-hood had given promise of becoming all that a religious

2

parent could desire. But her piety was then more of the head than of the heart ; it could not withstand the trial of the love professed for her by Sullivan, who was anything but a serious character, and like "the morning cloud and the early dew," her profession of religion vanished away, and as his wife she lost her relish for that in which she once had taken such delight. She was very happy in appearance, yet there was a sting in all her pleasures, and that was the craving of a spirit disquieted and restless from the secret though ever-present conviction that she had sinned in departing from the living God. By degrees these impressions deepened ; the Spirit of grace was at work within, and day after day was bringing to her memory the truths she had heard in childhood and was leading her back from her wanderings by a way which she knew not. A long conversation followed ; and that night saw the young couple kneeling for the first time in prayer at domestic worship.

The morning that witnessed the departure of the hunters was one of surpassing beauty. No cloud was to be seen upon the brow of William Sullivan. The bright beams of the early sun seemed to have dissipated the fears which had haunted him on the previous evening, and it required an earnest entreaty on the part of his wife to prevent his removing the feather from his cap. She held his hand while she whispered in his ear, and a slight quiver agitated his lips as he said, "Well, Mary dear, if you really think this feather will protect me from the redskins, for your sake I will let it remain." William then put on his cap, shouldered his rifle, and the hunters were soon on their way seeking for game.

The day wore away as is usual with people on such excursions. Many animals were killed, and at night the hunters took shelter in the cave of a bear, which one of the party was fortunate enough to shoot, as he came at sunset toward the bank of the river. His flesh furnished them with some excellent steaks for supper, and his skin spread upon a bed of leaves pillowed their heads through a long November night.

With the first dawn of morning, the hunters left their rude shelter and resumed the chase. William, in consequence of following a fawn too ardently, separated from his companions, and in trying to rejoin them became bewildered. Hour after hour he sought in vain for some mark by which he might thread the intricacy of the forest, the trees of which were so thick that it was but seldom that he could catch a glimpse of the sun; and not being much accustomed to the woodman's life, he could not find his way as one of them would have done, by noticing which side of the trees was most covered with moss or lichen. Several times he started in alarm, for he fancied that he could see the glancing eyeballs of some lurking Indian, and he often raised his gun to his shoulder, prepared to sell his life as dearly as he could.

Toward sunset the trees lessened and grew thinner, and by and by he found himself upon the outskirts of an immense prairie, covered with long grass, and here and there with patches of low trees and brushwood. A river ran through this extensive tract, and toward it Sullivan directed his lagging footsteps. He was both faint and weary, not having eaten anything since the morning. On the bank of the river there were many bushes, therefore Sullivan approached with caution, having placed his rifle at half-cock, to be in readiness against any danger that might present itself. He was yet some yards from its brink, when a rustling in the underwood made him pause, and the next instant out rushed an enormous buffalo. These animals usually roam through the prairies in immense herds, sometimes amounting to many thousands in number; but occasionally they are met with singly, having been separated from the main body either by some accident, or by the Indians, who show the most wonderful dexterity in hunting these formidable creatures. The buffalo paused for a moment, and then lowering his enormous head, rushed forward toward the intruder. Sullivan took aim; but the beast was too near to enable him to do so with that calmness and certainty which would have insured success, and though slightly wounded, it still came on with increased fury. Sullivan was a very powerful man, and though weakened by his long fast and fatiguing march, despair gave him courage and nerved his arm with strength, and with great presence of mind he seized the animal as it struck him on the side with its horn, drawing out his knife with his left hand, in the faint hope of being able to strike it into his adversary's throat. But the struggle was too unequal to be successful, and the buffalo had shaken him off, and thrown him to the ground, previous to trampling him to death, when he heard the sharp crack of a rifle behind him, and in another instant the animal sprang into the air, then fell heavily close by, and indeed partly upon, the prostrate Sullivan. A dark form in the Indian garb glided by a moment after, and plunged his hunting-knife deep into the neck of the buffalo, though the shot was too true not to have taken effect, having penetrated to the brain ; but the great arteries of the neck are cut, and the animal thus bled, to render the flesh more suitable for keeping a greater length of time.

The Indian then turned to Sullivan, who had now drawn himself from under the buffalo, and who, with mingled feelings of hope and fear, caused by his ignorance whether the tribe to which the Indian belonged was friendly or not, begged of him to direct him to the nearest white settlement.

" If the weary hunter will rest till morning, the eagle will show him the way to the nest of his white dove," was the reply of the Indian, in that figurative style so general among his people ; and then taking him by the hand he led him through the rapidly increasing darkness, until they reached a small encampment lying near the river, and under the cover of some trees which grew upon its banks. Here the Indian gave Sullivan a plentiful supply of hominy, or bruised Indian corn boiled to a paste, and some venison ; then spreading some skins of animals slain in the chase, for his bed, he signed to him to occupy it, and left him to his repose.

The light of dawn had not yet appeared in the east when the Indian awoke Sullivan ; and after a slight repast, they both started for the settlement of the whites. The Indian kept in advance of his companion, and threaded his way through the still darkened forest with a precision and a rapidity which showed him to be well acquainted with its paths and secret recesses. As he took the most direct way, with-

out fear of losing his course, being guided by signs unknown to any save some of the oldest and most experienced
hunters, they traversed the forest far more quickly than
Sullivan had done, and before the golden sun had sunk behind the summits of the far-off mountains, Sullivan once
more stood within view of his beloved home.  There it lay
in calm repose, and at a sight so dear he could not restrain
a cry of joy; then turning toward the Indian, he poured
forth his heartfelt thanks for the service he had rendered
him.

The warrior, who, till then, had not allowed his face to
be seen by Sullivan, except in the imperfect light of his
wigwam, now fronted him, allowing the sun's rays to fall
upon his person, and revealed to the astonished young man
the features of the very same Indian whom, five months
before, he had so cruelly repulsed.  An expression of dignified yet mild rebuke was exhibited in his face as he gazed
upon the abashed Sullivan; but his voice was gentle and
low as he said: "Five moons ago, when I was faint and
weary, you called me ' Indian dog,' and drove me from your
door.  I might last night have been revenged; but the
white dove fed me, and for her sake I spared her mate.
Carcoochee bids you to go home, and when hereafter you
see a red man in need of kindness, do to him as you have
been done by.  Farewell."

He waved his hand, and turned to depart, but Sullivan
sprang before him, and so earnestly entreated him to go
with him, as a proof that he had indeed forgiven his brutal
treatment, that he at last consented, and the humbled
farmer led him to his cottage.  There his gentle wife's sur-

prise at seeing him so soon was only equaled by her thankfulness at his wonderful escape from the dangers which had surrounded him, and by her gratitude to the noble savage who had thus repaid her act of kindness, forgetful of the provocation he had received from her husband. Carcoochee was treated not only as an honored guest, but as a brother; and such in time he became to them both.

Many were the visits he paid to the cottage of the once prejudiced and churlish Sullivan, now no longer so, for the practical lesson of kindness he had learned from the untutored Indian was not lost upon him. It was made the means of bringing him to a knowledge of his own sinfulness in the sight of God, and his deficiencies in duty toward his fellow men. He was led by the Holy Spirit to feel his need of Christ's atoning blood; and ere many months passed, Mary Sullivan and her husband both gave satisfactory evidence that they had indeed "passed from death unto life."

Carcoochee's kindness was repaid to him indeed a hundred fold. A long time elapsed before any vital change of heart was visible in him; but at length it pleased the Lord to bless the unwearied teaching of his white friends to his spiritual good, and to give an answer to the prayer of faith. The Indian was the first native convert baptized by the American missionary, who came about two years after to a station some few miles distant from Sullivan's cottage. After a lengthened course of instruction and trial the warrior, who once had wielded the tomahawk in mortal strife against both whites and redskins, went forth, armed with a far different weapon, "even the sword of the Spirit, which is the word of God," to make known to his heathen country-

men "the glad tidings of great joy," that "Christ Jesus
came into the world to save sinners." He told them that
"whosoever believeth on him should not perish, but have
everlasting life," whether they be Jews or Gentiles, bond or
free, white or red, for "we are all one in Christ." Many
years he thus labored, until, worn out with toil and age, he
returned to his white friend's home, where in a few months
he fell asleep in Jesus, giving to his friends the certain hope
of a joyful meeting hereafter at the resurrection of the just.

Many years have passed since then. There is no trace
now of the cottage of the Sullivans, who both rest in the
same forest churchyard, where lie the bones of Carcoochee;
but their descendants still dwell in the same township.
Often does the gray-haired grandsire tell this little history
to his rosy grandchildren, while seated under the stately
magnolia which shades the graves of the quiet sleepers of
whom he speaks. And the lesson which he teaches to his
youthful hearers, is one which all would do well to bear in
mind, and act upon; namely, "Whatsoever ye would that
men should do to you, do ye even so to them."

SPEAK not harshly—learn to feel
Another's woes, another's weal;
Of malice, hate, and guile, instead,
By friendship's holy bonds be led;
For sorrow is man's heritage
From early youth to hoary age.

# The Record.

*" The hours are viewless angels, that still go gliding by,*
*And bear each moment's record up to Him that sits on high."*

A MOTHER wrote a story about her daughter in which she represented her as making some unkind and rude remarks to her sister. Julia was a reader of the newspapers, and it did not escape her notice. The incident was a true one, but it was one she did not care to remember, much less did she like to see it in print.

" Oh! mother, mother," she exclaimed, " I do not think you are kind to write such stories about me. I do not like to have you publish it when I say anything wrong."

" How do you know it is you? It is not your name." Julia then read the story aloud.

" It is I. I know it is I, mother. I shall be afraid of you if you write such stories about me, I shall not dare to speak before you."

" Remember, my child, that God requireth the past, and nothing which you say, or do, or think, is lost to him."

Poor Julia was quite grieved that her mother should record the unpleasant and unsisterly words which fell from her lips. She did not like to have any memorial of her ill-nature preserved. Perhaps she would never have thought of those words again in this life; but had she never read this passage of fearful import, the language of Jesus Christ:

"But I say unto you that for every idle word that men shall speak, they shall give account thereof in the day of judgment"? Julia thought that the careless words which had passed her lips would be forgotten, but she should have known that every word and act of our lives is to be recorded and brought to our remembrance.

I have known children to be very much interested, and to be influenced to make a great effort to do right, by an account-book which was kept by their mothers. When such a book is kept at school, and every act is recorded, the pupils are much more likely to make an effort to perform the duties required of them. So it is in Sabbath-schools. I recently heard a Sabbath-school superintendent remark that the school could not be well sustained unless accounts were kept of the attendance, etc., of the pupils.

Many years ago a man, brought before a tribunal, was told to relate his story freely without fear, as it should not be used against him. He commenced to do so, but had not proceeded far before he heard the scratching of a pen behind a curtain. In an instant he was on his guard, for by that sound he knew that, notwithstanding their promise, a record was being taken of what he said.

Silently and unseen by us the angel secretaries are taking a faithful record of our words and actions, and even of our thoughts. Do we realize this? and a more solemn question is, What is the record they are making?

Not long ago I read of a strange list. It was an exact catalogue of the crimes committed by a man who was at last executed in Norfolk Island, with the various punishments he had received for his different offenses. It was written out in small hand by the chaplain, and was nearly three yards long.

What a sickening catalogue to be crowded into one brief life. Yet this man was once an innocent child. A mother no doubt bent lovingly over him, a father perhaps looked upon him in pride and joy, and imagination saw him rise to manhood honored and trusted by his fellow-men. But the boy chose the path of evil and wrong-doing regardless of the record he was making, and finally committed an act, the penalty for which was death, and he perished miserably upon the scaffold.

Dear readers, most of you are young, and your record is but just commenced. Oh, be warned in time, and seek to have a list of which you will not be ashamed when scanned by Jehovah, angels, and men. Speak none but kind, loving words, have your thoughts and aspirations pure and noble, crowd into your life all the *good* deeds you can, and thus crowd out *evil* ones.

We should not forget that an account-book is kept by God, in which all the events of our lives are recorded, and that even every thought will be brought before us at the day of judgment. In that day God will judge the secrets of men: he will bring to light the hidden things of darkness, and will make manifest the counsels of the heart.

There is another book spoken of in the Bible. The book of life, and it is said that no one can enter heaven whose name is not written in the Lamb's book of life.

Angels are now weighing moral worth. The record will soon close, either by death or the decree, " He that is unjust, let him be unjust still, and he which is filthy, let him be filthy still; and he that is righteous, let him be righteous still; and he that is holy let him be holy still." We have but one short, preparing hour in which to redeem the past and get ready for the future.   Our life record will soon be examined.   What shall it be!

## MOTHER.

THE silvery hairs are weaving
    A crown above her brow,
But surely mother never seemed
    One-half so sweet as now!

The love-light beams from out her eyes
    As clear, as sweet and true,
As when, with youthful beauty crowned,
    Life bloomed for her all new.

No thought of self doth ever cast
    A cloudlet o'er the light
That shines afar from out her soul,
    So steadfast, pure, and bright.

Her love illumes the darkest hour,
    Smooths all the rugged way,
Makes lighter every burden,
    Cheers through each weary day.

More precious than the rarest gem
    In all the world could be;
More sweet than honor, fame, and praise,
    Is mother's love to me.

# The Right Decision.

IT was the beginning of vacation when Mr. Davis, a friend of my father, came to see us, and asked to let me go home with him. I was much pleased with the thought of going out of town. The journey was delightful, and when we reached Mr. Davis' house everything looked as if I were going to have a fine time. Fred Davis, a boy about my own age, took me cordially by the hand, and all the family soon seemed like old friends. "This is going to be a vacation worth having," I said to myself several times during the evening, as we all played games, told riddles, and laughed and chatted merrily as could be.

At last Mrs. Davis said it was almost bedtime. Then I expected family prayers, but we were very soon directed to our chambers. How strange it seemed to me, for I had never before been in a household without the family altar "Come," said Fred, "mother says you and I are going to be bedfellows," and I followed him up two pair of stairs to a nice little chamber which he called his room; and he opened a drawer and showed me a box, and boat, and knives, and powder-horn, and all his treasures, and told me a world of new things about what the boys did there. He undressed first and jumped into bed. I was much longer about it, for a new set of thoughts began to rise in my mind.

When  my  mother  put  my  portmanteau  into  my  hand,
just  before  the  coach  started,  she  said  tenderly,  in  a  low
tone,  " Remember,  Robert,  that  you  are  a  Christian  boy."
I  knew  very  well  what  that  meant,  and  I  had  now  just  come
to  a  point  of  time  when  her  words  were  to  be  minded.    At
home  I  was  taught  the  duties  of  a  Christian  child ;  abroad
I  must  not  neglect  them,  and  one  of  these  was  evening
prayer.    From  a  very  little  boy  I  had  been  in  the  habit  of
kneeling  and  asking  the  forgiveness  of  God,  for  Jesus'  sake,
acknowledging  his  mercies,  and  seeking  his  protection  and
blessing.

" Why  do n't  you  come  to  bed,  Robert ?"  cried  Fred.
" What  are  you  sitting  there  for ?"    I  was  afraid  to  pray,
and  afraid  not  to  pray.    It  seemed  that  I  could  not  kneel
down  and  pray  before  Fred.    What  would  he  say ?    Would
he  not  laugh ?    The  fear  of  Fred  made  me  a  coward.    Yet
I  could  not  lie  down  on  a  prayerless  bed.    If  I  needed  the
protection  of  my  heavenly  Father  at  home,  how  much  more
abroad.    I  wished  many  wishes ;  that  I  had  slept  alone,
that  Fred  would  go  to  sleep,  or  something  else,  I  hardly
knew  what.    But  Fred  would  not  go  to  sleep.

Perhaps  struggles  like  these  take  place  in  the  bosom  of
every  one  when  he  leaves  home  and  begins  to  act  for  himself,  and  on  his  decision  may  depend  his  character  for  time,
and  for  eternity.    With  me  the  struggle  was  severe.    At
last,  to  Fred's  cry,  " Come,  boy,  come  to  bed,"  I  mustered
courage  to  say,  " I  will  kneel  down  and  pray  first ;  that  is
always  my  custom."    " Pray ?"  said  Fred,  turning  himself
over  on  his  pillow,  and  saying  no  more.    His  propriety  of
conduct  made  me  ashamed.    Here  I  had  long  been  afraid

of him, and yet when he knew my wishes he was quiet and left me to myself. How thankful I was that duty and conscience triumphed.

That settled my future course. It gave me strength for time to come. I believe that the decision of the "Christian boy," by God's blessing, made me the Christian man; for in after years I was thrown amid trials and temptations which must have drawn me away from God and from virtue, had it not been for my settled habit of secret prayer.

Let every boy who has pious parents, read and think about this. You have been trained in Christian duties and principles. When you go from home do not leave them behind you. Carry them with you and stand by them, and then in weakness and temptation, by God's help, they will stand by you. Take a manly stand on the side of your God and Saviour, of your father's God. It is by abandoning their Christian birthright that so many boys go astray, and grow up to be young men dishonoring parents, without hope and without God in the world.

> YES, we are boys, always playing with tongue or with pen,
> And I sometimes have asked, shall we ever be men?
> Will we always be youthful, and laughing and gay,
> Till the last dear companions drop smiling away?
> Then here's to our boyhood, its gold and its gray,
> The stars of its winter, the dews of its May.
> And when we have done with our life-lasting toys,
> Dear Father, take care of thy children, the boys.
> —*Oliver Wendall Holmes.*

# SUSIE'S PRAYER

IT was a half-holiday. The children were gathered on the green and a right merry time they were having.

"Come, girls and boys," called out Ned Graham, "let's play hunt the squirrel."

All assented eagerly, and a large circle was formed with Ned Graham for leader, because he was the largest.

"Come, Susie," said one of the boys, to a little girl who stood on one side, and seemed to shrink from joining them.

"Oh, never mind *her!*" said Ned, with a little toss of his head, "she's nobody, anyhow. Her father drinks."

A quick flush crept over the child's pale face as she heard the cruel, thoughtless words.

She was very sensitive, and the arrow had touched her heart in its tenderest place.

Her father *was* a drunkard, she knew, but to be taunted with it before so many was more than she could bear; and with great sobs heaving from her bosom, and hot tears filling her eyes, she turned and ran away from the playground.

Her mother was sitting by the window when she reached home, and the tearful face of the little girl told that something had happened to disturb her.

"What is the matter, Susie?" she asked, kindly.

"Oh mother," Susie said, with the tears dropping down her cheeks, as she hid her face in her mother's lap, "Ned Graham said such a cruel thing about me," and here the sobs choked her voice so that she could hardly speak; "He said that I wasn't anybody, and that father drinks."

"My poor little girl," Mrs. Ellet said, very sadly. There were tears in her eyes, too.

Such taunts as this were nothing new.

"Oh, mother," Susie said, as she lifted her face, wet with tears, from her mother's lap, "I can't bear to have them say so, and just as if *I* had done something wicked. I wish father wouldn't drink! Do you suppose he'll ever leave it off?"

"I hope so," Mrs. Ellet answered, as she kissed Susie's face where the tears clung like drops of dew on a rose. "I pray that he may break off the habit, and I can do nothing but pray, and leave the rest to God."

That night Mr. Ellet came home to supper, as usual. He was a hard-working man, and a good neighbor. So everybody said, but he had the habit of intemperance so firmly fixed upon him that everybody thought he would end his days in the drunkard's grave. Susie kissed him when he came through the gate, as she always did, but there was something in her face that went to his heart—a look so sad, and full of touching sorrow for one so young as she!

3

"What ails my little girl?" he asked as he patted her curly head.

"I can't tell you, father," she answered, slowly.

"Why?" he asked.

"Because it would make you feel bad." Susie replied.

"I guess not," he said, as they walked up to the door together.   "What is it, Susie?"

"Oh, father," and Susie burst into tears again as the memory of Ned Graham's words came up freshly in her mind, "I wish you wouldn't drink any more, for the boys and girls don't like to play with me, 'cause you do."

Mr. Ellet made no reply.   But something stirred in his heart that made him ashamed of himself; ashamed that he was the cause of so much sorrow and misery.   After supper he took his hat, and Mrs. Ellet knew only too well where he was going.

At first he had resolved to stay at home that evening, but the force of habit was so strong that he could not resist, and he yielded, promising himself that he would not drink more than once or twice.

Susie had left the table before he had finished his supper, and as he passed the great clump of lilacs by the path, on his way to the gate, he heard her voice and stopped to listen to what she was saying.

"Oh, good Jesus, please don't let father drink any more.   Make him just as he used to be when I was a baby, and then the boys and girls can't call me a drunkard's child, or say such bad things about me.   Please, dear Jesus, for mother's sake and mine."

Susie's father listened to her simple prayer with a great lump swelling in his throat.

And when it was ended he went up to her, and knelt down by her side, and put his arm around her, oh, so lovingly!

"God in Heaven," he said, very solemnly, "I promise to-night, never to touch another drop of liquor as long as I live. Give me strength to keep my pledge, and help me to be a better man."

"Oh, father," Susie cried, her arms about his neck, and her head upon his breast, "I'm *so* glad! I shan't care about anything they say to me now, for I know you won't be a drunkard any more."

"God helping me, I will be a *man!*" he answered, as, taking Susie by the hand he went back into the house where his wife was sitting with the old patient look of sorrow on her face.—the look that had become so habitual.

I cannot tell you of the joy and thanksgiving that went up from that hearthstone that night. I wish I could, but it was too deep a joy which filled the hearts of Susie and her mother to be described.

Was not Susie's prayer answered?

THERE is never a day so dreary,
But God can make it bright,
And unto the soul that trusts him
He giveth songs in the night.

There is never a path so hidden,
But God will show the way,
If we seek the Spirit's guidance,
And patiently watch and pray.

# Company Manners.

"WELL," said Bessie, very emphatically, "I think Russell Morton is the best boy there is, anyhow."

"Why so, pet?" I asked, settling myself in the midst of the busy group gathered around in the firelight.

"I can tell," interrupted Wilfred, "Bessie likes Russ because he is so polite."

"I do n't care, you may laugh," said frank little Bess; "that *is* the reason—at least, one of them. He's nice; he do n't stamp and hoot in the house—and he never says, 'Halloo Bess,' or laughs when I fall on the ice."

"Bessie wants company manners all the time," said Wilfred. And Bell added: "We should all act grown up, if she had her fastidiousness suited."

Bell, be it said in passing, is very fond of long words, and has asked for a dictionary for her next birthday present.

Dauntless Bessie made haste to retort, "Well, if growing up would make some folks more agreeable, it's a pity we can't hurry about it."

"Wilfred, what are company manners?" interposed I from the depths of my easy chair.

"Why—why—they're—It's *behaving*, you know, when folks are here, or we go a visiting."

"Company manners are good manners," said Horace.

"Oh yes," answered I, meditating on it. "I see; man-

36

ners that are *too* good—for mamma—but just right for Mrs. Jones."

"That's it," cried Bess.

" But let us talk it over a bit. Seriously; why should you be more polite to Mrs. Jones than to mamma? You do n't love her better?"

" Oh my! no indeed," chorused the voices.

"Well, then, I do n't see why Mrs. Jones should have all that's agreeable ; why the hats should come off, and the tones soften, and 'please,' and 'thank you,' and 'excuse me,' should abound in her house, and not in mamma's."

" Oh! that's very different."

" And mamma knows we mean all right. Besides, you are not fair, cousin ; we were talking about boys and girls —not grown up people."

Thus my little audience assailed me, and I was forced to a change of base.

" Well, about boys and girls, then. Can not a boy be just as happy, if, like our friend Russell, he is gentle to the little girls, does n't pitch his little brother in the snow, and respects the rights of his cousins and intimate friends? It seems to me that politeness is just as suitable to the play-ground as to the parlor."

" Oh, of course ; if you'd have a fellow give up all fun," said Wilfred.

" My dear boy," said I, "that is n't what I want. Run, and jump, and shout as much as you please ; skate, and slide, and snowball ; but do it with politeness to other boys and girls, and I'll agree you will find just as much fun in it. You sometimes say I pet Burke Holland more than any of my child-friends.  Can I help it ?  For though he is lively and sometimes frolicsome, his manners are always good.  You never see him with his chair tipped up, or his hat on in the house.  He never pushes ahead of you to get first out of the room.  If you are going out, he holds open the door ; if weary, it is Burke who brings a glass of water, places a chair, hands a fan, springs to pick up your hand-kerchief—and all this without being told to do so, or inter-fering with his own gaiety in the least.

"This attention is n't only given to me as the guest, or to Mrs. Jones when he visits her, but to mamma, Aunt Jennie, and little sister, just as carefully ; at home, in school, or at play, there is always just as much guard against rude-ness.  His courtesy is not merely for state occasions, but a well-fitting garment worn constantly.  His manliness is genuine loving-kindness.  In fact, that is exactly what real politeness is ; carefulness for others, and watchfulness over ourselves, lest our angles shall interfere with their com-fort."

It is impossible for boys and girls to realize, until they have grown too old to easily adopt new ones, how impor-tant it is to guard against contracting carelessness and awk-ward habits of speech and manners.  Some very unwisely think it is not necessary to be so very particular about these things except when company is present.  But this is a grave mistake, for coarseness will betray itself in spite of the most watchful sentinelship.

It is impossible to indulge in one form of speech, or have one set of manners at home, and another abroad, be-cause in moments of confusion or bashfulness, such as every young person feels sometimes who is sensitive and modest, the habitual mode of expression will discover itself.

It is not, however, merely because refinement of speech and grace of manners are pleasing to the sense, that our young friends are recommended to cultivate and practice them, but because outward refinement of any sort reacts as it were on the character and makes it more sweet and gentle and lovable, and these are qualities that attract and draw about the possessor a host of kind friends. Then again they increase self-respect.

The very consciousness that one prepossesses and pleases people, makes most persons feel more respect for themselves, just as the knowledge of being well dressed makes them feel more respectable. You can see by this simple example, how every effort persons make toward perfecting themselves brings some pleasant reward.

### BELIEVE AND TRUST.

BELIEVE and trust. Through stars and suns,
  Through life and death, through soul and sense,
His wise, paternal purpose runs;
  The darkness of his providence
  Is star-lit with benign intents.

O joy supreme! I know the Voice,
  Like none beside on earth and sea;
Yea, more, O soul of mine, rejoice!
  By all that he requires of me
  I know what God himself must be.

*—Whittier.*

# The Belle of the Ballroom.

O NLY this once," said Edward Allston, fixing a pair of loving eyes on the beautiful girl beside him—"only this once, sister mine. Your dress will be my gift, and will not, therefore, diminish your charity fund; and besides, if the influences of which you have spoken, do, indeed, hang so alluringly about a ballroom, should you not seek to guard me from their power? You will go, will you not? For me—for me?"

The Saviour, too, whispered to the maiden, "Decide for me—for me." But her spirit did not recognize the tones, for of late it had been bewildered with earthly music.

She paused, however, and her brother waited her reply in silence.

Beware! Helen Allston, beware! The sin is not lessened that the tempter is so near to thee. Like the sparkle of the red wine to the inebriate are the seductive influences of the ballroom. Thy foot will fall upon roses, but they will be roses of this world, not those that bloom for eternity. Thou wilt lose the fervor and purity of thy love, the promptness of thy obedience, the consolation of thy trust. The holy calm of thy closet will become irksome to thee, and thy power of resistance will be diminished many fold, for this is the first great temptation. But Helen will not beware. She forgets her Saviour. The melody of that rich

40

voice is dearer to her than the pleadings of gospel memories.

Two years previous to the scene just described, Helen Allston hoped she had been converted. For a time she was exact in the discharge of her social duties, regular in her closet exercises, ardent, yet equable, in her love. Conscious of her weakness, she diligently used all those aids, so fitted to sustain and cheer. Day by day, she rekindled her torch at the holy fire which comes streaming on to us from the luminaries of the past—from Baxter, Taylor, and Flavel, and many a compeer whose names live in our hearts, and linger on our lips. She was alive to the present also. Upon her table a beautiful commentary, upon the yet unfulfilled prophecies, lay, the records of missionary labor and success. The sewing circle busied her active fingers, and the Sabbath-school kept her affections warm, and rendered her knowledge practical and thorough. But at length the things of the world began insensibly to win upon her regard. She was the child of wealth, and fashion spoke of her taste and elegance. She was very lovely, and the voice of flattery mingled with the accents of honest praise. She was agreeable in manners, sprightly in conversation, and was courted and caressed. She heard with more complacency, reports from the gay circles she had once frequented, and noted with more interest the ever-shifting pageantry of folly. Then she lessened her charities, furnished her wardrobe more lavishly, and was less scrupulous in the disposal of her time. She formed acquaintances among the light and frivolous, and to fit herself for intercourse with them, read the books they read, until others became insipid.

Edward Allston was proud of his sister, and loved her, too, almost to idolatry.

They had scarcely been separated from childhood, and it was a severe blow to him when she shunned the amusements they had so long shared together. He admired indeed the excellency of her second life, the beauty of her aspirations, the loftiness of her aims, but he felt deeply the want of that unity in hope and purpose which had existed between them. He felt, at times, indignant, as if something had been taken from himself. Therefore, he strove by many a device to lure her into the path he was treading. He was very selfish in this, but he was unconscious of it. He would have climbed precipices, traversed continents, braved the ocean in its wrath, to have rescued her from physical danger, but, like many others, thoughtless as himself, he did not dream of the fearful importance of the result; did not know that the Infinite alone could compute the hazard of the tempted one. Thus far had he succeeded, that she had consented to attend with him a brilliant ball.

"It will be a superb affair," he said, half aloud, as he walked down the street. "The music will be divine, too. And she used to be so fond of dancing! 'T was a lovely girl spoiled, when the black-coated gentry preached her into their notions. And yet—and yet—pshaw!—all cant!—all cant! What harm can there be in it? And if she does withstand all this, I will yield the point that there is something—yes, a great deal in her religion.

So musing, he proceeded to the shop of Mrs. Crofton, the most fashionable dressmaker in the place, and forgot his momentary scruples in the consultation as to the proper materials for Helen's dress, which was to be a present from him, and which he determined should be worthy her grace and beauty.

The ball was over, and Helen stood in her festal costume, before the ample mirror in her chamber, holding in one hand a white kid glove she had just withdrawn. She had indeed been the belle of the ballroom. Simplicity of life, and a joyous spirit, are the wonder-workers, and she was irresistibly bright and fresh among the faded and hackneyed of heated assembly rooms. The most delicate and intoxicating flattery had been offered her, and wherever she turned, she met the glances of admiration. Her brother, too, had been proudly assiduous, had followed her with his eyes so perpetually as to seem scarcely conscious of the presence of another; and there she stood, minute after minute, lost in the recollections of her evening triumph.

Almost queenlike looked she, the rich folds of her satin robe giving fullness to her slender form, and glittering as if woven with silver threads. A chain of pearls lay on her neck, and gleamed amid the shading curls, which floated from beneath a chaplet of white roses. She looked up at length, smiled at her lovely reflection in the mirror, and then wrapping herself in her dressing-gown, took up a volume of sacred poems. But when she attempted to read, her mind wandered to the dazzling scene she had just quitted. She knelt to pray, but the brilliant vision haunted her still, and ever as the wind stirred the vines about the window, there came back that alluring music.

She rose with a pang of self-reproach. Instead of the confidence, the consciousness of protection, the holy serenity

with which she usually sought her pillow, she experienced
an excitement and restlessness which nothing could allay.
She attempted to meditate, but with every thought of duty
came memories of the festal garlands, and the blazing lamps,
and the flitting figures of the merry dancers.

An open Bible lay on the window-seat and as she passed
it she read: "Another parable put he forth unto them, saying: The kingdom of heaven is likened to a man which
sowed good seed in his field. But while he slept, his enemy
came and sowed tares among the wheat, and went his way."

Tears sprang to her eyes, and she exclaimed, "In the
field of my heart also hath the enemy sown tares." She
took up the book, and read again; then too soulful to remain quiet, she rapidly paced the chamber. Resolutely and
carefully she reviewed the past, back to her first faint trembling hope. Rigorously, as in the presence of her Maker,
she scanned her first departure from the narrow path; and
if her earlier convictions were pungent, tenfold more intense was the agony of this her second awakening.

In the solitude of his chamber, Edward thought with
less elation of his successful plan. He believed that Helen
would have yielded to no ordinary temptation, and felt that
he had been scarcely generous to enlist her affections against
her principles. His repeated, "It is but a trifle," did not
satisfy him; and when he had listened hour after hour to
her footfall, he could no longer restrain his inclination to
soothe her emotion. In vain he assayed all the arguments,
all the sophistry, which the world employs to attract the
lukewarm professor.

"Do not seek to console me," said Helen, "for such

WHILE HE SLEPT HIS ENEMY CAME AND SOWED TARES AMONG THE
WHEAT.

tears are salutary, my dear brother.   I have virtually said
that the joys of religion are fading and unsatisfactory ; I
must sometimes seek for others.   I have quieted more than
one uneasy conscience, by throwing the influence of a professing Christian into the scale of the world.   I have wandered from my Father's side to the society of his rebel subjects.   And yet I have cause to mourn less for this one
transgression, than for the alienation of heart, which led the
way to it.   Had I not fallen far, very far, from the strength
and purity of my earlier love, even your pleadings could not
have moved me."

"But the Bible says nothing about such amusements,
Helen."

"Not in words, perhaps, but in effect.   Put the case to
your own heart, Edward.   Would you have me choose for
my companions those who treat you with neglect?   Would
you wish me to frequent places, whence I should return,
careless and cold in my manner toward you?   Ah, brother!
I loved God once.   I saw his hand in everything around
me.   I felt his presence perpetually, and trusted, childlike,
to his protecting arm.   But now I regard him less, pray
less, read less, and give less."   And then she revealed to
her brother her beautiful experience—beautiful till she grew
negligent and formal—with a truth, an earnestness, a loving
simplicity, that for the first time gave him some insight into
the nature of true piety.

"And now, dear Edward," she said, "read to me
Christ's prayer to the people, that I may feel sure that they
prayed for me."

As she listened, the varying expressions of countenance indicated many and varied emotions. Submission, sorrow, love, and faith—all were there. When Edward had finished they knelt together, and Helen sorrowfully, yet hopefully, poured out her full soul in confession, and most touchingly she besought the divine compassion upon her erring brother.

The carol of the birds went up with the whispered amen of the penitent, the blossoms of the climbing honeysuckle sent in her fragrance, and the morning sun smiled on them as they rose from prayer. The face of Helen reflected her inward gladness, and restored peace shone in her dark eyes and tranquil countenance. "Thou art happier than I," said Edward, as he turned from the chamber.

### THE SHADOW OF THE CROSS.

"AYE, and the race is just begun,
The world is all before me now,
The sun is in the eastern sky,
And long the shadows westward lie;
In everything that meets my eye
A splendor and a joy I mind
A glory that is undesigned."
Ah! youth, attempt that path with care,
The shadow of the cross is there.

"I've time," he said, "to rest awhile,
And sip the fragrant wine of life,
My lute to pleasure's halls I'll bring
And while the sun ascends I'll sing,
And all my world without shall ring
Like merry chiming bells that peal
Not half the rapture that they feel."
Alas! he found but tangled moss,
Above the shadow of the cross.

# CHRIST OUR REFUGE

THERE were six cities in the land of Canaan which were set apart as places of refuge, to which a man might flee if he had, either by accident or design, killed another. These cities were easy of access. Three were on the west side of the river Jordan, and three on the east side. Every year the roads leading to them were examined, to see that they were in good condition, and that there was nothing in the way to stop the manslayer as he was running from his pursuer. At different points there were the guide-boards, and on them were written, REFUGE! REFUGE!

If any man by accident killed another, and reached one of these cities before his pursuer, he was allowed to stay there until the death of the high-priest who was then living. But if in anger a man had purposely killed another, then, although he sought refuge in one of these cities, he was given up to the avenger of blood to be slain. You will find more about these cities and their names if you will read the thirty-fifth chapter of Numbers, the nineteenth chapter of Deuteronomy, and the twentieth chapter of Joshua.

47

But what interest can boys and girls and all older persons have in these cities?

I will try to tell you.  God has different ways of teaching.  A great many things about which we read in the Old Testament are what is called types.  A type, in scripture language, means a pattern or a likeness to a person who is to come, or to an event which is to take place.  It is supposed to point forward to something more valuable than it self.  Thus, for example, the blood of the lamb which was slain on the Jewish altar was a type, or a foreshowing, of the crucifixion of Jesus Christ for our salvation.  Hence John the Baptist pointing to the Saviour, said to his disciples, "Behold the Lamb of God, which taketh away the sin of the world."  John 1:29.  The paschal lamb, which was slain to commemorate the deliverance of the Jews from the bondage of Egypt, and the lamb which was offered daily, both morning and evening, in the service of the temple, were representations of the greater sacrifice which Christ came from heaven to make for our salvation.

So the land of Canaan was a type of heaven.  The lifting up of the brazen serpent on a pole was a type of our Saviour's crucifixion ; and the cities of refuge were a beautiful type of Jesus Christ, who is the sinner's refuge.

You know, my dear children, that we have all sinned, and that we all need a place of safety.  The avenger says, "Thou shalt surely die."  Escape for thy life.  But that we may not die eternally, God has given us the Bible as our guide-board ; and the Bible is constantly pointing to Jesus Christ as the sinner's refuge.  He is our hiding-place.  It is to him Isaiah refers when he says, "And a man shall be as a hiding-place from the wind, and a covert from the tempest; as rivers of water in a dry place, as the shadow of a great rock in a weary land."

The way to our city of refuge is plain. "I am the way," is the Saviour's own direction. The gate is always open, and the assurance is, "Him that cometh to me I will in no wise cast out."

I want you to remember, dear children, that it is a great deal easier to run to this city of refuge when you are young, than it will be if you put it off until you are older. The promise of the Saviour is, "Those that seek me early shall find me." Will you not seek him when he may be found? How sad it will be if you neglect to do so. You will need a refuge when the tempest of God's judgments shall burst upon the wicked. Oh, then how glad you will be if you can say, as David said of his trust in God, "Thou art my hiding-place; thou shalt preserve me from trouble; thou shalt compass me about with songs of deliverance."

### THE MASTER'S HAND.

"In the still air the music lies unheard;
　In the rough marble beauty hides unseen;
To make the music and the beauty needs
　A master's touch, the sculptor's chisel keen.

Great Master, touch us with Thy skilled hand:
　Let not the music that is in us die!
Great Sculptor, hew and polish us, nor let
　Hidden and lost, Thy form within us lie!

Spare not the stroke! Do with us as thou wilt!
　Let there be naught unfinished, broken, marred;
Complete Thy purpose, that we may become
　Thy perfect image, Thou our God and Lord!"

# Tom's Trial.

T was a pleasant day in that particularly pleasant part of the summer time, which the boys call "vacation," when Tiger and Tom walked slowly down the street together. You may think it strange that I mention Tiger first, but I assure you Tom would not have been in the least offended by the preference. Indeed, he would have assured you that Tiger was a most wonderful dog, and knew as much as any two boys, though this might be called extravagant.

Nearly a year ago, on Tom's birthday, Tiger arrived as a present from Tom's uncle, and as he leaped with a dignified bound from the wagon in which he made his journey, Tom looked for a moment into his great, wise eyes, and impulsively threw his arms around his shaggy neck. Tiger, on his part, was pleased with Tom's bright face, and most affectionately licked his smooth cheeks. So the league of friendship was complete in an hour.

Tom had a pleasant, round face, and you might live with him a week, and think him one of the noblest, most generous boys you ever knew. But some day you would probably discover that he had a most violent temper. You would be frightened to see his face crimson with rage, as he stamped his feet, shook his little sister, spoke improperly to his mother, and above all, displeased his great Father in heaven.

Now I am going to tell you of one great trial on this account, which Tom never forgot to the end of his life. Tiger and Tom were walking down the street together, when they met Dick Casey, a school-fellow of Tom's.

"O Dick!" cried Tom, "I'm going to father's grain store a little while. Let's go up in the loft and play."

Dick had just finished his work in his mother's garden, and was all ready for a little amusement. So the two went up together, and enjoyed themselves highly for a long time. But at last arose one of those trifling disputes, in which little boys are so apt to indulge. Pretty soon there were angry words, then (Oh, how sorry I am to say it!), Tom's wicked passions got the mastery of him, and he beat little Dick severely. Tiger, who must have been ashamed of his master, pulled hard at his coat, and whined piteously, but all in vain. At last Tom stopped, from mere exhaustion.

"There, now!" he cried, "which is right, you or I?"

"I am," sobbed Dick, "and you tell a lie."

Tom's face flushed crimson, and darting upon Dick, he gave him a sudden push. Alas! he was near to the open door. Dick screamed, threw up his arms, and in a moment was gone. Tom's heart stood still, and an icy chill crept over him from head to foot. At first he could not stir; then—he never knew how he got there, but he found himself standing beside his little friend. Some men were raising him carefully from the hard sidewalk.

"Is he dead?" almost screamed Tom.

"No," replied one, "we hope not. How did he fall out?"

"He did n't fall," groaned Tom, who never could be so mean as to tell a lie, "I pushed him out."

"*You* pushed him, you wicked boy," cried a rough voice. "Do you know you ought to be sent to jail, and if he dies, maybe you'll be hung."

Tom grew as white as Dick, whom he had followed into the store, and he heard all that passed as if in a dream.

"Is he badly hurt?" cried some one.

"Only his hands," was the answer. "The rope saved him, he caught hold of the rope and slipped down; but his hands are dreadfully torn—he has fainted from pain."

Just then Tom's father came in, and soon understood the case. The look he gave at his unhappy son, so full of sorrow, not unmingled with pity, was too much for Tom, and he stole out, followed by the faithful Tiger. He wandered to the woods, and threw himself upon the ground. One hour ago he was a happy boy, and now what a terrible change! What has made the difference? Nothing but the indulgence of this wicked, violent temper. His mother had often warned him of the fearful consequences. She had told him that little boys who would not learn to govern themselves, grew up to be very wicked men, and often became murderers in some moment of passion. And now, Tom shuddered to think he was almost a murderer! Nothing but God's great mercy in putting that rope in Dick's way, had saved him from carrying that load of sorrow and guilt all the rest of his life. But poor Dick, he might die yet—how pale he looked—how strange! Tom fell upon his knees, and prayed God to "spare Dick's life," and from that time forth, with God's help, he promised that he would strive to conquer this wicked passion.

Then, as he could no longer bear his terrible suspense,

he started for Widow Casey's cottage. As he appeared at the humble door, Mrs. Casey angrily ordered him away, saying: "You have made a poor woman trouble enough for one day." But Dick's feeble voice entreated, "O mother, let him come in; I was just as bad as he."

Tom gave a cry of joy at hearing these welcome tones, and sprang hastily in. There sat poor Dick with his hands bound up, looking very pale, but Tom thanked God that he was alive.

"I should like to know how I am to live now," sighed Mrs. Casey. "Who will weed the garden, and carry my vegetables to market? I am afraid we shall suffer for bread before the summer is over," and she put her apron to her eyes.

"Mrs. Casey," cried Tom, eagerly, "I will do everything that Dick did. I will sell the potatoes and beans, and will drive Mr. Brown's cows to pasture."

Mrs. Casey shook her head incredulously, but Tom bravely kept his word. For the next few weeks Tom was at his post bright and early, and the garden was never kept in better order. And every morning Tiger and Tom stood faithfully in the market-place with their baskets, and never gave up, no matter how warm the day, till the last vegetable was sold, and the money placed faithfully in Mrs. Casey's hand.

Tom's father often passed through the market, and gave his little son an encouraging smile, but he did not offer to help him out of his difficulty, for he knew if Tom struggled on alone, it would be a lesson he would never forget. Already he was becoming so gentle and patient, that every one noticed the change, and his mother rejoiced over the sweet fruits of his repentance and self-sacrifice.

After a few weeks the bandages were removed from Dick's hands, but they had been unskilfully treated, and were drawn up in very strange shapes. Mrs. Casey could not conceal her grief. "He will never be the help he was before," she said to Tom, "he will never be like other boys, and he wrote such a fine hand, now he can no more make a letter than that little chicken in the garden."

"If we only had a great city doctor," said a neighbor, "he might have been all right. Even now his fingers might be helped if you should take him to New York."

"Oh, I am too poor, *too poor*," said she, and burst into tears.

"Tom could not bear it, and again rushed into the woods to think what could be done, for he had already given them all his quarter's allowance. All at once a thought flashed into his head, and he started as if he had been shot. Then he cried in great distress :—

"No, no, anything but that, I can't do *that !*"

Tiger gently licked his hands, and watched him with great concern. Now came a great struggle. Tom stroked him backward and forward, and although he was a proud boy, he sobbed aloud. Tiger whined, licked his face, rushed off into dark corners, and barked savagely at some imaginary enemy, and then came back, and putting his paws on Tom's knees, wagged his tail in anxious sympathy. At last Tom took his hands from his pale, tear-stained face, and looking into the dog's great honest eyes, he cried with a queer shake of his voice :—

"Tiger, old fellow! dear old dog, could you ever forgive me if I sold you?"

Then came another burst of sorrow, and Tom rose hastily, as if afraid to trust himself, and almost ran out of the woods. Over the fields he raced, with Tiger close at his heels, nor rested a moment till he stood at Major White's door, nearly two miles away.

"Do you still want Tiger, sir?"

"Why yes," said the old man in great surprise, "but do *you* want to sell him?"

"Yes, please," gasped Tom, not daring to look at his old companion. The exchange was quickly made, and the ten dollars in Tom's hand. Tiger was beguiled into a barn, and the door hastily shut, and Tom was hurrying off, when he turned and cried in a choking voice—

"You will be kind to him, Major White, won't you? Don't whip him, I never did, and he's the best dog—"

"No, no, child," said Major White, kindly; "I'll treat him like a prince, and if you ever want to buy him back, you shall have him." Tom managed to falter, "Thank you," and almost flew out of hearing of Tiger's eager scratching on the barn door.

I am making my story too long, and can only tell you in a few words that Tom's sacrifice was accepted. A friend took little Dick to the city free of expense, and Tom's money paid for the necessary operation. The poor crooked fingers were very much improved, and were soon almost as good as ever. And the whole village loved Tom for his brave, self-sacrificing spirit, and the noble atonement he had made for his moment of passion.

A few days after Dick's return came Tom's birthday, but he did not feel in his usual spirits. In spite of his great delight in Dick's recovery, he had so mourned over the matter, and had taken Tiger's loss so much to heart, that he had grown quite pale and thin. So, as he was permitted to spend the day as he pleased, he took his books and went to his favorite haunt in the woods.

"How different from my last birthday," thought Tom. "Then Tiger had just come, and I was so happy, though I did n't like him half so well as I do now." Tom sighed heavily; then added more cheerfully, "Well, I hope some things are better than they were last year. I hope I have begun to conquer myself, and with God's help I will never give up trying while I live. Now if I could only earn money enough to buy back dear old Tiger." While Tom was busied with these thoughts he heard a hasty, familiar trot, a quick bark of joy, and the brave old dog sprang into Tom's arms.

"Tiger, old fellow," cried Tom, trying to look fierce, though he could scarcely keep down the tears, "how came you to run away, sir?"

Tiger responded by picking up a letter he had dropped in his first joy, and laying it in Tom's hand:—

"MY DEAR CHILD: Tiger is pining, and I must give him a change of air. I wish him to have a good master, and knowing that the best ones are those who have learned to govern *themselves*, I send him to you. Will you take care of him and greatly oblige

"Your old friend, MAJOR WHITE."

Tom then read through a mist of tears—

"P. S.  I know the whole story.  Dear young friend,
'Be not weary in well-doing.'"

## WHAT COUNTS.

DID you tackle the trouble that came your way,
  With a resolute heart and cheerful,
Or hide your face from the light of day
  With a craven face and fearful.

O, a trouble's a ton, or a trouble's an ounce.
  A trouble is what you make it.
It is n't the fact that you're hurt that counts,
  But only, HOW DID YOU TAKE IT?

You are beaten to the earth? Well, what of that?
  Come up with a smiling face.
It's nothing against you to fall down *flat*;
  But to LIE THERE—that's disgrace.

The harder you're thrown, the higher you'll bounce,
  Be proud of your blackened eye.
It is n't the fact that you're licked that counts,
  But, HOW did you fight, and WHY?

And though you be down to death, what then?
  If you battled the best that you could,
If you played your part in the world of men,
  The *Critic* will call it good.

Death comes with a crawl, or comes with a pounce,
  And whether he's slow or spry,
It is n't the fact that you're DEAD that counts,
  But only HOW DID YOU DIE?

                              *—Cooke.*

# The Premium.

"I THINK I am sure of one premium at least," said Edward, as he placed himself upon the form among his school-fellows.

It was examination day, and many a young heart was beating quick with the hope of approbation and reward, or with the fear of disgrace. Some had looked forward to this day, and applied to their tasks, knowing how carefully they should be examined, and commended or punished according to their deservings. Others had chosen to forget that such a day must come, and idled away the time which they would now have given a great deal to have at their disposal again.

In the center of the schoolroom was placed a long table, covered with books of various sizes and of different value. There were Bibles and Testaments, both large and small, the histories of Rome, of Greece, and of England. There were volumes elegantly bound and pamphlets just stitched together. The school was extensive, and it was wished that every one who had exerted himself to the best of his ability, however little that might be, should carry home with him some mark of encouragement, to remind him that diligence and perseverance were not overlooked.

Like the servants to whom the Lord entrusted the talents, some had five, and some had but one, yet these last could not be excused for hiding and neglecting it because it was small; even the youngest and the simplest child at school may make something of the reason and opportunities which the Lord has given him to improve.

With anxious hearts and busy faces the boys arranged themselves around the table; and were examined with great care and patience by their teachers, as to the progress they had made in their studies.

Now, Edward had set his heart on one particular premium, the Roman History, neatly bound, and making two very pretty volumes, which he thought would handsomely fill up a vacant space on his little book-shelves. He allowed himself to think of this until no other prize was of any value in his sight, a great fault, often committed by children, and grown people, too; who instead of thankfully receiving whatever the bounty of Providence assigns them, would choose for themselves; and become discontented and unhappy in the midst of blessings, because the wisdom of God sees fit to withhold some one thing that their folly deems necessary to their happiness.

Edward passed his examination with much credit, and one of the first premiums was adjudged to him; but instead of the Roman History, a very neat Bible, in excellent large type, was placed in his hands. Many of his schoolmates had wished for that Bible, but Edward regarded it not; and the eyes of the foolish boy filled with tears, as he saw the elegant history of Rome presented to another, who, perhaps, would gladly have exchanged with him.

The next day Edward returned home and related his disappointment to his parents, who thought his desire for the Roman History a mark of great learning and taste;

but since he had distinguished himself so well they did not much care what prize he received.

Edward's father lived in the country, not far from the seaside, in a most delightful and healthy situation; and at this time his mother's brother, who was in a very sickly state, had just arrived there to enjoy the benefit of the sea-breezes, and rest a little from the toil and bustle of his employments in London.

Mr. Lewis was a young man of the most pleasing manners and appearance. He was very gentle and serious, but not at all gloomy or severe. His bad health only served to show forth his patience in enduring it without a murmuring word or discontented look; and Edward, who was really a kind-hearted and affectionate boy, soon became very much attached to his uncle, who had not seen him since he was an infant, and who was much pleased at the attentions his nephew delighted to pay him.

Young hearts are soon won; and it was only three days after Edward's return from school, that he went bounding over the grounds in search of his uncle, whose society he already preferred to his hoop and ball.

Mr. Lewis was seated under a fine old oak-tree, the high and knotted roots of which served as a seat; while the soft moss, interspersed with many delicate little flowers, was like a carpet beneath his feet. A rich and extensive tract of country lay spread before his eyes; and, at a distance the mighty ocean bounded the prospect, whose deep green waters were seen in beautiful contrast with the pale yellow cliff, that with a graceful, yet abrupt curve, interrupted the view to the right. Thin clouds were floating

past the sun every now and then, and threw all the varieties of light and shade upon the lovely scene below.

Mr. Lewis had a book in his hand, into which he frequently looked, and then raised his eyes again to gaze upon
the varieties that surrounded him ; and so intent he seemed,
that Edward doubted whether he ought to disturb him,
until his uncle, seeing him at some little distance, kindly
beckoned him to come near.

"Is not this a pretty place, uncle?" said Edward, as
he seated himself beside him; "and do you not find the
breeze from the water very refreshing?"

"It is beautiful indeed, my dear boy; and I am deriv-
ing both refreshment and instruction while I look around
me."

"Is that a Bible, uncle?"

"Yes. It is God's word, which I always find the best
commentary upon his works; they explain each other."

"I love the Bible too, uncle," said Edward, "and I got
much credit for my answering on Scripture questions last
half-year."

"And which, Edward, afforded you the greater satisfaction, the Scriptures, or the credit you got for studying
them?"

Edward looked a little embarrassed and did not immediately reply.

"It is quite right to take pleasure in the well-earned
approbation of your teachers," continued Mr. Lewis, "and
I was glad to hear that you obtained a premium at the last
examination also."

"Yes, uncle, but not the prize I wished for. There

was a Roman History that I should have liked better, and it was just of equal value with the Bible that I got."

"How of equal value, Edward?"

"I mean that it was not reckoned a higher prize, and it would have been a nicer book for me."

"Then you had a Bible already?"

"Why, no, uncle, not of my own, but it is easy to borrow one on the Sabbath; and I had gone through all my Scripture proofs, and do not want it on other days."

"Read these four verses for me," said Mr. Lewis, pointing to the sixth chapter of Deuteronomy "commencing with the sixth verse."

Edward read: "And these words which I command thee this day, shall be in thine heart; and thou shalt teach them diligently unto thy children, and shalt talk of them when thou sittest in thine house, and when thou walkest by the way, and when thou liest down, and when thou risest up; and thou shalt bind them for a sign upon thine hand, and they shall be as frontlets between thine eyes, and thou shalt write them upon the posts of thine house, and on thy gates."

"To whom was this command given, Edward?"

"To the Jews, uncle."

"Yes; and the word of God, which cannot pass away, is as much binding on us as on them, in everything excepting the sacrifices and ceremonies, which foreshowed the coming of the Lord Jesus Christ, and which were done away with, by his death's fulfilling all those types and shadows."

"Then," said Edward, "we are commanded to write the Bible on our hands and on our door-posts."

"No, my dear boy, not literally, but in a figure of speech; as the Lord, when declaring he never will forget Zion, says, 'I have graven thee upon the palms of my hands; thy walls are continually before me.' The meaning of the passage you first read is that we must have the word of God as continually present to our minds as anything written on our hands, and on every object around us, would be to our bodily sight. And how are we to get our thoughts so occupied by it, Edward?"

"By continually reading it, I suppose," replied Edward, rather sullenly.

"By reading it often, and meditating on it much," said his uncle; "and that we can do without interfering with our other business. Without prayer you cannot obtain any spiritual blessing, nor maintain any communion with God; and without reading the Scriptures you will have but little desire to pray. We are like people wandering in the dark, while the Bible is as a bright lamp held out to direct us in the only safe path. You cannot be a child of God if you do not his will; you cannot do it unless you know it, and it is by the Bible he is pleased to communicate that knowledge. Do you begin to see, Edward, that the Bible is more suitable to be an every-day book than your profane history?"

"Why, yes, uncle; but the Bible is a grave book, and if I read it so constantly I never should be merry."

"There is no merriment among the lost, Edward; and that dreadful lot will be your portion if you neglect the great salvation which the Scriptures set forth. Besides, there is no foundation for what you suppose to be the effect of reading the Bible.  I have known people naturally melancholy and discontented, to become cheerful and happy by studying it; but I never in my life saw an instance of a person's becoming unhappy because he had a good hope of going to heaven."

Edward paused a moment, and then said, "Uncle, I remember it is written concerning wisdom, that 'her ways are ways of pleasantness, and all her paths are peace.'"

"Most true, my dear boy, 'quietness and assurance forever' is the portion of God's people.  'Rejoice in the Lord alway, and again I say, rejoice.'  'The ransomed of the Lord shall return, and come to Zion with songs and everlasting joy upon their heads; they shall obtain joy and gladness; and sorrow and sighing shall flee away.'  Are such expressions as these likely to make us gloomy, Edward?"

"O, no, uncle; and I often wonder that you, who suffer so much pain, and read the Bible constantly, are not melancholy."

"How can I be melancholy, Edward, when the Bible tells me that all these things are working together for my spiritual good?  that He who spared not his own Son, but delivered him up for us all, will with him also freely give us all things?  When I think of what my sins deserve, and see the Lamb of God bearing the chastisement that should fall on me, how can I be melancholy?  When I feel that the Spirit of God is bringing these things to my remembrance, and enabling me to love the Lord Jesus, who has done so much for me, must I not rejoice?  I know that in me, that is, in my flesh, dwelleth no good thing; and since

God has promised forgiveness to all who seek that blessing
through his Son; and since I feel assured that I have
sought that blessing, and feel peace and joy in believing,
surely the song of praise, not the moan of lamentation, becomes me. Yet I do lament, Edward, daily lament, my
many offenses against God; but I am assured that Christ's
blood cleanseth from all sin, and that in him I have a powerful and all-prevailing Advocate with the Father. I know
in whom I have believed, and that he will never cast off nor
forsake me. I am sinking into the grave, but I do not
shrink from that prospect, because the bitterness of death
is taken away by my Saviour, who died for my sins, and
rose again for my justification; and though this body returns to dust, I shall live again, and enter into the presence
of my Redeemer, and rejoice there evermore."

Edward looked at the animated countenance of his
uncle, and then cast down his eyes; they were full of tears.
At last he said, "Uncle, indeed I am a very sinful boy,
neglecting the Bible, because I know it would show me my
sin, and the consequences of it. But I will trifle no more
with God's displeasure. I will get that precious Bible,
worth a thousand Roman histories, and I will read it daily,
with prayer, that I may be wise unto salvation."

Mr. Lewis did not live long after this. He died, rejoicing in hope of eternal life; and as often as Edward was
permitted to return home from his school, he was to be
seen under the old oak, with the Bible in his hand, from
which he learned more and more the will of his God and
Saviour—the utter sinfulness of his own nature—his inability to help himself; and from this holy word he learned

to place all his dependence on the righteousness of his Saviour—to follow the example of his Saviour, in prayer, in resignation, and in doing good to the poor around him.

He often thought of his dear uncle, and counted that day happy when he sat to listen to his kind advice, which, as a means, brought him to a knowledge of himself and of his heavenly Father.


### OUR NEIGHBORS.

" Somebody near you is struggling alone
   Over life's desert sand;
Faith, hope, and courage together are gone;
   Reach him a helping hand;
Turn on his darkness a beam of your light;
Kindle, to guide him, a beacon fire bright;
Cheer his discouragement, soothe his affright,
   Lovingly help him to stand.

Somebody near you is hungry and cold;
   Send him some aid to-day;
Somebody near you is feeble and old,
   Left without human stay.
Under his burdens put hands kind and strong;
Speak to him tenderly, sing him a song;
Haste to do something to help him along
   Over his weary way.

Dear one, be busy, for time fleeth fast,
   Soon it will all be gone;
Soon will our season of service be past,
   Soon will our day be done.
Somebody near you needs now a kind word;
Some one needs help, such as you can afford;
Haste to assist in the name of the Lord;
   There may be a soul to be won."

# A Kind Word.

Within each soul the God above
Plants the rich jewel,—human love.
The fairest gem that graces youth
Is love's companion,—fearless truth.

WILLIAM and Henry were clerks in a large wholesale establishment. They met one morning on their way to the store and proceeded together. After talking awhile on various subjects, the following dialogue took place :—

"By the way, William," said Henry, "I understand you were last evening at ——'s," naming a fashionable billiard saloon.

"A mistake, Henry. I was never in a billiard saloon."

"Well, I thought it very strange when I heard it."

"Why so?"

"Why?" said Henry in astonishment. "Why, because you are a religious young man and a church member."

"Do you ever visit such places, Henry?"

"Oh, yes; but that is quite a different matter. I don't profess to be a Christian, you know."

"You would think it wrong for me to be there?"

"Of course I should."

"And right for you?"

"Well, yes; there's no harm in my being there."

"*Why* not?"

"Why, because—because I do not profess to be bound by the same obligations that you are."

"And who has released you from those same obligations and imposed them upon me?"

"Oh, well, now, there's no use in talking, William; you know that Christians do not and ought not to engage in what they consider pernicious amusements."

"I certainly do know that they ought not; but I wish to know why it is wrong for them and right for others."

"You know the fact that it is so."

"No, I do not know that it is; and I wish to call your attention to the truth that the obligation to refrain from evil rests upon every rational human being in a Christian land, for God has commanded *all* men to love and obey him; also, to the fact that the difference between the Christian and the sinner is that one acknowledges the obligation, while the other denies it; and that the denial does not remove the obligation. God has not invited you to love him if you prefer to do so; but he has absolutely commanded you and me to love and obey him. I have the right, if you have, to engage in any kind of amusement, and to follow my inclinations in all things; and it is your duty, equally with mine, to honor our Master's law by shunning every wicked way. Think of this, friend Henry, I entreat you, and acknowledge the responsibility which you cannot remove; and from which, after accepting, you will not desire to be released."

They had arrived at the store, and each went to his own department. These young men had entered the employment of A. B. & Sons at the same time, about two years before the above conversation occurred. William had gained the confidence of his employers, and had risen in position. The senior partner intended retiring from business, and was looking about for a Christian young man of ability and energy to propose as a partner for his sons ; and had lately been thinking of William as a suitable person. He had observed him closely, and thought he saw in him the habits and qualifications necessary to make a successful business man.

He had also been watching Henry's course. He had heard of him at places where a young man who aspires to positions of truth and honor will never be seen, and was about proposing his discharge to the other members of the firm. He knew that a clerk whose style of living requires more money than his salary gives him will be very likely, indeed almost sure, to resort to dishonest practices to make up the deficiency. Instances of this kind are every day occurring in our cities ; and as long as we meet, as we may every morning and evening in the Broadway stages, dainty looking young men, dressed in finer and fresher broadcloth than their employers wear, with heavy gold chains, fine chronometers, and diamond pins and rings, we may expect to hear of a great many more.

That morning's conversation made a deep impression upon Henry's mind. The subject had never been presented to him in that light before. He had imagined, as young persons are apt to suppose, that no moral responsibility rested upon him till he assumed it publicly by uniting with the church. Henry did not mean to die a sinner. Oh, no ; he fully intended, after he had enjoyed what he considered the pleasures of youth, to settle down into Christian manhood. After this talk with William he could not get rid of the idea of accountability to his God. His wicked amusements and extravagant habits appeared to him as they never had done before, and he began to see their inevitable tendency. The result was an entire change in his aims and conduct. This was so marked that it very soon became known to all of his associates, and, of course, to his employers.

He remained in that house; gradually rising to the highest clerkship, and, finally, becoming the junior partner of the firm of which William had for some time been a member. His happiness and prosperity he always attributed to the word kindly spoken at the right time by his fellow clerk. He has been successful not only as a merchant, but as a Christian, exerting a powerful influence for good upon all about him, but particularly upon the young men employed in his house.

> " LIVE for something! All created
>   Nature doth reciprocate
> Her kindness. Should the animated
>   This great law invalidate?
> Rather show thy grateful praises
>   To thy God who reigns above,
> In acts that Sorrow's soul releases—
>   ' Words of kindness,' ' deeds of love.' "

# ANOTHER COMMANDMENT

A NEW presiding elder, Mr. N., was expected in the district; and as all the ministers stopped with Brother W. and his wife, every preparation was made to give him a cordial reception. The honest couple thought that religion in that part consisted in making parade, and therefore the parlor was put in order, a nice fire was made, and the kitchen replenished with cake, chickens, and every delicacy, preparatory to cooking. While Mr. W. was out at the wood-pile, a plain-looking, coarsely dressed, but quiet-like pedestrian, came along and asked the distance to the next town. He was told it was three miles. Being very cold, he asked permission to enter and warm himself. Assent was given very grudgingly, and both went into the kitchen. The wife looked daggers at this untimely intrusion, for the stranger had on cowhide boots, an old hat, and a threadbare, but neatly patched coat. At length she gave him a chair beside the Dutch oven which was baking nice cakes for the presiding elder, who was momentarily expected, as he was to preach the next day at the church a mile or two beyond.

The stranger, after warming himself, prepared to leave, but the weather became inclement, and as his appetite was aroused by the viands about the fire, he asked for some little refreshment ere he set out for a cold walk to the town beyond. Mrs. W. was displeased, but on consultation with her husband, cold bacon and bread were set out on an old table, and he was somewhat gruffly told to eat. It was growing dark, and hints were thrown out that the stranger had better depart, as it was three long miles to town.

The homely meal was at last concluded—the man thanked him kindly for the hospitality he had received, and opened the door to go. But it was quite dark and the clouds denoting a storm filled the heavens.

"You say it is full three miles to D——?"

"I do," said Mr. W. coldly. "I said so when you first stopped, and you ought to have pushed on, like a prudent man. You could have reached there before it was quite dark."

"But I was cold and hungry, and might have fainted by the way."

His manner of saying this touched the farmer's feelings a little.

"You have warmed and fed me, for which I am thankful. Will you now bestow another act of kindness upon one in a strange place, who if he goes out into the darkness, may lose himself and perish in the cold?"

The particular form in which this request was made, and the tone in which it was uttered, put it out of the farmer's heart to say no.

"Go in there and sit down," he answered, pointing to

the kitchen, "and I will see my wife and hear what she says."

And Mr. W. went into the parlor where the supper table stood, covered with snow-white cloth, and displaying his wife's set of blue-sprigged china, that was brought out only on special occasions.

The tall mold candles were burning thereon, and on the hearth blazed a cheerful fire.

"Has n't that old fellow gone yet?" asked Mrs. W. She heard his voice as he returned from the door.

"No, and what do you suppose, he wants us to let him stay all night."

"Indeed, we will do no such thing. We cannot have the likes of him in the house now. Where could he sleep?"

"Not in the best room, even if Mr. N. did not come."

"No, indeed!"

"But really I do n't see, Jane, how we can turn him out of doors. He does n't look like a strong man, and it's full three miles to D——."

"It's too much; he ought to have gone on while he had daylight, and not lingered here, as he did, till it got dark."

"We can't turn him out of doors, Jane, and it's no use to think of it. He'll have to stay somehow."

"But what can we do with him?"

"He seems like a decent man at least; and does n't look as if he had anything bad about him. We might make a bed on the floor."

When Mr. W. returned to the kitchen, where the stranger had seated himself before the fire, he informed him that he had decided to let him stay all night. The man expressed in few words his grateful sense of their kindness, and then became silent and thoughtful. Soon after the farmer's wife, giving up all hope of Mr. N.'s arrival, had supper taken up, which consisted of coffee, warm shortcake, and broiled chicken. After all was on the table, a short conference was held as to whether it would do not to invite the stranger to take supper. It was true they had given him as much bread and bacon as he could eat, but then, as long as he was going to stay all night, it looked too inhospitable to sit down to the table and not ask him to join them. So, making a virtue of necessity, he was kindly asked to come to supper—an invitation which he did not decline. Grace was said over the meal by Mr. W., and the coffee poured, and the bread helped, and the meat carved.

There was a fine little boy, six years old, at the table, who had been brightened up and dressed in his best, in order to grace the minister's reception. Charles was full of talk, and the parents felt a mutual pride in showing him off, even before their humble guest, who noticed him particularly, though he had not much to say. "Come, Charley," said Mr. W., after the meal was over, and he sat leaning in his chair, "can't you repeat the pretty hymn mamma taught you last Sabbath?"

Charley started off without any further invitation, and repeated very accurately two or three verses of a camp-meeting hymn, that was then popular.

"Now let us hear you say the commandments, Charley," spoke up the mother, well pleased with her son's performance.

And Charley repeated them with a little prompting.

"How many commandments are there?" asked the father.

The child hesitated, and then looking at the stranger, near whom he sat, said innocently:—

"How many are there?"

The man thought for some moments, and said, as if in doubt,

"Eleven, are there not?"

"Eleven!" ejaculated Mrs. W. in unfeigned surprise.

"Eleven?" said her husband with more rebuke than astonishment in his voice. "Is it possible, sir, that you do not know how many commandments there are? How many are there, Charley? Come, tell me—you know, of course."

"Ten," replied the child.

"Right, my son," returned Mr. W., looking with a smile of approval on the child. "Right, there is n't a child of his age in ten miles who can't tell you there are ten commandments."

"Did you ever read the Bible, sir?" addressing the stranger.

"When I was a boy I used to read it sometimes. But I am sure I thought that there were eleven commandments. Are you not mistaken about there being ten?"

Sister W. lifted her hands in unfeigned astonishment, and exclaimed:—

"Could any one believe it? such ignorance of the Bible!"

Mr. W. did not reply, but rose, and going to the corner of the room where the good book lay upon the stand, he put it on the table before him, and opened to that portion in which the commandments are recorded.

"There," he said, placing his finger upon the proof of the stranger's error, "There, look for yourself."

The man came around from his side of the table and looked over the stranger's shoulder.

"There, do'ye see?"

"Yes, it does say so," replied the man, "and yet it seems to me there are eleven. I'm sure I always thought so."

"Doesn't it say ten here?" inquired **Mr. W.** with marked impatience in his voice.

"It does, certainly."

"Well, what more do you want? Can't you believe the Bible?"

"Oh, yes, I believe the Bible; and yet it strikes me somehow that there must be eleven commandments. Hasn't one been added somewhere else?"

Now this was too much for Brother and Sister W. to bear. Such ignorance of sacred matters they felt to be unpardonable. A long lecture followed, in which the man was scolded, admonished, and threatened with divine indignation. At its close he modestly asked if he might have the Bible to read for an hour or two before retiring for the night. This request was granted with more pleasure than any of the preceding ones.

Shortly after supper the man was conducted to the little spare room, accompanied by the Bible. Before leaving him alone, Mr. W. felt it to be his duty to exhort him to spirit-

CHRIST BLESSING LITTLE CHILDREN

ual things, and he did so most earnestly for ten or fifteen minutes. But he could not see that his words made much impression, and he finally left his guest, lamenting his obduracy and ignorance.

In the morning he came down, and meeting Mr. W., asked if he would be so kind as to lend him a razor, that he might remove his beard, which did not give his face a very attractive appearance. His request was complied with.

" We will have prayers in about ten minutes," said Mr. W., as he handed him the razor and shaving box.

The man appeared and behaved with due propriety at family worship. After breakfast he thanked the farmer and his wife for their hospitality, and parting went on his journey.

Ten o'clock came, but Mr. N. had not arrived. So Mr. and Mrs. W. started for the meeting-house, not doubting they would find him there. But they were disappointed. A goodly number of people were inside the meeting-house, and a goodly number outside, but the minister had not arrived.

" Where is Mr. N——?" inquired a dozen voices, as a crowd gathered around the farmer.

" He has n't come yet. Something has detained him. But I still look for him—indeed, I fully expected to find him here."

The day was cold, and Mr. W., after becoming thoroughly chilled, concluded to keep a good lookout for the minister from the window near which he usually sat. Others, from the same cause, followed his example, and the little meeting-house was soon filled, and one after another came dropping in. The farmer, who turned towards the door each time it was opened, was a little surprised to see his guest of the previous evening enter, and come slowly down the aisle, looking on either side, as if searching for a vacant seat, very few of which were now left. Still advancing, he finally got within the little enclosed altar, and ascended to the pulpit, took off his old grey overcoat and sat down.

By this time Mr. W. was by his side, and had his hand upon his arm.

"You must n't sit here. Come down and I will show you a seat," he said, in an excited tone.

"Thank you," replied the man in a composed voice. "It is very comfortable here." And the man remained immovable.

Mr. W., feeling embarrassed, went down, intending to get a brother "official" to assist him in making a forcible ejection of the man from the place he was desecrating. Immediately upon his doing so, however, the man rose, and standing up at the desk, opened the hymn-book. His voice thrilled to the finger ends of Brother W. as in a distinct and impressive manner he gave out the hymn beginning:

> "Help us to help each other, Lord,
>     Each other's cross to bear;
>   Let each his friendly aid afford,
>     And feel a brother's care."

The congregation rose, after the stranger had read the entire hymn, and had repeated the first two lines for them to sing. Brother W. usually started the tunes. He tried this time, but went off on a long meter tune. Discovering his mistake at the second word, he balked and tried it again, but now he stumbled on short meter. A musical brother came to his aid and led off with a tune that suited the measure in which the hymn was written. After singing, the congregation knelt, and the minister—for no one doubted his real character—addressed the throne of grace with much fervor and eloquence. The reading of a chapter in the Bible succeeded. Then there was a deep pause throughout the room in anticipation of the text, which the preacher prepared to announce.

The dropping of a pin might have been heard. Then the fine, emphatic tones of the preacher filled the room:—

*"A new commandment I give unto you, that* ye *love one another."*

Brother W. had bent forward to listen, but now he sunk back in his seat. This was the eleventh commandment.

The sermon was deep, searching, yet affectionate and impressive. The preacher uttered nothing that could in the least wound the brother and sister of whose hospitality he had partaken, but he said much that smote upon their hearts, and made them painfully conscious that they had not shown as much kindness to the stranger as he had been entitled to receive on the broad principles of humanity. But they suffered more from mortification of feeling. To think that they had treated the presiding elder of the district after such a fashion was deeply humiliating; and the idea of the whole affair getting abroad interfered sadly with their devotional feelings throughout the whole period of service.

At last the sermon was over, the ordinance administered

and the benediction pronounced.   Brother W. did not know
what was best for him to do.   He never was more at a loss
in his life.   Then Mr. N. descended from the pulpit; but
he did not step forward to meet him.   How could he do
that?   Others gathered around him, but still he lingered
and held back.

"Where is Brother W.?" he at length heard asked.   It
was the voice of the minister.

"Here he is," said one or two, opening the way to
where the farmer stood.

The preacher advanced, and catching his hand, said:—

"How do you do, Brother W., I am glad to see you.
And where is Sister W.?"

Sister W. was brought forward, and the preacher shook
hands with them heartily, while his face was lit up with
smiles.

"I believe I am to find a home with you," he said, as
if it was settled.

Before the still embarrassed brother and sister could
make reply, some one asked:—

"How came you to be detained so late?   You were expected last night.   And where is Brother R.?"

"Brother R. is sick," replied Mr. N., "and I had to
come alone.   Five miles from this my horse gave out, and
I had to come the rest of the way on foot.   But I became
so cold and weary, that I found it necessary to ask a farmer
not far from here, to give me a night's lodging, which he
was kind enough to do.   I thought I was still three miles
off, but it happened that I was very much nearer my journey's end than I supposed."

This explanation was satisfactory to all parties, and in due time the congregation dispersed, and the presiding elder went home with Brother and Sister W

## THE TEN COMMANDMENTS.

### I

THOU shalt have no other gods before me.

### II

Thou shalt not make unto thee any graven image, or any likeness of any thing that is in heaven above, or that is in the earth beneath, or that is in the water under the earth: thou shalt not bow down thyself to them, nor serve them: for I the Lord thy God am a jealous God, visiting the iniquity of the fathers upon the children unto the third and fourth generation of them that hate me; and showing mercy unto thousands of them that love me, and keep my commandments.

### III

Thou shalt not take the name of the Lord thy God in vain; for the Lord will not hold him guiltless that taketh his name in vain.

### IV

Remember the Sabbath day, to keep it holy.   Six days shalt thou labor, and do all thy work; but the seventh day is the Sabbath of the Lord thy God: in it thou shalt not do any work, thou, nor thy son, nor thy daughter, thy manservant, nor thy maidservant, nor thy cattle, nor thy stranger that is within thy gates: for in six days the Lord made heaven and earth, the sea, and all that in them is, and rested the seventh day: wherefore the Lord blessed the Sabbath day, and hallowed it.

6

### V

Honor thy father and thy mother: that thy days may be long upon the land which the Lord thy God giveth thee.

### VI

Thou shalt not kill.

### VII

Thou shalt not commit adultery.

### VIII

Thou shalt not steal.

### IX

Thou shalt not bear false witness against thy neighbor.

### X

Thou shalt not covet thy neighbor's house, thou shalt not covet thy neighbor's wife, nor his manservant, nor his maidservant, nor his ox, nor his ass, nor any thing that is thy neighbor's.

# Make It Plain.

ON the sixteenth day after the battle of Gettysburg, I entered the room where a young wounded colonel was apparently near to death. As I entered, he was roused from his stupor and beckoned me to his bedside, and threw his feeble arms around my neck.

"O my father, how glad I am to see you. I was afraid you would not come till it was too late. I am too feeble to say much, though I have a great many things to say to you; you must do all the talking. Tell me all about dear mother and sister."

I soon perceived by the appearance of those in the house, that there was no hope entertained of his recovery. But as I could no longer endure the agony of suspense, I at last inquired of the doctor, "Doctor, what do you think of my son's case?"

"Entirely hopeless."

"But is there nothing more that can be done to save him?"

"No, sir. Every thing that human skill and kindness can do has been done. Your son has been a brave and very successful officer; has been a great favorite in the army; has won the highest esteem of all who have known him, but he now must die. Immediately after the amputation the gangrene set in, and defies all efforts to arrest it."

83

"Well, Doctor, how long do you think he can live?"

"Not more than four days. He may drop away at any hour. We are constantly fearing that an artery will give way, and then it is all over with the colonel. What you wish to do in reference to his death, you had better do at once."

"Have you, or has any one, told him of his real condition?"

"No. We have left that painful duty for you to do, as we have been expecting your arrival for several days."

As I entered the room with the dreadful message of death pressing on my heart, the eyes of my son fastened on me.

"Come, sit by my side, father. Have you been talking with the doctor about me?"

"Yes."

"What did he tell you? Does he think I shall recover?"

There was a painful hesitation for a moment.

"Don't be afraid to tell me just what he said."

"He told me you must die."

"How long does he think I can live?"

"Not to exceed four days, and that you may drop away any hour,—that an artery may slough at any moment which you cannot survive."

With great agitation he exclaimed,

"Father, is that so? Then I must die! I cannot. I must not die! Oh! I am not prepared to die now. Do tell me how I can get ready? Make it so plain that I can get hold of it.. Tell me, in a few words, if you can, so that

I can see it plainly. I know you can, father, for I used to hear you explain it to others."

'T was no time now for tears, but for calmness and light, by which to lead the soul to Christ, and both were given.

"My son, I see you are afraid to die."

"Yes, I am."

"Well, I suppose you feel guilty."

"Yes, that is it. I have been a wicked young man. You know how it is in the army."

"You want to be forgiven, don't you?"

"Oh, yes! That is what I want. Can I be, father?"

"Certainly."

"Can I know it before I die?"

"Certainly."

"Well now, father, make it so plain that I can get hold of it."

At once, an incident which occurred during the school days of my son, came to my mind. I had not thought of it before for several years. Now it came back to me, fresh with its interest, and just what was wanted to guide the agitated heart of this young inquirer to Jesus.

"Do you remember while at school in —— you came home one day, and I having occasion to rebuke you, you became very angry and abused me with harsh language?"

"Yes, father, I was thinking it all over a few days ago, as I thought of your coming to see me, and felt so bad about it, that I wanted to see you, and once more ask you to forgive me."

"Do you remember, how, after the paroxysm of your anger had subsided, you came in, and threw your arms around my neck, and said, 'My dear father, I am sorry I abused you so. It was not your loving son that did it. I was very angry. Won't you forgive me?'"

"Yes, I remember it very distinctly."

"Do you remember what I said to you as you wept upon my neck?"

"Very well. You said, 'I forgive you with all my heart,' and kissed me. I shall never forget those words."

"Did you believe me?"

"Certainly. I never doubted your word."

"Did you then feel happy again?"

"Yes, perfectly; and since that time I have loved you more than ever before. I shall never forget how it relieved me when you looked upon me so kindly, and said, 'I forgive you with all my heart.'"

"Well, now, this is just the way to come to Jesus. Tell him you are sorry just as you told me, and ten thousand times quicker than a father's love forgave you, will he forgive you. He says he will. Then you must take his word for it, just as you did mine."

"Why, father, is this the way to become a Christian?"

"I don't know of any other."

"Why, father, I can get hold of this. I am so glad you have come to tell me how."

He turned his head upon his pillow for rest. I sank into my chair and wept freely, for my heart could no longer suppress its emotions. I had done my work, and committed the case to Christ. He, too, I was soon assured had done his. The broken heart had made its confession, had heard what it longed for, "I forgive you," and believed it. It was but a few moments of silence, but the new creation had taken place, the broken heart had made its short, simple prayer, and believed, and the new heart had been given.  A soul had passed out from nature's darkness into marvelous light, and from the power of sin and Satan unto God

I soon felt the nervous hand on my head, and heard the word "father," in such a tone of tenderness and joy, that I knew the change had come.

"Father, my dear father, I don't want you to weep any more, you need not.  I am perfectly happy now.  Jesus has forgiven me.  I know he has, for he says so, and I take his word for it, just as I did yours.  Wipe your tears.  I am not afraid to die now.  If it is God's will, I should like to live to serve my country, and take care of you and mother, but if I must die, I am not afraid to now, Jesus has forgiven me.  Come, father, let us sing,—

"'When I can read my title clear,'"

And we did sing.

"Now, father, I want you should pray, and I will follow you."

We did pray, and Jesus heard us.

"Father, I am very happy.  Why, I believe I shall get well.  I feel much better."

From that hour all his symptoms changed—pulse went down, and countenance brightened.  The current of life had changed.

The doctor soon came in and found him cheerful and happy—looked at him—felt his pulse, which he had been watching with intense anxiety, and said,—

"Why, Colonel, you look better."

"I am better, Doctor.   I am going to get well.   My
father has told me how to become a Christian, and I am
very happy.   I believe I shall recover, for God has heard
my prayer.   Doctor, I want you should become a Christian,
too.   My father can tell you how to get hold of it."

In the evening three surgeons were in consultation, but
saw no hope in the case, and one of them took his final
leave of the colonel.

Next morning the two surgeons, who had been in constant attendance, came in and began as usual to dress the
wound.

On opening the bandage, they suddenly drew back, and
throwing up their arms, exclaimed,—

"Great God, this is a miracle!   The gangrene is ar-
rested, and the colonel will live!   God has heard your
prayers!"

"Why, Doctor," replied the colonel, ' I told you yesterday, that I believed I should get well, for I asked Jesus
that I might live to do some good.   I knew he heard my
prayer, and now you see he has.   Bless the Lord with me,
Doctor."

Meanwhile, *"Our son must die,"* had gone over the
wires, and made sadness at home.   Next day, *"Our son will
live, and is happy in Christ,"* followed, and joy came again
to the loved ones.

After his recovery, the colonel returned to the people
whose sons he had led with honor through fifteen hard-
fought battles.   They, in return, gave him the best office
in the gift of a loyal and grateful people.   Among them he
now lives in prosperity and honor, he is a member of the

church of Christ, and the father of a happy family growing up around him, and consecrated to the service of his Redeemer.

I, too, was made a better man and better minister by that scene, where this dear son, struggling with his guilt and fear of death, was led to Jesus, and found the pardon of his sins. I there resolved never to forget that charge he made me, in his extremity: *"Make it so plain that I can get hold of it."*

I have made this the motto of every sermon I have preached, and God has blessed the effort.

### A CHRISTIAN LIFE.

" A CHRISTIAN life, have you ever thought
　How much is in that name?
A life like Christ, and all he taught
　We must follow, to be the same.

How little of ease the Saviour knew
　With his life of labor and love!
And if we would walk in his footsteps too,
　We must look not to earth, but above.

The darkest hour the Christian knows
　Is just before the dawn;
For as the night draws to its close,
　It will bring in the morn.

So if you trust, though shadows fall,
　And dark your pathway be,
The light, which shines from heaven for all,
　Will surely fall on thee."

# A RETIRED MERCHANT

A LONDON merchant engaged in Mediterranean commerce, had successfully prosecuted his business, and amassed what all merchants desire, an ample fortune. His, indeed, was a princely one. He had purchased a large and beautiful estate in the country, and had built and furnished a splendid mansion in town, on the Surrey side of the river, and now that he was verging towards sixty, he concluded to retire and enjoy the remnant of his life in peaceful leisure.

He negotiated for the sale of his abundance-making business, and sold it for another fortune. He then retired. He was a bachelor. He had his halls, his parlors, dining-rooms, and drawing-rooms, his library and cabinets of curiosities. The floors were covered with the most mosaic specimens of Brussels and Turkey carpetings, the furniture was of the most complete and exquisite selections, the walls were adorned with splendid mirrors and with classic paintings, and fine linen decorated all.

Carriages, horses, grooms, and servants were at his com-

mand.   Books, pictures, and engravings were at hand to interest him.   The daily and the weekly papers, and the
periodicals, brought to his table all the news of the great
world, and his friends and his acquaintances paid him homage.   How happy must the man be who has all this!

*He* was not happy.   He had no aim, no motive.   The
zest with which he read the papers when he was a merchant,
he had lost now he had ceased to be engaged in commerce.
A storm, a fleet, a pestilence along the Mediterranean
shores, was full of interest to him before, because he had
investments there.   Now, they were of no consequence to
him.   The views and aims of government were watched by
him before with searching scrutiny, because his destiny was
bound up with theirs.   The parliamentary debates were of
the greatest consequence before, as indicating British policy ,
but that to him now ceased to be an object of importance.
His fortune was achieved, his course was run, his destiny
fulfilled.

Soon, every thing and place appeared to him one uni-
form and universal blank.   His beautiful apartments were
unused, his carriage and horses unemployed, his books un-
read, his papers unopened, his meals untasted, and his
clothes unworn.   He had lost all enjoyment of life, and con-
templated suicide.

Saturday night arrived, and he resolved on Sunday
morning early, before the busy populace were stirring, he
would make his way to Waterloo bridge and jump into the
river, or tumble off.

At three o'clock, he set out on his final expedition, and
had nearly reached the bridge, the shadows of the night

protecting him from observation, when a figure stood before him. Amazed at being seen by any one, he turned out of the path, when the figure crouching low before him, revealed a tattered, miserable man, baring his head in abjectness.

"What are you doing here?" inquired the retired merchant.

"I have a wife and family, whom I can't help from starving, and I am afraid to go and see them. Last night I knew they would be turned into the streets," replied the man.

"Take that," replied the merchant, giving him his purse, with gold and silver in it—thinking to himself, "how much more useful this will be to him, than in my pockets in the water."

"God bless you, sir—God bless you, sir," exclaimed the man several times, kneeling before the astonished merchant.

"Stop," said the merchant, "do not overwhelm me so with your thanksgivings—but tell me where you live."

"In Lambeth, sir."

"Then why are you *here* this morning?" said the merchant.

"I do not like to tell you," said the man. "I am ashamed to tell a gentleman like you."

"Why so?" replied the merchant.

"Well, sir," replied the man, "as I had not a single penny, and did not know how to get one, I came here to drown myself, although I knew 't was wicked!"

The merchant was astonished and appalled, and after a long silence, said, "Sir, I am overwhelmed with wealth, and yet I am so miserable that I came here this morning for the same purpose as yourself. There's something more in this than I can understand at present. Let me go with you to see your family."

The man made every excuse to hinder the merchant, but he would go.

"Have you lost your character?" said the merchant.

"No, sir," replied the man, "but I am so miserably poor and wretched—and, for anything I know, my wife and children may be turned into the street."

"Why are you out of work and pay?" resumed the merchant.

"I used to groom the horses of the stage-coaches," said the man, "but since the railroads are come up the coaches are put down, and many men, like me, have no employ-ment."

They plodded on their way, two miles of brick and mortar piled on either side. At last they came to a third-rate house, when a rough, common looking woman opened the door and shutter. As soon as she saw the man, she let loose her tongue upon him for all the villainy in the world, but something which passed from his hand to hers hushed her in an instant; and observing the merchant, she courte-sied to him civilly.

The man ran up-stairs, leaving the merchant and woman together, which gave the former an opportunity to make in-quiries. Having satisfied himself that want was the crime of the family, he told the woman who he was, promised to see her paid, and induced her to set on and cook a break-fast for the family, and supply them with any thing which they needed.

The man returned, and the merchant went up-stairs to see, for the first time, the wretched family in rags, dirt, and misery. He comforted them with hope of better days, and bidding the man take a hasty meal below, took him with him, and helped with his own hands to load a cart with bed, bedding, clothes, furniture, and food for the family.

The man was gone, and the merchant for the first moment, reflected on all that had passed. He was relieved of his misery by doing something for another, and out of mere selfishness he resolved on doing good to others, to prevent the necessity for drowning himself.

He employed the man in his stable, removed the family near, and placed them in a cottage, sending the children to school. Soon he sought out misery to relieve, and was led to consider the cause of all misery—sin. He turned to God and found him, and sought to turn his fellow sinners.

He aided every good word and work, and was the humble teller of his own humbling story. He had been a merchantman seeking goodly pearls, and having found the pearl of great price, he went and sold all that he had, and bought it ; and the retired earthly merchant became an active heavenly merchant.

> " BETTER the valley with peace and love
>   Than the desolate heights some souls attain;
> Lonely is life on the hills above
>   The valley lands and the sunny plain.
> What is fame to love? Can it satisfy
>   The longing and lonely hearts of men?
> On the heights they must hunger and starve and die,
>   Come back to the valley of peace again ! "

# EFFECT *of* NOVEL READING

ON the romantic borders of a beautiful river, in one of our Northern States, there is situated an elegant mansion. Spacious grounds surround the dwelling, and, what is not usual in this country, it has a terraced garden. This is a hill, situated at the side of the house, presenting a mass of living verdure. You ascend gradually, step by step, each platform, as it were, richly embroidered with brilliant flowers.

In this retreat of elegance and retirement, lived Mr. and Mrs. M., their daughter, and a French governess. No expense or labor had been spared to make this daughter an accomplished woman; but not one thought was ever bestowed upon the immortal interests of her soul. At the age of sixteen, she was beautiful and intelligent, but utterly destitute of all religious principle. Enthusiastically fond of reading, she roamed her father's spacious library, and selected whatever books best pleased her. Of an imaginative turn, earnest and impassioned, hers was the very mind that

95

required the strong, controlling hand of a matured judgment. Yet it was left to feed at will upon the poisoned
fruits that lie scattered around. She naturally turned to
the novels that stored the library shelves; and at sixteen
was as much at home in the pages of Bulwer as she was in
her French grammar. The ridiculous romances of Mrs.
Radcliffe were laid aside with disgust, and Bulwer, James,
and others, took their place. But she descended a step,
many steps lower, and, supplied by the governess, eagerly
devoured the very worst fictions of Eugene Sue and George
Sand. Next she was heard discussing and excusing the
most heinous crimes of which human nature can be guilty.

Her parents heard with horror her freely expressed
sentiments, and wondered where she had inhaled such lax
ideas. They never thought of looking into her library for
the cause, or at the unprincipled governess. The poison
began to do its work; she could no longer live this tame
life; she must have something more exciting, more exhilarating. The resolution was formed; with a beating heart she
collected her mother's jewels; took one long look at her indulgent parents; bade a silent farewell to the scenes of her
happy childhood, and left the house forever. No warning
voice implored her to return; no hand was stretched out to
save. On, on she went, until she reached the far-off city.
Its lights dazzled her, its noise confused her, but she never
regretted the peaceful home she had so culpably deserted.
Her plan was to go on the stage, and become a renowned
actress, like the heroine of one of her French novels. But
this was not so easily achieved as she imagined; and after
a most unsuccessful attempt, she was compelled to act only

in subordinate parts. She had lost home, happiness, and respectability, and had not gained that fame for which she had sacrificed so much.

But it would be too painful to follow her through all her wretched life, and tell how each succeeding year she grew more degraded and more miserable, until at length having run a fearful career of vice she sank into a dishonored and early grave. No mother's hand wiped the cold death-dew from her brow; no kind voice whispered hope and consolation. Alone, poor, degraded, utterly unrepentant, she will appear before the judgment-seat of Christ; we pause; for we dare not follow it further.

The sound of her name never echoed through the halls of her childhood. Her father, stern and silent, buried all memories of his guilty child deep within his heart; whilst the mother, wan, broken-hearted, hopeless, wept in secret those tears of bitter agony whose fountain was perpetually welling afresh.

It is "to point a moral" that we have opened these annals of the past; and we would have the young ponder well the lesson that this history teaches. There *is* a danger in novel reading; it vitiates the taste, enervates the understanding, and destroys all inclination for spiritual enjoyment. The soul that is bound in fetters of this habit, *cannot* rise to the contemplation of heavenly things. It has neither the inclination nor the power. We knew one, who, even with death in view, turned with loathing away from the only Book that could bring her peace and salvation, to feed greedily on the pages of a foolish romance. It matters not that some of the finest minds have given their powers

to this style of writing; that bright gems of intellect flash
along their pages.   The danger is so much the greater; for
the jewels scattered by Genius, blind even while they dazzle.
"Some of the greatest evils of my life," said a remarkable
woman, "I trace to the eager perusal of what are called
'well-written novels.'   I lived in a world of delusion.   I
had no power to separate the false from the real.   My Bible
lay covered with dust; I had no desire for its pages."   Oh,
then, if the young would reach a heavenly haven; if they
would be guided unto "the still waters" of everlasting bliss,
let them avoid the dangerous rock of novel reading, upon
which so many souls have been shipwrecked and utterly
lost.

### TO-DAY'S FURROW.

Sow the shining seeds of service
  In the furrows of each day,
Plant each one with serious purpose,
  In a hopeful, tender way.
Never lose one seed, nor cast it
  Wrongly with an hurried hand;
Take full time to lay it wisely,
  Where and how thy God hath planned.

This the blessed way of sharing
  With another soul your gains,
While, though losing life, you find it
  Yielding fruit on golden plains;
For the soul which sows its blessings
  Great or small, in word or smile,
Gathers as the Master promised,
  Either here or afterwhile.

# Be Just Before Generous.

**M**Y friend Peyton was what is called a "fine, generous fellow." He valued money only as a means of obtaining what he desired, and was always ready to spend it with an acquaintance for mutual gratification. Of course, he was a general favorite. Every one spoke well of him, and few hesitated to give his ears the benefit of their good opinion. I was first introduced to him when he was in the neighborhood of twenty-two years of age. Peyton was then a clerk in the receipt of six hundred dollars a year. He grasped my hand with an air of frankness and sincerity, that at once installed him in my good opinion. A little pleasure excursion was upon the tapis, and he insisted on my joining it. I readily consented. There were five of us, and the expense to each, if borne mutually, would have been something like one dollar. Peyton managed everything, even to paying the bills; and when I offered to pay him my proportion, he said:—

"No, no!"—pushing back my hand—"nonsense!"

"Yes; but I must insist upon meeting my share of the expense."

"Not a word more. The bill's settled, and you need n't trouble your head about it," was his reply; and he seemed half offended when I still urged upon him to take my por, tion of the cost.

"What a fine, generous fellow Peyton is!" said one of the party to me, as we met the next day.

"Did he also refuse to let you share in the expense of our excursion?" I asked.

"After what he said to you, I was afraid of offending him by proposing to do so."

"He certainly is generous—but, I think, to a fault, if I saw a fair specimen of his generosity yesterday."

"We should be just, as well as generous."

"I never heard that he was not just."

"Nor I. But I think he was not just to himself. And I believe it will be found to appear in the end, that, if we are not just to ourselves, we will, somewhere in life, prove unjust to others. I think that his salary is not over twelve dollars a week. If he bore the whole expense of our pleasure excursion, it cost him within a fraction of half his earnings for a week. Had we all shared alike, it would not have been a serious matter to any of us."

"Oh! as to that, it is no very serious matter to him. He will never think of it."

"But, if he does so very frequently, he may *feel* it sooner or later," I replied.

"I'm sure I don't know anything about that," was returned. "He is a generous fellow, and I cannot but like him. Indeed, every one likes him."

Some days afterwards I fell in with Peyton again, and, in order to retaliate a little, invited him to go and get some refreshments with me. He consented. When I put my hand in my pocket to pay for them, his hand went into his. But I was too quick for him. He seemed uneasy about it.

He could feel pleased while giving, but it evidently worried him to be the recipient.

From that time, for some years, I was intimate with the young man. I found that he set no true value upon money. He spent it freely with every one; and every one spoke well of him. "What a generous, whole-souled fellow he is!" or, "What a noble heart he has!" were the expressions constantly made in regard to him. While "Mean, stingy fellow!" and other such epithets, were unsparingly used in speaking of a quiet, thoughtful young man, named Merwin, who was clerk with him in the same store. Merwin appeared to set a due value upon time and money. He rarely indulged himself in any way, and it was with difficulty that he could every be induced to join in any pleasures that involved much expense. But I always observed that when he did so, he was exact about paying his proportion.

About two years after my acquaintance with Peyton began, an incident let me deeper into the character and quality of his generosity. I called one day at the house of a poor widow woman who washed for me, to ask her to do up some clothes, extra to the usual weekly washing. I thought she looked as if she were in trouble about something, and said so to her.

It's very hard, at best," she replied, "for a poor woman, with four children to provide for, to get along, if she has to depend upon washing and ironing for a living. But when so many neglect to pay her regularly"—

"Neglect to pay their washerwoman!" I said, in a tone of surprise, interrupting her.

"Oh, yes. Many do that!"

"Who?"

"Dashing young men, who spend their money freely, are too apt to neglect these little matters, as they call them."

"And do young men for whom you work really neglect to pay you?"

"Some do. There are at least fifteen dollars now owed to me, and I do n't know which way to turn to get my last month's rent for my landlord, who has been after it three times this week already. Mr. Peyton owes me ten dollars and I can't "—

"Mr. Peyton? It can't be possible!"

"Yes, it is though. He used to be one of the most punctual young men for whom I washed. But lately he never has any money."

"He's a very generous-hearted young man."

"Yes, I know he is," she replied. "But something is wrong with him. He looks worried whenever I ask him for money; and sometimes speaks as if half angry with me for troubling him. There's Mr. Merwin—I wish all were like him. I have never yet taken home his clothes, that I did n't find the money waiting for me, exact to a cent. He counts every piece when he lays out his washing for me, and knows exactly what it will come to; and then, if he happens to be out, the change is always left with the chambermaid. It's a pleasure to do anything for him."

"He is n't liked generally so well as Mr. Peyton is," said I.

"Is n't he? It's strange!" the poor woman returned, innocently.

On the very next day, I saw Peyton riding out with an acquaintance in a buggy.

"Who paid for your ride yesterday?" I said to the latter, with whom I was quite familiar, when next we met.

"Oh, Peyton, of course. He always pays, you know. He's a fine, generous fellow. I wish there were more like him."

"That you might ride out for nothing a little oftener, hey?"

My friend colored slightly."

"No, not that," said he. "But you know there is so much selfishness in the world; we hardly ever meet a man who is willing to make the slightest sacrifice for the good of others."

"True. And I suppose it is this very selfishness that makes us so warmly admire a man like Mr. Peyton, who is willing to gratify us at his own charge. It's a pleasant thing to ride out and see the country, but we are apt to think twice about the cost before we act once. But if some friend will only stand the expense, how generous and whole-souled we think him! It is the same in everything else. We like the enjoyment, but can't afford the expense; and he is a generous, fine-hearted fellow, who will squander his money in order to gratify us. Isn't that it, my friend?"

He looked half convinced, and a little sheepish, to use an expressive Saxonism.

On the evening succeeding this day, Peyton sat alone in his room, his head leaning upon his hand, and his brow contracted. There was a tap at his door. "Come in." A poorly clad, middle-aged woman entered. It was his washerwoman.

The lines on the young man's brow became deeper.

"Can't you let me have some money, Mr. Peyton? My landlord is pressing hard for his rent, and I cannot pay him until you pay me."

"Really, Mrs. Lee, it is quite impossible just now. I am entirely out of money. But my salary will be due in three weeks, and then I will pay you up the whole. You must make your landlord wait until that time. I am very sorry to put you to this trouble. But it will never happen again."

The young man really did feel sorry, and expressed it in his face as well as in the tone of his voice.

"Can't you let me have one or two dollars, Mr. Peyton? I am entirely out of money."

"It is impossible—I haven't a shilling left. But try to wait three weeks, and then it will all come to you in a lump, and do you a great deal more good than if you had it a dollar at a time."

Mrs. Lee retired slowly, and with a disappointed air. The young man sighed heavily as she closed the door after her. He had been too generous, and now he could not be just. The buggy in which he had driven out with his friend on that day had cost him his last two dollars—a sum which would have lightened the heart of his poor washerwoman.

"The fact is, my salary is too small," said he, rising and walking about his room uneasily. "It is not enough to support me. If the account were fully made up, tailor's bill, bootmaker's bill, and all, I dare say I should find myself at least three hundred dollars in debt."

Merwin received the same salary that he did, and was

just three hundred dollars ahead. He dressed as well, owed no man a dollar, and was far happier. It is true, he was not called a "fine, generous fellow," by persons who took good care of their own money, while they were very willing to enjoy the good things of life at a friend's expense. But he did not mind this. The want of such a reputation did not disturb his mind very seriously.

After Mrs. Lee had been gone half an hour, Peyton's door was flung suddenly open. A young man, bounding in, with extended hand came bustling up to him.

"Ah, Peyton, my fine fellow! How are you? how are you?" And he shook Peyton's hand quite vigorously.

"Hearty!—and how are you, Freeman?"

"Oh, gay as a lark. I have come to ask a favor of you."

"Name it."

"I want fifty dollars."

Peyton shrugged his shoulders.

"I must have it, my boy? I never yet knew you to desert a friend, and I don't believe you will do so now."

"Suppose I haven't fifty dollars?"

"You can borrow it for me. I only want it for a few days. You shall have it back on next Monday. Try for me—there's a generous fellow!"

"There's a generous fellow," was irresistible. It came home to Peyton in the right place. He forgot poor Mrs. Lee, his unpaid tailor's bill, and sundry other troublesome accounts.

"If I can get an advance of fifty dollars on my salary to-morrow, you shall have it."

"Thank you! thank you! I knew I shouldn't have to ask twice when I called upon Henry Peyton. It always does me good to grasp the hand of such a man as you are."

On the next day, an advance of fifty dollars was asked and obtained. This sum was lent as promised. In two weeks, the individual who borrowed it was in New Orleans, from whence he had the best of reasons for not wishing to return to the North. Of course, the generous Henry Peyton lost his money.

An increase of salary to a thousand dollars only made him less careful of his money. Before, he lived as freely as if his income had been one-third above what it was; now, he increased his expenses in like ratio. It was a pleasure to him to spend his money—not for himself alone, but among his friends.

It is no cause of wonder, that in being so generous to some, he was forced to be unjust to others. He was still behindhand with his poor washerwoman—owed for boarding, clothes, hats, boots, and a dozen other matters—and was, in consequence, a good deal harrassed with duns. Still, he was called by some of his old cronies, "a fine, generous fellow." A few were rather colder in their expressions. He had borrowed money from them, and did not offer to return it, and he was such a generous-minded young man, that they felt a delicacy about calling his attention to it.

"Can you raise two thousand dollars?" was asked of him by a friend, when he was twenty-seven years old. "If you can, I know a first-rate chance to get into business."

"Indeed! What is the nature of it?"

The friend told him all he knew, and he was satisfied

that a better offering might never present itself.    But two thousand dollars were indispensable.

"Can't you borrow it?" suggested the friend.

" I will try."

" Try your best.    You will never again have such an opportunity."

Peyton did try, but in vain.    Those who could lend it to him considered him "too good-hearted a fellow" to trust with money ; and he was forced to see that tide, which if he could have taken it at the flood, would have led him on to fortune, slowly and steadily recede.

To Merwin the same offer was made.    He had fifteen hundred dollars laid by, and easily procured the balance. No one was afraid to trust him with money.

"What a fool I have been!" was the mental exclamation of Peyton, when he learned that his fellow-clerk had been able, with his own earnings, on a salary no larger than his own, to save enough to embrace the golden opportunity which he was forced to pass by.    " They call Merwin *mean* and *selfish*—and I am called a *generous fellow*.    That means, he has acted like a wise man, and I like a fool, I suppose.    I know him better than they do.    He is neither mean nor selfish, but careful and prudent, as I ought to have been.    His mother is poor, and so is mine.    Ah, me!" and the thought of his mother caused him to clasp both hands against his forehead.    " I believe two dollars of his salary have been sent weekly to his poor mother.    But I have never helped mine a single cent.    There is the mean man, and here is the generous one.    Fool! fool! wretch! He has fifteen hundred dollars ahead, after having sent his mother one hundred dollars a year for five or six years, and I am over five hundred dollars in debt. A fine, generous fellow, truly!"

The mind of Peyton was, as it should be, disturbed to its very center. His eyes were fairly opened, and he saw just where he stood, and what he was worth as a generous man.

"They have flattered my weakness," said he, bitterly, "to eat and drink and ride at my expense. It was very easy to say, 'how free-hearted he is,' so that I could hear them. A cheap way of enjoying the good things of life, verily! But the end of all this has come. One year from to-day, if I live, I will owe no man a dollar. My kind old mother, whom I have so long neglected, shall hear from me at once—ten dollars every month I dedicate to her. Come what will, nothing shall touch that. This agreement with myself I solemnly enter into in the sight of Heaven, and nothing shall tempt me to violate it."

"Are you going to ride out this afternoon, Peyton?" inquired a young friend, breaking in upon him at this moment.

"Yes, if you'll hire the buggy," was promptly returned.

"I can't afford that."

"Nor I either. How much is your salary?"

"Only a thousand."

"Just what mine is. If you can't, I am sure I cannot."

"Of course, you ought to be the best judge. I knew you rode out often, and liked company."

"Yes, I have done so; but that's past. I've been a 'fine, generous fellow' long enough to get into debt and

mar my prospects for life, perhaps; but I am going to assume a new character.   No doubt the very ones who have
had so many rides, oyster suppers, and theater tickets at
my expense, will all at once discover that I am as mean and
selfish as Merwin, who has refrained from not only injuri-
ous, expensive indulgences, but even denied himself many
innocent pleasures to save time and money for better purposes.   I now wish I had been as truly noble and generous
in the right direction as he has been."

Peyton went to work in the matter of reform in right
good earnest, but he found it hard work; old habits and inclinations were very strong.   Still he had some strength of
mind, and he brought this into as vigorous exercise as it
was possible for him to do, mainly with success, but sometimes with gentle lapses into self-indulgence.

His mother lived in a neighboring town, and was in
humble circumstances.   She supported herself by keeping
a shop for the sale of various little articles.   The old lady
sat behind her counter, one afternoon, sewing, and thinking
of her only son.

"Ah, me!" she sighed, "I thought Henry would have
done something for himself long before this; but he is a
wild, free-hearted boy, and spends everything as he goes."

"Here's a letter for you at last, Mrs. Peyton," said the
well-known voice of the postman, breaking in upon her just
at this moment.

With trembling hands, Mrs. Peyton broke the seal; a
bank-bill crumpled in her fingers as she opened the letter.
A portion of its contents read:—

"DEAR MOTHER: I have had some very serious thoughts

of late about my way of living. You know I never liked
to be considered mean; this led me to be, what seemed to
everybody, very generous. Everybody was pleased to eat,
and drink, and ride at my expense; but no one seemed inclined to let me do the same at his expense. I have been
getting a good salary for six or seven years, and for a part
of that time, as much as a thousand dollars. I am ashamed
to say that I have not a farthing laid by; nay, what is
worse, I owe a good many little bills. But, dear mother,
I think I have come fairly to my senses. I have come to a
resolution not to spend a dollar foolishly; thus far I have
been able to keep my promise to myself, and, by the help
of Heaven, I mean to keep it to the end. My first thought,
on seeing my folly, was of my shameful disregard to my
mother's condition. In this letter are ten dollars. Every
month you will receive from me a like sum—more, if you
need it. As soon as I can lay by a sufficient amount, I
will look around for some means of entering into business,
and, as soon after as possible, make provision for you, that
your last days may be spent in ease and comfort."

"God bless the dear boy!" exclaimed Mrs. Peyton,
dropping the letter, while the tears gushed from her eyes.
The happy mother wept long for joy. With her trembling
hand she wrote a reply, and urged him, by the tenderest
and most sacred considerations, to keep to his good resolutions.

At the end of a year Peyton examined his affairs and
found himself freed from debt; but for nearly one hundred
dollars of his wages he could not account. He puzzled
over it for two or three evenings, and made out over fifty
dollars spent foolishly.

"No doubt the rest will have to be passed to that account," said he at last, half angry with himself. "I'll have to watch closer than this. At the end of the next year, I'll not be in doubt about where one hundred dollars have gone"

It was but rarely, now, that you would hear the name of Peyton mentioned. Before, everybody said he was a "fine, generous fellow;" everybody praised him. Now, he seemed to be forgotten, or esteemed of little consideration He felt this; but he had started to accomplish a certain end, and he had sufficient strength of mind not to be driven from his course.

In a few years he entered into business and succeeded beyond his expectations. He provided a home for his mother, and no one who saw her during the remaining ten years of her life would have called her unhappy.

I know Peyton still. He is not now, by general reputation, "a fine, generous fellow." But he is a good and respected citizen, and was a good son while his mother lived with him. He has won the means of really benefiting others, and few are more willing than he is to do it, when it can be done in the right way. He is still "generous"— but wisely so.

### CONSOLATION.

"Unto those who sit in sorrow, God has sent this precious word:
Not an earnest prayer or impulse of the heart ascends unheard.
He who rides upon the tempest, heeds the sparrow when it falls,
And with mercies crowns the humblest, when before the throne he calls."

# CAUGHT in the QUICKSAND

VICTOR HUGO gives the following impressive description of a death in the quicksand off certain coasts of Brittany, or Scotland. He says:—

It sometimes happens that a man, traveler or fisherman, walking on the beach at low tide, far from the bank, suddenly notices that for several minutes he has been walking with some difficulty. The strand beneath his feet is like pitch; his soles stick to it; it is sand no longer—it is glue.

The beach is perfectly dry, but at every step he takes, as soon as he lifts his foot the print which it leaves fills with water. The eye, however, has noticed no change; the immense strand is smooth and tranquil; all the sand has the same appearance; nothing distinguishes the surface which is solid from that which is no longer so; the joyous little cloud of sand fleas continue to leap tumultuously over the wayfarer's feet. The man pursues his way, goes forward, inclines to the land, endeavors to get nearer the upland. He is not anxious. Anxious about what? Only he feels somehow as if the weight of his feet increases with every step he takes. Suddenly he sinks in.

He sinks in two or three inches. Decidedly he is not on the right road; he stops to take his bearings. All at once he looks at his feet. They have disappeared. The sand covers them. He draws them out of the sand; he will retrace his steps; he turns back; he sinks in deeper. The sand comes up to his ankles; he pulls himself out and throws himself to the left; the sand is half-leg deep. He throws himself to the right; the sand comes up to his shins. Then he recognizes with unspeakable terror that he is caught in the quicksand, and that he has beneath him the fearful medium in which man can no more walk than the fish can swim. He throws off his load if he has one, lightens himself like a ship in distress; it is already too late; the sand is above his knees. He calls, he waves his hat or his handkerchief; the sand gains on him more and more. If the beach is deserted, if the land is too far off, if there is no help in sight, it is all over.

He is condemned to that appalling burial, long, infallible, implacable, and impossible to slacken or to hasten, which endures for hours, which seizes you erect, free, and in full health, and which draws you by the feet, which at every effort that you make, at every shout you utter, drags you a little deeper, sinking you slowly into the earth while you look upon the horizon, the sails of the ships upon the sea, the birds flying and singing, the sunshine and the sky. The victim attempts to sit down, to lie down, to creep; every movement he makes inters him; he straightens up, he sinks in; he feels that he is being swallowed. He howls, implores, cries to the clouds, despairs.

Behold him waist deep in the sand. The sand reaches his breast; he is now only a bust. He raises his arm, utters furious groans, clutches the beach with his nails, would hold by that straw, leans upon his elbows to pull himself out of this soft sheath, sobs frenziedly; the sand rises. The sand reaches his shoulders; the sand reaches his neck; the face alone is visible now. The mouth cries, the sand fills it; silence. The eyes still gaze, the sand shuts them; night. Now the forehead decreases, a little hair flutters above the sand; a hand comes to the surface of the beach, moves, and shakes, and disappears. It is the earth-drowning man. The earth filled with the ocean becomes a trap. It presents itself like a plain, and opens like a wave.

Could anything more graphically describe the progress of a young man, from the first cup of wine to the last?

## "ONCE AGAIN."

Lord, in the silence of the night,
　Lord, in the turmoil of the day;
In time of rapture and delight,
　In hours of sorrow and dismay;
Yea, when my voice is filled with laughter,
　Yea, when my lips are thinned with pain;
For present joy, and joy hereafter,
　Lord, I would thank thee once again.

—*Elmer James Bailey.*

# "What Shall It Profit?"

**W**HY, Archie Allen, you are not ready for church yet; we shall surely be late," said the young wife as she entered the elegant library where her husband sat reading a choice volume of poetry. It was Clara's first Sabbath in her new home. She had but lately left the sheltering roof of a kind great-uncle, who had taken her to his home when a lonely orphan, and reared her very tenderly, surrounding her with every comfort and many of the elegancies of life. A gentleman some years her senior had won her heart's affection, and now she was installed as mistress of his beautiful city home. Six months before she had publicly professed her love for the Saviour, but she was yet in the morning of her religious life. She needed the fostering care of an experienced, devoted Christian. Would she meet with such aid from him who was to be her future companion and protector? "Marry only in the Lord," was the advice of an aged friend to the young girl.

"Archie is not a professor of religion," she reasoned with herself; "but he respects religion, I know, and who can tell what influence I may exert over him?"

"You are not really going to church to-day, Clara, dear, cold as it is?" said the young man dropping his book and looking up with a smile.

"Why, who ever heard of such a thing as staying at home from church unless one was ill!"

"I think I am not very well, Clara. Won't you stay at home and take care of me? Read me some poetry and sing a few of your sweet songs."

Clara looked at him a moment a little incredulously and then replied, "You are quite well, I know by your laughing. I think it is very wrong to stay at home from church; indeed I do, Archie. Won't you go with me?"

"But where shall we go, my good wife?"

"Wherever you are accustomed to."

"I am accustomed to attend that cozy little brick church down by your uncle's, and I thought I had done duty so well there I should be considered religious enough for the rest of my days. But don't look so sad, Clara. I will go anywhere to please you. I know of a splendid marble church on the Avenue. We will drive there if you like, though I really have no idea of what persuasion it is. I will order the carriage and be ready in a few minutes," and he left the room gaily humming the fragment of an opera air.

It was an elegant, stately church. The brilliant light which flowed through the stained windows almost dazzled the sight of the young girl, accustomed only to the plain green shades of the humble village church. The voice of the deep-toned organ rolled through the marble hall and then burst forth into a light, gay air, which, to her unaccustomed ears, sounded strangely in a house of worship. God seemed nearer in the little church at home, which, nestled down among the grassy mounds and moss-grown headstones, seemed always pointing to a life beyond.

When the minister arose she marked well his graceful

air, the polished words and sentences which flowed so smoothly from his lips as he read them from the page before him. But, alas!

> " So coldly sweet, so deadly fair,
> We start, for soul is wanting there."

Clara felt that her soul had not been fed, as the carriage rolled away from the marble church; but there was much around her to attract the gaze of one who had never before spent a Sabbath in the city. Her husband was glad to be released from the sound of " the prosy old doctor's essay." and was in quite good humor with himself for his act of self-denial in going to church. So the drive home was quite a pleasant one, though considerably longer than the one to church.

When they reached home a note was brought in containing an invitation from a fashionable friend of Mr. Allen's to take a little drive out to the new park grounds that afternoon. The carriage would call at three o'clock.

Clara was greatly shocked at such a disregard of the sanctity of God's holy day, and her husband employed a great deal of skillful rhetoric and much more subtle sophistry before she could be brought even to entertain such a project.

" You know I went to church to please you this morning. I am sure you will be kind enough to oblige me by accepting my friend's invitation. I know he would be seriously offended if we did not."

Alas for youth, when the counselors it relies on " counsel to do wickedly"! Clara yielded, though with sad misgivings, and dressed herself for the ride.

The lady beside her was very courteous and attentive, and the gay conversation turned on various frivolous worldly subjects, till in the pleasant excitement of the drive Clara almost forgot the day. When they turned back again Mrs. Harvey insisted that they should dine with her, and the carriage stopped at their residence. A gay evening was spent, Clara being prevailed upon to play some of her choicest music and join her new acquaintance in singing some popular songs, which she did with most exquisite grace and expression. Her dark eye grew brighter and her fair cheek flushed softly, as she felt the proud, admiring glance of her husband bent upon her. But underneath all her pleasure was a dull sense of pain and a consciousness of wrong-doing, which was a very serpent trail among her fragrant flowers. When she reached her home again a flood of regretful sorrow overwhelmed her heart, and she wept bitterly. Her husband sought most tenderly to soothe her grief, and secretly resolved to undermine the "superstition which caused the dear girl so much unhappiness."

"You have done nothing wrong, dear Clara, that you should reproach yourself so bitterly. You have only spent a pleasant afternoon and evening with a friend. We must have dined somewhere, and what difference whether at their house or our own! what is life given us for except to make it just as full of happiness as we can, and to make others around us happy! Just think how much pleasure your sweet singing gave my friends and me. Harvey said it was better than the finest opera he ever heard. Religion ought to make people happy. I am afraid yours has

not to-day, Clara, so I cannot think it is just the right sort
for you. Now, really, did not the drive to and from church
do you more good than the sermon? I am quite sure it
did; so I always intend to take a good long road to church
in the future."

It was some consolation to know that her husband intended to go to church with her in the future; so Clara
dried her eyes and listened to a little gem of poetry he had
selected to read to her that morning.

Little by little the rock of her faith was worn away, and
she was fast learning to look on happiness as the true end
of existence instead of *holiness*, "without which no man
shall see the Lord." And, alas! many whose associations
are far less worldly make this mistake, and look mainly for
a great deal of joy and exalted happiness in their religious
life. Because they do not attain it they go mourning all
their days, looking with weeping eyes on those whom they
regard as more favored of God, because the light of gladness shines upon their pathway. Desponding heart! there
is no true happiness in religion where that alone is the end
you seek. Holiness must be the end and aim of your whole
course, or your joy will be like the "hope of the hypocrite,
but for a moment." "Be ye holy, for I am holy," is the
divine command.

How strange that a truly loving heart could enter upon
such a task as that which Mr. Allen now commenced—the
work of loosing a trusting nature from its only safe moor-
ings, leaving it to drift without a compass or a guiding star
upon a sea abounding with fearful rocks and angry breakers.
But such is the hatred of the natural heart to the humbling

doctrine of the cross and salvation alone through Him who was crucified upon it.

Clara was fond of reading, and her husband took care to place in her way certain fascinating writers, then quite popular, whose frequent merry flashes and sarcastic allusions to the "orthodoxy" tended more surely than serious reasoning would have done to make her think lightly of the faith in which she had been trained. The old-fashioned Bible was skilfully tortured out of its plainest meaning by these so-called reformers, or utterly ignored where it could not be distorted to suit their views. What their opinions of its inspiration were could never be clearly seen by others, if, indeed, they had ever given such a trifling matter any consideration whatever. Instead of the sure foundation which has Jesus Christ for its corner-stone, and a religion which teaches faith, humility, self-denial, earnest labor for souls, and all lowly virtues, they profess to throw wide open the doors of a "broad church," which should gather in all mankind as brothers, which should teach them the dignity and excellence of humanity, and give every one a free pass at last on the swift train over the celestial railway. In their great harvest-field they claimed the tares to be as valuable as the wheat, and never gave thought to the "harvest day." But, alas! calling the tares wheat will not avail when "the Lord of the harvest" comes and the command is given, "Bind them in bundles to burn them."

But the form in which the fatal error was clothed was fair and pleasing, especially so when her husband would

> "Lend to the charm of the poet
> The music of his voice."

There was one favorite writer who seemed to possess a magic power in painting every shady nook and mossy way-side spring of the human heart. No old, gray rock or fathomless shadow of feeling seemed to escape that observ ing eye. And there were clear, bold strokes sometimes which showed a strength not often given to a woman's hand. Through all her writings ran a thread of light re-flected from God's word, though bent out of its own right line by the prism through which it flowed. Much was said of the love and tender mercy of God, but the fact that he is also a just God, and will in nowise clear the guilty, was set aside as a hard doctrine. The gay scoffer, the one who despises Christ's tender offers of love and pardon, provided he is amiable and pleasant among his friends and associates, must not be given over to a just retribution. God is too loving a Father to see such a lovely scorner perish. It is " so incongruous " to think of the one with whom we have had such pleasant converse here being forever lost. The sophistry gradually wrought its work ; the more readily, as poor Clara, in the whirl of fashion and gaiety, failed to bring it to the test of " the law and the testimony.''

Time rolled on, and Clara was becoming more thought-ful and studious. Various philosophical works which her husband admired, and which he often read and discussed with her, were becoming favorite volumes. There was something grand in the old philosopher's views of life and its little ills and joys. There was something wonderful in their curious speculations respecting the mysteries of the world beyond. Her husband delighted in leading her mind through all their fantastic windings as they groped for the truth so clearly revealed to us. He praised his wife for her appreciation of such intellectual food, and rejoiced that he had been so successful in winning the affection of a truly intellectual woman. Her self-love was gratified, and her diligence in diving deeper into his favorite works daily increased.

In her own home circle her heart had room to expand its choicest tendrils. A noble boy three summers old was prattling at her feet, and all the demands of fashion could not make her forget a mother's duties. Still they were only the duties that pertained to his temporal welfare, for the flame of devotion had smoldered to ashes on the hearthstone of her heart.

The rain was dashing against the closed shutters one November night as an anxious group gathered in Mrs. Allen's chamber. They were standing on either side of a beautiful rosewood crib, whose hangings of azure gauze were closely drawn aside. There lay a little form tossing and restless, his little face and throat seemed scarlet as they rested on the snowy pillow, and his little hand moved restlessly to and fro, as if vainly striving to cool the burning heat. It was the mother's hand that tirelessly bathed the scarlet brow and burning limbs. Servants were constantly in waiting, but no hand but her husband's was allowed to take her place.

"Do you think there is hope, doctor?" was the question she longed to ask, but could not frame it into words It came at length from her husband's lips. The answer was only a straw to grasp at.

"He is in a very critical state, indeed. If I had been

at home when he was first taken ill I think the fever would not have reached such a height. But everything almost depends on the first steps. We must do what we can now to make up for lost hours."

But all that the best medical skill could do proved useless. The little sufferer lingered through the long night watch, and when the morning dawned seemed once more to know them all. "My mamma," were the first words which fell from his lips, sending a thrill of joy to all their hearts. It was bliss to see the smile of recognition light once more those sweet blue eyes, and the parents grasped each other's hand in silent joy. The old physician alone looked grave and sorrowful. The little light was fast fading out, and this was its dying flicker.

"Mamma, please take Bertie," said the little one, holding up the dimpled hands. Very tenderly was he lifted up and laid in her arms.

"Good night, papa, it's most dark now; Bertie is going to sleep."

His mother's tearful face bent over him, and as the strange hand of Death was laid upon his heart-strings he clasped her closely about the neck, as if she were a refuge from every danger.

They took the little one gently from her arms and laid him on his couch again. Her husband could not even strive to comfort her. He saw the joy and pride of his existence, the heir of his name and fortune, around whom so many fair hopes clustered, "taken away by a stroke," and his soul seemed crushed within him. He bowed his head upon his hands, and, regardless of other eyes, the proud man groaned, and sobbed, and wept as never in his life he had done before. Both were too deeply stricken to utter words of comfort. Clara felt her bleeding heart torn from her bosom. Yet no tears came to her relief. Her brain seemed bursting with the pressure upon it. Where was the sustaining power of boasted philosophy in this hour of darkness?

Ah, when the afflictions of life come home to "the bone and marrow of our own households" they are far different to us from those which concern only our neighbors. It is an easy thing to look on pleasure philosophically, or even the afflictions of others, but when our turn to suffer comes we shall feel our need of a strong staff to lean upon, a sure support that can keep us in perfect peace, even in the furnace. Clara had sought to pray when the agony of fear was upon her, but God seemed too far away to listen.

"I cannot give him up, my husband!" was the agonized cry of the mother as they stood for the last time by his side before he was to be taken forever from their chamber. "I cannot give him up," was the despairing language of both their hearts. There can be no true resignation where a loving Father's hand is not recognized in the affliction; where this poor world is allowed to bound the spirit's vision. But at last the precious dust was borne away to be seen no more by mortal eye till the resurrection morning.

Time, the great healer, wore away the sharpness of the bereavement, but Clara could never again delight in her former pursuits. How like very dust and ashes seemed the food she had been seeking to nourish her soul upon! A softened melancholy rested upon her heart, and she would

CHRIST THE GOOD SHEPHERD.

wander about her house looking at the relics of her lost one. And day by day the roses faded from her cheek, her step grew lighter on the stair, and she rapidly declined, till at length she was startled at the shadowy form and face her mirror revealed to her. Her long-neglected Bible was once more sought for, and she read with all the desperate eagerness of a drowning man, who catches at every chance of safety. It was her mother's Bible, and along the margin were delicate pencil tracings, pointing to many precious passages. How eagerly she read them over! and when she was too weary herself, she gave the book into her husband's hand. Still he could give her no advice in her spiritual distress, and looked upon it with compassion as the result of her disease. He gave her the tenderest worldly consolation, but it brought no peace to her anxious soul. Was there no one to offer a word of true counsel? From a very humble source came the advice she so much needed. The kind nurse, Margaret, whom little Bertie had loved next to his parents, was an earnest, humble Christian. It was from her lips he had learned to lisp his morning and evening prayer, and her low, gentle voice that told him over and over the sweet story he never tired of hearing—the story of the Babe of Bethlehem.

Plainly and simply she pointed Clara's mind to the Lamb of God as the only Saviour, praying hourly in her heart that God would bring home the truth with power to her.

At length a little light broke in upon her mind. "It may be he will receive even such a wandering sheep as I," she said, "oh, I will cast myself upon his mercy only, for I can do nothing to make myself better!"

The thin hands were folded over the Bible, the eyes closed wearily, a faint motion of the lips told of the silent prayer her heart was offering, as gently she breathed her life away.

A few months later Mr. Allen became a wanderer in many lands.

Do you ever sigh and disquiet your heart, Christian pilgrim, because God has not given you wealth and worldly ease? Remember the words of One who never gave a needless caution nor spoke an untruthful word—"How hardly shall they that have riches enter into the kingdom of heaven!"

It is a dangerous step indeed for a young heart to form a life-long union with one who is a stranger to its hopes of heaven. "Be ye not unequally yoked together with unbelievers," is a command which may not be lightly broken. Where all of this world, and very probably the world to come, are at stake, the cost should be well counted. "What shall it profit a man if he gain the whole world and lose his own soul?" Even the most devoted affection the world can bestow will be no substitute for God's loving favor. "What shall a man give in exchange for his soul?"

> "Jesus, my all in all thou art,
>   My rest in toil, my ease in pain;
> The healing of my broken heart,
>   In strife my peace, in loss my gain;
> My smile beneath the tyrant's frown,
> In shame my glory and my crown."

# Live Within Your Means.

THIS is pleasant!" exclaimed a young husband, taking his seat in the rocking-chair as the supper things were removed. The fire glowing in the grate, revealed a pretty and neatly furnished sitting-room, with all the appliances of comfort. The fatiguing business of the day was over, and he sat enjoying what he had all day been anticipating, the delights of his own fireside. His pretty wife, Esther, took her work and sat down by the table.

"It is pleasant to have a home of one's own," he again said, taking a satisfactory survey of his little quarters. The cold rain beat against the windows, and he thought he felt really grateful for all his present comforts.

"Now if we only had a piano!" exclaimed the wife.

"Give me the music of your own sweet voice before all the pianos in creation," he observed, complimentarily ; but he felt a certain secret disappointment that his wife's thankfulness did not happily chime with his own.

"Well, we want one for our friends," said Esther.

"Let our friends come to see *us*, and not to hear a piano," exclaimed the husband.

"But, George, everybody has a piano now-a-days—we don't go anywhere without seeing a piano," persisted the wife.

"And yet I don't know what we want one for—you will

have no time to play on one, and I don't want to hear it."

"Why, they are so fashionable—I think our room looks nearly naked without one."

"I think it looks just right."

"I think it looks very naked—we want a piano shockingly," protested Esther emphatically.

The husband rocked violently.

"Your lamp smokes, my dear," said he, after a long pause.

"When are you going to get a camphene lamp? I have told you a dozen times how much we need one," said Esther pettishly.

"These are very pretty lamps—I never can see by a camphene lamp," said her husband. "These lamps are the prettiest of the kind I ever saw."

"But, George, I do not think our room is complete without a camphene lamp," said Esther sharply. "They are so fashionable! Why, the Morgans, and Millers, and many others I might mention, all have them; I am sure we ought to."

"We ought not to take pattern by other people's expenses, and I don't see any reason in that."

The husband moved uneasily in his chair.

"We want to live as well as others," said Esther.

"We want to live within our means, Esther," exclaimed George.

"I am sure we can afford it as well as the Morgans, and Millers, and Thorns; we do not wish to appear mean."

George's cheek crimsoned.

"Mean! I am not mean!" he cried angrily.

"Then we do not wish to appear so," said the wife. "To complete this room, and make it look like other people's we want a piano and camphene lamps."

"We want—we want!" muttered the husband, "there's no satisfying woman's wants, do what you may," and he abruptly left the room.

How many husbands are in a similar dilemma? How many houses and husbands are rendered uncomfortable by the constant dissatisfaction of a wife with present comforts and present provisions! How many bright prospects for business have ended in bankruptcy and ruin in order to satisfy this secret hankering after fashionable superfluities! Could the real cause of many failures be known, it would be found to result from useless expenditures at home—expenses to answer the demands of fashion and "what will people think?"

"My wife has made my fortune," said a gentleman of great possessions, "by her thrift, and prudence, and cheerfulness, when I was just beginning."

"And mine has lost my fortune," answered his companion, "by useless extravagance and repining when I was doing well."

What a world does this open to the influence which a wife possesses over the future prosperity of her family! Let the wife know her influence, and try to use it wisely and well.

Be satisfied to commence on a small scale. It is too common for young housekeepers to begin where their mothers ended. Buy all that is necessary to work skilfully with; adorn your house with all that will render it comfortable. Do not look at richer homes, and covet their costly furniture. If secret dissatisfaction is ready to spring up, go a step further and visit the homes of the suffering poor ; behold dark, cheerless apartments, insufficient clothing, and absence of all the comforts and refinements of social life, and then turn to your own with a joyful spirit. You will then be prepared to meet your husband with a grateful heart, and be ready to appreciate the toil of self-denial which he has endured in the business world to surround you with the delights of home ; and you will be ready to co-operate cheerfully with him in so arranging your expenses, that his mind will not be constantly harassed with fears lest his family expenses may encroach upon public payments. Be independent ; a young housekeeper never needed greater moral courage than she does now to resist the arrogance of fashion. Do not let the A.'s and B.'s decide what you must have, neither let them hold the strings of your purse. You know best what you can and ought to afford It matters but little what people think, provided you are true to yourself and family.

### THE DARK FIRST.

Not first the glad and then the sorrowful—
　But first the sorrowful, and then the glad;
Tears for a day—for earth of tears is full:
　Then we forget that we were ever sad.

Not first the bright, and after that the dark—
　But first the dark, and after that the bright;
First the thick cloud, and then the rainbow's arc:
　First the dark grave, and then resurrection light.

　　　　　*—Horatius Bonar.*

# OUT of THE WRONG POCKET

**M**R. TAGGARD frowned as he observed the pile of bills by his plate, placed there by his prudent, economical wife, not without an anxious flutter at the heart, in anticipation of the scene that invariably followed. He actually groaned as he read the sum total.

"There must be some mistake, Mary" he said, pushing back his plate, with a desperate air: "it is *absolutely impossible* for us to have used all these things in one month!"

"The bills are correct, John," was the meek response; "I looked them over myself."

"Then one thing is certain, provisions are either wasted, thrown out the window, as it were, or stolen. Jane has relatives in the place, and I haven't the least doubt but that she supports them out of what she steals."

Mrs. Taggard's temper was evidently rising; there were two round crimson spots upon her cheeks, and she tapped her foot nervously upon the floor.

"I am neither wasteful, nor extravagant, John. And

as for Jane, I know her to be perfectly honest and trust-worthy."

"It is evident that there is a leak somewhere, Mary; and it is your duty as a wife, to find out where it is, and stop it. Our bills are perfectly enormous; and if this sort of thing goes on much longer, I shall be a bankrupt."

Mrs. Taggard remained silent, trying to choke down the indignant feelings that struggled for utterance.

You will have to order some coal," she said, at last; "we have hardly sufficient for the day."

"Is there anything more, Mrs. Taggard?" inquired her husband; ironically.

"Yes; neither I nor the children are decently or comfortably clothed; all need an entire new outfit."

"Go on, madam. As I am a man of unlimited means, if you have any other wants, I hope you won't be at all backward about mentioning them."

"I don't intend to be," was the quiet, but spirited reply. "I wouldn't do for another what I do for you, for double my board and clothing. Both the parlor and sitting-room need refurnishing; everything looks so faded and shabby, that I am ashamed to have any one call. And the stairs need recarpeting, the blinds and gate need repairing, and the fence needs painting."

"That can't be all, Mrs. Taggard. Are you sure that there isn't something else?"

"I don't think of anything else just now, Mr. Taggard; though if there should be a few dollars over and above what these will cost, they won't come amiss. I should like to have a little change in my pocket, if only for the novelty of the thing. You needn't fear its being wasted."

Mr. Taggard was evidently not a little astonished at this sudden outbreak in his usually quiet and patient wife, but who, like most women of that stamp, had considerable spirit when it was aroused.

"Now that you are through, Mrs. Taggard, perhaps you will let me say a word. Here is all the money I can spare you this month; so you can make the most of it."

Laying a roll of bills on the table, Mr. Taggard walked to the door; remarking, just before he closed it, that he should leave town on the next train, to be absent about a week.

The reverie into which Mrs. Taggard fell, as she listened to the sound of his retreating steps, was far from being a pleasant one.   Aside from her natural vexation, she felt grieved and saddened by the change that had come over her once kind, indulgent husband.   He seemed to be entirely filled with the greed of gain, the desire to amass money—not for the sake of the good that it might enable him to enjoy, or confer, but for the mere pleasure of hoarding it.   And this miserly feeling grew upon him daily, until he seemed to grudge his family the common comforts of life.   And yet Mrs. Taggard knew that he was not only in receipt of a comfortable income from his business, but had laid by a surplus, yearly, ever since their marriage.

She had taxed her ingenuity to save in every possible way, but when the monthly bills were presented the same scene was enacted, only it grew worse and worse.

And this penuriousness extended to himself.   He grudged himself, as well as wife and children, clothing suitable to his means and station, and went about looking so

rusty and shabby that Mrs. Taggard often felt ashamed of
him, inwardly wondering if he could be the same man who
had wooed and won her.

With a heavy sigh Mrs. Taggard took up the roll of bills
upon the table, hoping to find enough to pay what was already due—she did not look for more.

An ejaculation of astonishment burst from her lips as
she unrolled the paper in which it was folded. It contained $500 in bills, and a check for $500 more.

With a look of quiet determination in her eyes, Mrs.
Taggard arose to her feet. "The family should now have
some of the comforts to which they were entitled, if they
never did again."

First, she settled every bill; a heavy weight being lifted
from her heart as she did so; besides getting a fresh supply of fuel and other comforts. Her next move was to
order new furniture for the sitting-room and parlor, have
the hall recarpeted and papered, the broken door-step
mended, and the fence and blinds repaired and painted.
She then took the children out, and got them new garments
from hats to shoes. She bought herself three new dresses;
a neat gingham for morning wear, a delaine for afternoons,
and something nicer for best. And before going home she
took the children into a toy-shop; delighting the boy with
the skates he had so often asked for, and giving the girl
the chief wish of her heart, a doll and doll's wardrobe—not
forgetting some blocks for the baby. For, like a wise, as
well as kind, mother, Mrs. Taggard desired to make their
childhood a happy one; something to look back upon with
pleasure through their whole life. Neither was John for-

gotten ; by the aid of some old garments, for a pattern, she got him an entire new suit, together with stuff for dressing-gown and slippers.

The day on which Mrs. Taggard expected her husband's return was a very busy one ; but at last the carpets were down, the paper hung, and everything in the best of order.

He was expected on the five o'clock train, and Mrs. Taggard set the children, attired in their pretty new dresses, at the window to watch for papa, while she went below to assist Jane in preparing something extra for supper.    She had just returned when Mr. Taggard was seen approaching the house.

It looked so different from what it did when he left, that he stared at it in amazement, and would have hesitated about entering, had it not been for the name on the newly burnished door-plate.    But he was still more astonished when he entered.

"Am I in my own house, or somebody else's ?" he ejaculated, as he looked around the bright and pleasant room.

" It is the new furniture I have been buying," said his wife, smiling.    " How do you like it ? "

" Have you been running me in debt, Mary ? "

" Not in the least, John, it was all bought with the money you so generously left me when you went away."

Mr. Taggard clapped his hand into one of his pockets.

" My goodness ! " he exclaimed, in an agitated tone and manner, " I gave it to you out of the wrong pocket ! "

Mrs. Taggard did not look at all astonished or disturbed at this announcement ; on the contrary, her countenance wore a very smiling and tranquil aspect.

"You do n't mean to say that you've spent it?" inquired Mr. Taggard, desperately.

"Why, what else should I do with it, John? You told me to make the most of it; and I rather think I have."

"I am a ruined man!" groaned Mr. Taggard.

"Not a bit of it, my dear husband," said his wife, cheerfully; you would n't be ruined if you had given me twice that amount. Besides, I have saved enough for our housekeeping expenses, for three months, at least. I think you had better give me an allowance for that purpose in future; it will save us both much annoyance."

The children, who had been led to consider what their mother had bought them as "presents from papa," now crowded eagerly around him.

Mr. Taggard loved his children, and it would be difficult for any one having the kind and tender heart that he really possessed, to turn away from the innocent smiles and caresses that were lavished upon him.

It was a smiling group that gathered round the cheerful supper-table. And as Mr. Taggard glanced from the gleeful children to the smiling face of his wife, who certainly looked ten years younger, attired in her new and becoming dress, he came to the conclusion that though it might cost something to make his family comfortable, on the whole, it paid.

We do not mean to say that Mr. Taggard was entirely cured; a passion so strong is not so easily eradicated. But when the old miserly feeling came over him, and he began to dole out grudgingly the means with which to make his family comfortable, his wife would pleasantly say: "You are taking it out of the wrong pocket, John ! "—words which seemed to have a magical effect upon both heart and purse-strings.

"Let us not deprive ourselves of the comforts of life," she would often say, "nor grudge our children the innocent pleasures natural to youth, for the purpose of laying up for them the wealth that is, too often, a curse rather than a blessing."

### AN INFINITE GIVER.

THINK you, when the stars are glinting,
　　Or the moonlight's shimmering gleam
Paints the water's rippled surface
　　With a coat of silvered sheen—
Think you then that God, the Painter,
　　Shows his masterpiece divine?
That he will not hang another
　　Of such beauty on the line?

Think you, when the air is trembling
　　With the birds' exultant song,
And the blossoms, mutely fragrant,
　　Strive the anthem to prolong—
Think you then that their Creator,
　　At the signal of his word,
Fills the earth with such sweet music
　　As shall ne'er again be heard?

He will never send a blessing
　　But have greater ones in store,
And each oft recurring kindness
　　Is an earnest of still more.
If the earth seems full of glory
　　As his purposes unfold,
There is still a better country—
　　And the half has not been told !

# "My House" and "Our House."

THESE houses are opposite each other in a beautiful suburban town. "My house" is large and handsome, with a cupola, and has a rich lawn before it. It is surrounded by a broad piazza, and graced and shaded by ancestral elms and huge buttonwood trees. Its barns and stables are large and well-filled; its orchards are gorgeous with fruit, in the season, and the fields around it seem alive with golden grain that waves in the wind. Everything about the place tells of long-continued prosperity. The rich old squire who lives there rides about with fine horses, and talks a great deal to his neighbors about "my house, my orchards, and my horses."

His wife is evidently the lady of the region. She was a model housekeeper and dairywoman in the days when they worked the farm, and is now an oracle on many questions. She, too, talks of "my house, my horses, and my estate."

These persons each brought property to the other, and the two interests have, unfortunately, never flowed together and formed one estate as they should have done; so there are always two separate interests in the house.

Of course the property belongs, legally, to both; but as each has a snug little fund laid away, the question is always to be settled, if repairs are to be made, or horses or furniture bought, who shall pay for it.

It seems but proper to the husband that carpets, and sofas, etc., shall be bought by his wife; also the cows, as the lady is at the head of the house. But she says, " You walk on the carpets, sit on the sofas, and eat the cream and butter just as much as I do, and I see no reason why you should not, at least, help to pay for them."

Such discussions often occur, but, on the whole, each upholds the interest of the other against outsiders, and gets along without open rupture. They ride about in better dress than their neighbors, they receive and return visits, and are called the leading family in town.

But "my house," as some have named the great square mansion, is nobody's house but its owners'. No guest who can not return hospitality in equal style is asked to tarry for a night there. All ministers sojourning in the place are directed by them to the humble parsonage for entertainment. Every weary, homeless wanderer is pointed to the distant almshouse; and a neighbor's horse or cow which has strayed from its own enclosure, is at once put into the pound by the squire's man.

If an appeal is made for any benevolent object the squire says, "Go to my house and ask my wife to give you something." She, in turn, points the applicant to the field or the orchard, and says, "Go down there and ask my husband to give you something." So one puts it on the other, and nothing is given; and neither the town nor the world is the better for their living.

This is the way things are done at "my house."

Across the street, under the shadow of two wide-spreading elms, stands a very modest cottage nestled in vines and flowers, with curtains drawn up to let in the light of God's blessed sun, and an ever-open door with a great chair in full view, holding out its time-worn arms, as if to invite and welcome in the weary passer-by. The birds are always remembered here in their times of scarcity, and so in token of their gratitude, they gather in the trees and carol out sweet and merry songs by way of paying their bills.

God's peace, as well as his plenty, rests on this place, and while its owners call it, in their hearts, "God's house," they speak of it to others, always as "our house."

Twenty-five years ago a sturdy, brave-hearted young mechanic bought this one acre of land, and with his own hands dug and walled a cellar, at times when he had no work to do for others. When he had earned an additional hundred or two dollars he bought lumber and began to build a house. People asked him what he was going to do with it, and he replied that if he should live to finish it, he was going to live in it.

Well, in two years the house was finished, to the last nail and hook. Then he went away, as it was thought, for a wife. In a week he returned, bringing with him some neat household furniture, and three persons instead of only one.

He did bring a wife—a bright-eyed, merry-hearted young girl—and also two aged women, "our mothers," as he called them.

The first night in the house they dedicated their humble home—"our house" to God, and in the name of the Lord they set up their banner, praying that ever after this his banner over them might be love.

Many a family moves into a new home and asks God to come in and prosper them, and take up his abode there; but they do nothing to draw him thither. They begin for self, and go on for self; and sometimes God leaves them to themselves.

But the young owners of "our house"—the children of "our mothers"—made their little home His home and the home of His poor and feeble ones. "Our mothers" now laid down the weapons of toil over which they had grown gray, and came out of the vale of honest poverty into the sunshine of plenty. Their hearts grew warm in this gift of double love. They renewed their youth.

In their first days at their children's home, one of "our mothers" spoke of "Henry's new house," when he checked her, saying, "Never call this my house again. I built it for God and for all of you, and I want it always called 'our house.' There is yet one thing I want done here before I shall feel that I have made my thank-offering to God for the health and strength and the work which have enabled me to build and pay for this house. I promised then that no stranger or wanderer should ever go hungry or weary from this door. You have made sure of a neat and sunny room for our friends. Now I want a bed, a chair, and a table put in the shed-chamber for such strangers as we cannot ask into the house. I want also to fill the little store-closet under the back stairway with provisions to give the needy. They will then not be our own; and if at any time we should be short of money, we will not be tempted to say, 'I have nothing to give.' I want to live for more than self, and I know you all share the feeling. I want to feel that God is here, and to live as if we saw him and were all under his actual guidance and care, and to realize that he sees and approves our way in life."

Thus was "our house" opened, and thus was it kept— a home sanctified to humanity and to God.

The years rolled away, not without changes, but peace and plenty still reign in the modest home whose owners are looked up to by all the town's people—rich as well as poor —as friends and benefactors; for all men alike need human sympathy and comfort.

The young carpenter of twenty-five years ago, is now a prosperous builder in the great city near his home. He could afford to erect and occupy a house worth four times what the cottage cost. But he loves the place, and cannot tear himself from it. He has added more than one L to it, and he has refurnished it, and brought into it many articles of taste and luxury.

When asked why he does not build a house more in accordance with his means, he replies :—

"No house could be built which would be like 'our house.' I can never forget the night we and our mothers dedicated it to God in prayer and simple trust; and ever since that night I have felt as if we were dwelling in the secret of his tabernacle, under the shadow of the Almighty. We might have a larger and more fashionable house, but it would bring a weight of care on its mistress, and steal the time she has made sacred to others. No other house could have the memories this one has; no other house be hallowed as this house has been by the prayers of the holy and the blessings of the poor."

And so the family still live on and are happy in "our house." Still the pastor's weary wife is relieved of church company, for, from force of habit, all ministers and others on errands of good, draw up their horses before the well-filled stable, and ring, for themselves, at this open door. Still the poor are fed from that store-closet under the back stairway; still the wanderer—though he be a wanderer in a double sense—rests his weary head in that shed-chamber.

The squire wonders at the builder, because he lives in such a modest way compared with his means, and says, "If I were he, I'd be ashamed of that cottage which was all well enough when he was a young journeyman."

The builder wonders what the squire does with all that great house, and why, when half a dozen rooms are empty there, he does n't allow himself the pleasure of company, and of sheltering strangers and getting the blessing they bring.

The squire's wife peeps through her fine curtains, and says, "I wonder that pretty and intelligent woman has n't more taste. She might live like a lady if she pleased, and dress as I do; but she pokes on just as she began, and dresses no better than the minister's wife, and has a rabble of poor, forlorn creatures whom I would n't let into my house, nor into my wood-shed, running after her for food and clothing, and nobody knows what."

So you see, "my house" is literally "my house," and "our house" is God's house.

# A MOUNTAIN PRAYER MEETING

WILL you go to meeting with me this afternoon, Mabel? Come; this is your last day here; do go once before you leave the White Mountains." "What do you do in 'meeting'?" asked the gay, beautiful, "High Church" New York belle, with just a shade of contemptuous inflection in her voice.

"Well,—there will be no sermon; there never is in the afternoon. The good minister sits in the aisle, in front of the pulpit, and invites any one he likes to make a prayer. Any other one, who feels the need of it, may request that he or she be mentioned personally in the petition; and those who wish it may relate their experience."

"How very funny! All the old women 'speakin' in meetin',' and scaring themselves dreadfully. I'll go. I dare say I shall have a good laugh, if I don't fall asleep."

So we walked through the long, hilly street of Bethlehem, in the pleasant hour before sunset, in the sweet, warm, hazy air of early autumn. The glory of the Lord shone round about us; for all the mountains were burnished, splendid, gorgeous, in purple and crimson and gold. Mabel's deep gray eyes grew large and luminous as her artist-soul drank in the ineffable beauty.

The building was so crowded with the villagers and many visitors that it was with difficulty we obtained seats, apart from each other. Mabel found a place next to a young, sweet-faced country woman, and looked, with her flower-like face and French costume, like some rare exotic by the side of a humble mountain daisy.

The minister opened the services with a few fervent, simple words, and then said, " Brother ——, will you lead in prayer ? "

A plain old country farmer knelt in the aisle before us. His prayer—sincere, and, I doubt not, as acceptable, because sincere, as if it had been offered in polished language —made Mabel shake with laughter.

He rose, and there was utter silence for a moment. Then a high, sweet woman's voice, far in front of us, sang out, clear as a bell,—

> " Sweet hour of prayer ! sweet hour of prayer !
> That calls me from a world of care,
> And bids me at my Father's throne
> Make all my wants and wishes known."

The congregation joined in ; only one verse was sung, and again the strange, solemn silence fell upon us.

It was broken by the sudden rising of a lank, awkward boy, who uttered a few words in a frightened nasal whine.

This time Mabel was convulsed with laughter ; but the sweet singer, who saw in this utterance only the contrite soul of the speaker, burst forth triumphantly with—

"Oh, gift of gifts! oh, grace of faith!
  My God, how can it be
That thou, who hast discerning love,
  Shouldst give that gift to me?"

Only one verse, as before. Then the pure notes, high above all the other voices, died away, and a strange-looking woman arose.

"I haven't any gift of language," said she, "but I want to give in my testimony. I've always been a wicked woman; I've always gone against my conscience. I've made my folks at home miserable for many a long year; and that's the reason God poured trouble after trouble down on me, till I was about to take my own life, when some one—it must have been one of God's angels—went singing through the woods. Shall I ever forget the words?—

"'With tearful eyes I look around;
  Life seems a dark and stormy sea;—'"

She stopped, her voice breaking into a hoarse sob, when the other sweet voice immediately went on—

"Yet, mid the gloom, I hear a sound,—
  A heavenly whisper,—'Come to me.'

"Oh, voice of mercy! voice of love!
  In conflict, grief, and agony,
Support me, cheer me from above!
  And gently whisper—'Come to me.'"

I looked at Mabel. She was not laughing. A strange, awed expression rested upon her features; her head was bowed down as the sweet-faced woman at her side rose, and, turning to the last speaker, said, in a low, gentle voice,—

" My sister, we all thank our heavenly Father that he
put his strong arm of protection about you while it was yet
time ; and since you have joined with us in profession of
your faith, there has been no one more earnest in those
good works without which faith is nothing."

Then reverently kneeling, she prayed that God would
strengthen her dear sister, and give them all love and charity, one for another, and his peace, which passeth all understanding.

Out rang the sweet voice,—

> " Haste thee on, from grace to glory,
>     Armed by faith, and winged by prayer!
> Heaven's eternal day's before thee,
>     God's own hand shall guide thee there."

Mabel was now silently crying, and big tears were
blinding my eyes, when a grand old man rose from his seat.
Bent and feeble now, I could see that he had once been
tall and stately, looking as the Puritan fathers must have
looked when they first stepped upon " the stern and rock-
bound coast " at Plymouth. Fine, clean-cut features, and
eyes still blue and piercing remained, but his voice trembled painfully as he said,—

" I am ninety-four years old, and most of those I love
have gone to the graveyard before me ; I have lived all
these years in Bethlehem, and, boy and man, have tried to
serve the Lord: and I owe my blessed hope in my Saviour
to the teaching and example of my good and pious mother."
Then, with aged, trembling hands uplifted, he prayed that
all the children present might be brought up in the nurture
and admonition of the Lord.

Near us was a handsome, well-dressed man, past middle age, who had listened with absorbed attention to all that had been said, and who now seemed strangely agitated. In a moment he arose, and then he spoke.

"I presume that no one here remembers a poor boy who nearly fifty years ago left this place to seek his fortune. Fatherless, motherless, with no claim upon any one here, I wandered away with a heavy heart to earn my bread Many a time have I been exhausted, discouraged, almost hopeless; but my mother had taught me to pray—her dying gift to me was her own Bible. It has gone round the world with me, and God has never forsaken me. I have long been a rich man, and I have come once more to these grand hills—my childhood's home—to testify my gratitude to my Maker for all his goodness. I never intended to speak as I am now doing; but after what I have heard and witnessed, I should be most ungrateful if I did not give my testimony and belief in the abounding love and mercy of God. O friends! take me back! Let me be one with you in this most sweet and touching service, and when I leave you, pray that I may never be ungrateful for the earthly blessings he has heaped upon me, and for the far more priceless gift of his Son, Jesus Christ."

Every one had listened to the stranger in deep silence. Every heart had thrilled responsive to his words. It seemed as if the very breath of Heaven had entered into the little church, cleansing and purifying each soul present, and filling it with inexpressible devotion, when, like a soft, trembling wave, the pure young voice came floating down the aisles, and we heard the solemn acknowledgment,—

> "A charge to keep I have,
>   A God to glorify;
> A precious, blood-bought soul to save,
>   And fit it for the sky."

She sang alone; a feeling too deep for utterance had prevented the rest from joining in, and many heads were bent in silent prayer and thanksgiving.

But oh! what did I see? Pale as death, her eyes dilated, her whole frame quivering like an aspen, Mabel arose and essayed to speak. The muscles of her mouth refused to obey her will, but with a painful effort she faltered in low, broken tones, "Pray for me," and sank down upon her knees.

It was the voice of God that spoke in those three little words, "*Pray for me*," uttered so low, yet distinctly heard in every part of the church. Joyful tears were streaming down many women's faces, as for the first time the singer's voice trembled, broke, and at last sobbed through the humble entreaty,—

> "Just as I am—without one plea,
>   But that thy blood was shed for me,
> And that thou bid'st me come to thee,
>   O Lamb of God, I come."

As she finished, a young minister who was living in the same house with us, and whose life had been nearly sacrificed in missionary labors, bowed in prayer. The radiance of Heaven was upon his face, and God spoke through him to the awakened soul of Mabel in a way I had never heard before. The words poured out in an inspired flood, carrying her soul resistless upon its mighty waves to repentance, faith, prayer, praise, love, joy, peace, and at last heaven!

With a solemn benediction the services were ended; and when we had come out, it seemed as if the very heavens were rejoicing over the tidings which had gone up of the soul that day redeemed. All that was gorgeous and beautiful in color had taken possession of the sky. The clouds, like great gold and crimson banners, were moving high over our heads, furling and unfurling, as if carried by exultant angels, marching and singing their triumphant allelujahs.

And Mabel, still white as an Easter lily, but with her deep gray eyes full of a new happiness, a steadfast resolution to live henceforth for Christ, walked by my side, watching the great glory of the heavens, with her arm lovingly entwined in mine. We did not speak; we had no need, for our thoughts were in perfect accord. I had witnessed the wonderful mystery of her instantaneous " change of heart;" I knew it was well with her.

Beautiful, gay, fashionable, the pet of society, I knew her also to be a staunch upholder of all that was noble, good, and pure, and I felt a thorough conviction that she had indeed given herself up body and soul to Him who had chosen to send his Holy Spirit into her heart, as she was going out of the little village which bore the blessed name of *Bethlehem.*

> However it be, it seems to me,
> 'T is only noble to be good.
> Kind hearts are more than coronets,
> And simple faith than Norman blood.

# Only a Husk.

OM DARCY, yet a young man, had grown to be a very hard one. Although naturally kind-hearted, active, and intelligent, he lacked strength of will to resist temptation, and had therefore fallen a victim to intemperance. He had lost his place as foreman of the great machine-shop, and what money he now earned came from odd jobs of tinkering which he was able to do here and there at private houses; for Tom was a genius as well as a mechanic, and when his head was steady enough, he could mend a clock or clean a watch as well as he could set up and regulate a steam-engine, and this latter he could do better than any other man ever employed by the Scott Falls Manufacturing Company.

One day Tom was engaged to mend a broken mowing-machine and reaper, for which he received five dollars; and on the following morning he started for his old haunt, the village tavern. He knew that his wife sadly needed the money, and that his two little children were absolutely suffering for want of clothing, and that morning he held a debate with the better part of himself, but the better part had become weak, and the demon of appetite carried the day.

So away to the tavern Tom went, where, for two or three hours, he felt the exhilarating effects of the alcoholic draught, and fancied himself happy, as he could sing and laugh; but, as usual, stupefaction followed, and the man

died out.   He drank while he could stand, and then lay
down in a corner, where his companions left him.

It was almost midnight, when the landlord's wife came
to the barroom to see what kept her husband up, and she
quickly saw Tom.

"Peter," said she, not in a pleasant mood, "why don't
you send that miserable Tom Darcy home?   He's been
hanging around here long enough."

Tom's stupefaction was not sound sleep.   The dead
coma had left his brain, and the calling of his name stung
his senses to keen attention.   He had an insane love of
rum, but he did not love the landlord.   In other years,
Peter Tindar and he had wooed the same maiden,—
Ellen Goss,—and he had won her, leaving Peter to take up
with the sharp-tempered damsel who had brought him the
tavern, and Tom knew that lately the tapster had gloated
over the misery of the woman who had once discarded him.

"Why don't you send him home?" demanded Mrs.
Tindar, with an impatient stamp of her foot.

"Hush, Betsey, he's got money.   Let him be, and he'll
be sure to spend it before he goes home.   I'll have the
kernel of that nut, and his wife may have the husk."

Betsey turned away, and shortly afterward Tom Darcy
lifted himself up on his elbow.

"Ah, Tom, are you awake?"

"Yes."

"Then rouse up and have a warm glass."

Tom got upon his feet and steadied himself.

"No; I won't drink any more to-night."

"It won't hurt you, Tom—just one glass."

"I know it won't!" said Tom, buttoning up his coat by the solitary button left. "I know it won't!"

And with this he went out into the chill air of midnight. When he got away from the shadow of the tavern, he stopped and looked up at the stars, and then he looked down upon the earth.

"Aye," he muttered, grinding his heel in the gravel, "Peter Tindar is taking the kernel, and leaving poor Ellen the worthless husk,—a husk more than worthless! and I am helping him do it. I am robbing my wife of joy, robbing my dear children of honor and comfort, and robbing myself of love and life—just that Peter Tindar may have the kernel, and Ellen the husk! We'll see!"

It was a revelation to the man. The tavern-keeper's speech, not meant for his ears, had come on his senses as fell the voice of the Risen One upon Saul of Tarsus.

"We'll see!" he said, setting his foot firmly upon the ground; and then he wended his way homeward.

On the following morning he said to his wife, "Ellen, have you any coffee in the house?"

"Yes, Tom." She did not tell him that her sister had given it to her. She was glad to hear him ask for coffee, instead of the old, old cider.

"I wish you would make me a cup, good and strong."

There was really music in Tom's voice, and the wife set about her work with a strange flutter at her heart.

Tom drank two cups of the strong fragrant coffee, and then went out, with a resolute step, and walked straight to the great manufactory, where he found Mr. Scott in his office.

"Mr Scott, I want to learn my trade over again."

"Eh, Tom, what do you mean?"

"I mean that it's Tom Darcy come back to the old place, asking forgiveness for the past, and hoping to do better in the future."

"Tom," cried the manufacturer, starting forward and grasping his hand, "are you in earnest? Is it really the old Tom?"

"It's what's left of him, sir, and we'll have him whole and strong very soon, if you'll only set him at work."

"Work! Aye, Tom, and bless you, too. There is an engine to be set up and tested to-day. Come with me."

Tom's hands were weak and unsteady, but his brain was clear, and under his skilful supervision the engine was set up and tested; but it was not perfect. There were mistakes which he had to correct, and it was late in the evening when the work was complete.

"How is it now, Tom?" asked Mr. Scott, as he came into the testing-house and found the workmen ready to depart.

"She's all right, sir. You may give your warrant without fear."

"God bless you, Tom! You don't know how like music the old voice sounds. Will you take your old place again?"

"Wait till Monday morning, sir. If you will offer it to me then, I will take it."

At the little cottage, Ellen Darcy's fluttering heart was sinking. That morning, after Tom had gone, she found a dollar bill in the coffee-cup. She knew that he left it for

her. She had been out and bought tea and sugar, and
flour and butter, and a bit of tender steak ; and all day long
a ray of light had been dancing and glimmering before her,
—a ray from the blessed light of other days. With prayer
and hope she had set out the tea-table, and waited ; but the
sun went down and no Tom came. Eight o'clock—and
almost nine.

Hark ! The old step ! quick, strong, eager for home.
Yes, it was Tom, with the old grime upon his hands, and
the odor of oil upon his garments.

"I have kept you waiting, Nellie."

"Tom !"

"I did not mean to, but the work hung on."

"Tom ! Tom ! You have been to the old shop !"

"Yes, and I'm bound to have the old place, and ——"

"Oh, Tom !"

And she threw her arms around his neck, and pressed
a kiss upon his lips.

"Nellie, darling, wait a little, and you shall have the
old Tom back again."

"Oh, I have him now ! God bless you, my husband !"

It was a banquet, that supper—with the bright angels
of peace, and love, and joy, spreading their wings over the
board.

On the following Monday morning, Tom resumed his
place at the head of the great machine-shop, and those who
thoroughly knew him had no fear of his going back into the
slough of joylessness.

A few days later, Tom met Peter Tindar on the street.

"Eh, Tom, old boy, what's up ?"

"I am up, right side up."

"Yes, I see; but I hope you haven't forsaken us, Tom."

"I have forsaken only the evil you have in store, Peter. The fact is, I concluded that my wife and little ones had fed on husks long enough, and if there was a good kernel left in my heart, or in my manhood, they should have it."

"Ah, you heard what I said to my wife that night."

"Yes, Peter; and I shall be grateful to you for it as long as I live. My remembrance of you will always be relieved by that tinge of warmth and brightness."

### SONG OF THE RYE.

I WAS made to be eaten,
  And not to be drank;
To be thrashed in a barn,
  Not soaked in a tank.
I come as a blessing
  When put through a mill,
As a blight and a curse
  When run through a still.

Make me up into loaves,
  And the children are fed;
But if into drink,
  I'll starve them instead.
In bread I'm a servant,
  The eater shall rule;
In drink I am master,
  The drinker a fool.

# Ruined at Home.

T is at home that the ruin of a soul begins."
"At home!" We hear the response in tones
of pained surprise or indignant denial from
many voices. "It is a hard saying and cruel."
"It may hurt like a blow many sad hearts; but if it be
true—what then?"

"It is not true! I can point to you a dozen cases
within my own range of observation to disprove the assertion—to young men who have gone astray in spite of the
careful training and good example of religious homes—in
spite of all the best of mothers and the wisest of fathers
could do."

Yes, we hear such things said every day; but feel certain there is an error somewhere, a defect in your observation. Were you in the homes of these young men from
the beginning? Did you observe the personal bearing of
their parents toward them—know their walk and conversation? If nay, then you are not competent, with your
instances, to disprove our assertion.

A small error at the beginning of a series of calculations
in applied mechanics may lead to a great disaster; the
slightest variation from a right line at the beginning will
throw a projectile hundreds of yards away from its object.
It is in the little things at home, the almost unnoticed de-
partures from order and good government, the neglects

arising from parental self-indulgence, the weakness of love that fails to nip a fault in the bud; and many other things that might be instanced, which turn the young feet into ways of life that, as the years go by, lead farther and farther from safety and happiness.

The Bible, experience, and reason all declare that the future of a child depends upon his early training. If this is bad, the chances are nearly all against him.

"But," we hear it said, "children raised under the worst influences often make good and useful men."

The cases are exceptional, and stand out in strong contrast to the general rule. And so we go back to what was declared in the beginning, that the ruin of a soul begins at home. How many instances crowd upon the memory! Let us take a few at this time for their lesson and their warning.

Not long ago, in one of our principal cities, an almost broken-hearted mother parted from her son in the court-house, and was taken fainting to her home, while he was thrust into a van and conveyed to prison. His crime was stealing. Society held up its hands in pity and amazement, for the young man's father and mother were highly respectable people, and good church members, as the saying is. The father's business reputation stood high. People said of him: "His word is as good as his bond." And yet his son was a condemned thief. He had stolen from his employer.

Did the ruin in this case begin at home?—Yes! It was at home the son learned to be dishonest, and he learned it from his mother! Let us rehearse a few of the lessons, in precept and example, that were given to the boy. We begin when he was just five years of age. The boy, Karl, was standing near his mother, Mrs. Omdorff, one day, when he heard her say to his aunt: "Barker has cheated himself. Here are four yards of ribbon, instead of three. I asked for three yards, and paid for only three; but this measures full four yards."

The boy listened and waited for what was to come next. He loved his mother, and trusted in her.

"What are you going to do about it?" inquired the aunt.

"Keep it, of course," answered Mrs. Omdorff; "Barker will never be the wiser. He makes enough out of us, dear knows." And she rolled the ribbon about her fingers.

Karl was a little surprised. It did not seem like his mother, nor in accordance with what she had often said to him about truth and honesty, but he had faith in her, and was sure that she could do nothing wrong. His Aunt Ruth, of whom he was very fond, and who had great influence over him, was a weak woman in some respects, and much more inclined to take the current of other's opinions than to give herself the trouble of opposition. Her innate sense of honor was a little disturbed at her sister's views of the case; but she failed to say the right words which were in her thoughts, and which, if spoken, might have helped the boy to see what was just and right.

A day or two afterward, Karl heard his mother say: "I saved a car ticket this morning."

"How?" inquired her sister.

"The conductor forgot to ask for it."

"Why did n't you give it to him, mamma?" asked Karl.

"It was his business to look after his passengers," replied Mrs. Omdorff, who felt rather uncomfortable at this question from her little boy. "It will teach him a lesson."

Karl thought a moment, and then said: "But he won't know anything about it."

"Oh, you're too sharp!" exclaimed his mother, with a laugh. "I was n't talking to you, anyhow."

"Little pitchers have big ears," said Aunt Ruth, echoing her sister's laugh.

And so the matter was pushed aside, neither mother nor aunt imagining that the bright and beautiful boy they both loved so tenderly had received a lesson in dishonesty not soon to be forgotten.

"I do believe," said Mrs. Omdorff, not long afterward, as she sat counting over some money, "that Poole has given me the wrong change."

"Karl was in the room and heard her remark.

"Let me see," she added, going over the money again. "Two and a half, three, four and three-quarters. It's a fact; I gave him a ten-dollar bill, and here are four and three-quarters change."

"What did the goods amount to?" asked her sister.

"There were eleven yards of muslin at eighteen; that's a dollar and ninety-eight cents. Two yards of silk at a dollar and a half, and an eighth of a yard of velvet one dollar—making just five dollars and ninety-eight cents. If it had come to six dollars, my right change would have been four; but he has given me four and three-quarters."

Then, in a tone of satisfaction, she added: "I'm that much richer, you see, Ruth."

Her sister smiled, but did not utter the disapproval that was in her heart. Karl listened and took all in. A little while afterward Mrs. Omdorff got up and rang the bell, saying, as she did so, with a short gurgling laugh, that seemed ashamed of itself: "I guess we'll have a little ice-cream—at Poole's expense."

Aunt Ruth shook her finger, and said feebly: "Oh, that's too bad!" But Karl was not able to see whether she approved or disapproved. The ice-cream was sent for, and enjoyed by the child. While the sweet taste was yet on his tongue, he heard his mother say: "I'm very much obliged to Poole for his treat—it's delicious."

Is it strange that the boy's perception of right and wrong should be obscured? or that, in a day or two afterward, he should come in from the street with an orange in his hand, and, on being questioned about it, reply: "A woman let it drop from her basket, and I picked it up. She didn't see it drop, mamma."

"But why didn't you call after her?" asked Aunt Ruth.

"'Cause I didn't want to," answered the child. "She dropped it. I didn't knock it off."

Mrs. Omdorff was not satisfied with the conduct of her child; and yet she was amused at what she called his cuteness, and laughed instead of reproving him for an act that was in spirit a theft.

So the child's education for crime was begun—his ruin initiated  The low moral sense of his mother was perpetually showing itself in some disregard for others' rights. A mistake made in her favor was never voluntarily corrected, and her pleasure at any gain of this kind was rarely concealed. "He cheated himself," was a favorite saying, heard by Karl almost every week; and as he grew older he understood its meaning more clearly.

Mr. Omdorff was a man of higher integrity than his wife, and just in dealing to the smallest fraction. "Foolish about little things—more nice than wise," as she often said, when he disapproved of her way of doing things, as was sometimes the case. Mrs. Omdorff had learned to be guarded in her speech when he was at home; and so he remained in ignorance of the fatal perversions going on in the mind of his child.

As the boy grew up his father's supervision became more direct. He was careful about his associates, and never permitted him to be away from home without knowing where and with whom he was. He knew but too well the danger of evil association; and guarded his boy with jealous solicitude.

Alas! he dreamed not of the evil influences at home; never imagined that the mother was destroying in her son that nice sense of honor without which no one is safe; nor that she had taught him to disregard the rights of others, to take mean advantages, and to appropriate what did not belong to him whenever it could be done with absolute certainty of concealment.

We do not mean to say that such were the direct and purposed teachings of his mother. She would have been horror stricken at the mere suggestion. But she had so taught him by example. In heart she was not honest; and in many of her transactions she was as much a thief as if she had robbed a till. Retaining what belongs to another, simply because it has come into our hands by mistake, is as much a theft in its spirit as purposed stealing; and the fine lady who keeps the change to which she is not entitled, or the yard of ribbon measured to her in error, is just as criminal, as the sneak-thief who gets into her hall through a neglected door and steals her husband's overcoat. The real quality of an act lies in the intent.

Is it any wonder that amid such home influences the boy did not show, as he advanced toward maturity, a high sense of honor? That he should be mean and selfish and dishonest in little things? "As the twig is bent the tree is inclined." Evil seed will produce evil fruit.

Society punished and execrated the unhappy young man, and pitied his wretched mother, little dreaming that by her hand his prison doors had been opened.

Another instance of the baneful influence that may exist at home is to be found in the ruin of a young man who recently died in one of the lowest and vilest haunts of the city. He had been well educated, and grew to manhood with a fine sense of honor. His mother was a woman of rare culture, and beloved by every one in the circle where she moved. All the moral sentiments of her son had been carefully fostered and developed, and when he reached manhood no one showed a fairer promise.

But it was not long before a shadow fell across his life. He had learned one thing at home that was destined to work his ruin—he had learned to love the taste of wine.

His father belonged to a class of men who considered wine drinking a mark of good breeding. He knew all about wines, and had a weak vanity in being thought a

connoisseur.   If he had a friend to dinner, he would bring
out two or three kinds, and discuss them through half the
meal.   He called the men who were ranging themselves
against the terrible evil of intemperance, and seeking to
stay its baleful course, "poor fanatics."   He talked of pure
wines and liquors as harmless, and gave them to his son at
suitable times and occasions, *moderately;* only guarding
him by warnings against excess.

But these warnings went for nothing as appetite increased.   At twelve years of age the boy was content with
a single glass of light wine at his dinner ; at eighteen he
wanted two glasses, and at twenty-one three.   By this time
he had acquired convivial habits, and often drank freely
with other young men of his age.   His mother was the first
to take the alarm ; but his father was slow to believe that
his son was in danger.   The sad truth broke upon him at
last in a painful humiliation.   At a large party in his own
house the young man became so badly intoxicated that he
had to be removed from the company.

From that unhappy period wine was banished from the
father's table.   But it was too late !   The work of ruin had
progressed too far.   At twenty-seven the wretched young
man died, as we have said, in one of the lowest and vilest
dens of the city.

We could give many instances like this.   Here, at
home, is the chief source of that wide-spread ruin by intemperance, that is every year robbing society of thousands
of young men, who, by education, culture, and social standing are fitted for useful and honorable positions.   They are
ruined at home.   Not in one case in ten does a young man

acquire the taste for drink in a saloon or tavern, but at home—if not in his own home, in that of some friend. We fear that the drinking saloons men set up in their drawing-rooms, and to which they invite the young and old of both sexes, do more to deprave the taste and lead to intemperance than all the licensed taverns in the land. It is here that the appetite is formed and fostered—here that the apprenticeship to drunkenness is served. Year by year the sons of our wealthiest and most intelligent and influential citizens are tempted and led astray by the drinking customs of society—ruined at home. How few of the sons of successful men rise to the level their fathers have gained. How many, alas! sink so far below this level that the eyes ache to look down upon them!

### GOOD-BYE—GOD BLESS YOU!

I LOVE the words—perhaps because
   When I was leaving mother,
Standing at last in solemn pause,
   We looked at one another;
And I—I saw in mother's eyes
   The love she could not tell me,
A love eternal as the skies,
   Whatever fate befell me.

She put her arms about my neck,
   And soothed the pain of leaving,
And though her heart was like to break,
   She spoke no word of grieving;
She let no tear bedim her eye,
   For fear that might distress me;
But, kissing me, she said good-bye,
   And asked our God to bless me.

# HOW IT WAS BLOTTED OUT

FOR many years I had been a follower of strange gods, and a lover of this world and its vanities. I was self-righteous, and thought I had religion of my own which was better than that of the Bible. I did not know God, and did not serve him. Prayer was forgotten, public worship neglected ; and worldly morality was the tree which brought forth its own deceptive fruit.

But when I shared parental responsibility, and our boy was growing up, our love for him made us anxious about his welfare and future career. His questions often puzzled me, and the sweet and earnest manner in which he inquired of his poor sinful father to know more about his Heavenly Father, and that "happy land, far, far away," of which his nurse had taught him, proved to me that God had given me a great blessing in the child.

A greater distrust of myself, and a greater sense of my inability to assure my boy of the truth contained in the simple little prayers that I had learned from my mother in

166

childhood, gradually caused me to reflect. Still, I never went to church; had not even a Bible in the house. What was I to teach my boy,—Christ and him crucified, or the doctrines I had tried to believe?

One of his little friends died, then another, then his uncle. All these deaths made an impression on the boy. He rebelled against it; wanted to know "why God had done it?" It was hard that God should take away his friends; he wished he would not do it. I, of course, had to explain the best I could. One evening he was lying on the bed partly undressed; my wife and I were seated by the fire. She had been telling me that Willie had not been a good boy that day, and I had reproved him for it. All was quiet, when suddenly he broke out in a loud crying and sobbing, which surprised us. I went to him, and asked him what was the matter.

"I don't want it there, father; I don't want it there," said the child.

"What, my child, what is it?"

"Why, father, I don't want the angels to write down in God's book all the bad things I have done to-day. I don't want it there; I wish it could be wiped out;" and his distress increased. What could I do? I did not believe, but yet I had been taught the way. I had to console him, so I said,—

"Well, you need not cry; you can have it all wiped out in a minute if you want."

"How, father, how?"

"Why, get down on your knees, and ask God, for Christ's sake, to wipe it out, and he will do it."

I did not have to speak twice.  He jumped out of bed, saying, "Father, won't you come and help me?"

Now came the trial.  The boy's distress was so great, and he pleaded so earnestly, that the man who had never once bowed before God in spirit and in truth, got down on his knees beside that little child, and asked God to wipe away his sins; and perhaps, though my lips did not speak it, my heart included my own sins too.  We then rose, and he lay down in his bed again.  In a few moments more he said,—

"Father, are you sure it is all wiped out?"

Oh, how the acknowledgment grated upon my unbelieving heart, as the words came to my mouth,—"Why, yes, my son; the Bible says that if from your heart you ask God for Christ's sake to do it, and if you are really sorry for what you have done, it shall be all blotted out."

A smile of pleasure passed over his face, as he quietly asked,—

"What did the angel blot it out with?  With a sponge?"

Again was my whole soul stirred within me, as I answered,—

"No, but with the precious blood of Christ.  The blood of Christ cleanseth from all sin."

The fountains had at last burst forth.  They could not be checked, and my cold heart was melted within me.  I felt like a poor guilty sinner, and, turning away, said,—

"My dear wife, *we* must first find God, if we want to show him to our children.  We cannot show them the way, unless we know it ourselves."

And in the silent hour of the night I bowed beside that

dear boy, and prayed, " Lord, I believe, help thou mine unbelief!" My wife, too, united with me, and we prayed
jointly for ourselves and our child. And God heard our
prayers, and received us, as he always does those who seek
him with the whole heart.

## THE WAY TO OVERCOME.

WHEN first from slumber waking,
  No matter what the hour,
If you will say, " Dear Jesus,
  Come, fill me with thy power,"
You'll find that every trouble
  And every care and sin
Will vanish, surely, fully,
  Because Christ enters in.

It may be late in morning,
  Or in the dark before,
When first you hear his knocking;
  But open wide the door,
And say to him, " Dear Jesus,
  Come in and take the throne,
Lest Satan with his angels
  Should claim it for his own."

For we are weak and sinful,
  " Led captive at his will."
But thou canst " bind the strong man,"
  Our heart with sweetness fill.
So would we have " thy presence "
  From our first waking hour;
All through the swift day's moments,
  Dwell thou with us in power.

# Never Indorse.

I SHALL not soon forget the family of Israel Day, who lived neighbor to my father when I was a boy. Mr. Day was working out as a laborer, and as he had a large family dependent upon his earnings for support, and sometimes it was difficult in our neighborhood to find employment, the family was poor, and the strictest economy had to be practiced to furnish the bare necessities of life.

I often wondered how it happened that such a man as Mr. Day should be so poor. He had no intemperate or extravagant habits, and was a man of more than common education, and there was an air of intelligence and refinement about the entire family that commanded the respect of their neighbors. Mr. Day was industrious, but always seemed to me a man who had no ambition in life, and who expected and desired no more than a mere subsistence for his family. No one in the neighborhood knew anything of his history. The family had come from another State a few years previous, and while polite and friendly, they were very uncommunicative as to their former life, and there was something about them that forbade inquisitiveness.

I was at this time sixteen years old, and on very intimate terms with Mr. Day's family. At the time of my story he was helping my father on the farm for a few days and boarding with us. One day when we came in from our forenoon work, we found 'Squire Black was to take dinner with us, and as he was reputed to be the wealthiest man in the township, we felt quite honored. He was a very genial man and an excellent talker, and had an adroit way of flattering and making every one feel easy in his company.

On this occasion he made himself very agreeable; he praised the neat appearance of the farm and buildings, complimented mother on her good cooking, called me a fine, manly fellow, gave some small change to the children, and by the time dinner was over had gained the good will of the entire family.

After dinner Mr. Black asked to see the stock and examine the arrangement of the barn and outbuildings, and as father took pride in having good, well-fed stock and one of the most conveniently arranged barns in the county, he was glad to show him around, and was much pleased with the hearty commendation which Mr. Black bestowed upon them.

He finally made known the object of his visit; he had found a piece of very desirable property for sale, low, so that there was no question that within less than a year he could clear several thousand dollars on it, but he must pay all cash down and he lacked two thousand dollars of having enough money to pay for it. He wished father to become security for him for one year, as he had found a party who was willing to lend him the amount if his signature could be had to the note.

He did not give father time to think or scarcely to answer his questions, but took out his pocketbook and handed him a paper, supposing it to be the note which he had drawn up, and signed by himself, all ready for father's signature. I verily believe that if the paper had been what Squire Black thought it to be, father could not have refused to sign it; but it so happened that he had made a mistake and left the note at home and had substituted for it another paper.

A shade of vexation passed over the 'Squire's face when he discovered the mistake, but he at once recovered his good humor and said, "Never mind; I will call again this evening," and hastily mounted his horse and rode away.

Father looked troubled, and turning to me, said, "I do not like to indorse for any one, but 'Squire Black will be insulted if I refuse, and as he is rich I suppose there can be no risk about it. It is only complying with a legal form, and I suppose I shall be obliged to do it; but I wish he had not asked me to do so."

Before I could reply, the barn door opened and Mr. Day came out; he was pale and deeply agitated, and when he spoke I should not have recognized his voice. Calling my father by name, he said, "I believe that you are in danger, and if you will listen to me I will give you a chapter from my own history that I had never intended should be known to any in this neighborhood."

Father motioned for me to leave, thinking that Mr. Day wished to speak to him alone. He noticed it, however, and said, "No, let him stay, for one cannot learn too soon the lesson that my experience teaches. I would be willing that it should be published to the world if thereby some could be saved from my bitter experience. I overheard, as you know, what 'Squire Black said to you. Listen to my story

PAUL AT ATHENS.

and then decide as to whether you will put your name on his note.

"Fifteen years ago, when I was married, I was not the poor man that you now know me to be. My father gave me as my share of his property two thousand dollars, which I had increased to three, and my wife received as her wedding portion one thousand dollars. We were both strong and willing to work, and ambitious to succeed in the world, and we bought a good farm, running in debt a few hundred dollars. For several years we were greatly prospered. We had good health, and the seasons were favorable, so that we grew heavy crops and obtained fair prices for them.

"At the end of five years we had paid off our debt and had nearly one thousand dollars in the bank, and we felt that it would be safe to build a new house, although we expected to put more than the amount of money on hand into it.

"In the meantime there had come into the neighborhood one of the most companionable men I ever met. He was familiarly known as Capt. Cole. He had been a lawyer, but had been appointed by the General Government to a lucrative office which he held for some years, and had the reputation of being very wealthy. He lived in good style, and was a general favorite in all the community.

"When my house was finished I found myself in debt seven hundred dollars, and as I had given the contract to a carpenter, he to furnish everything, he needed all his money. I went to the bank to borrow the amount until I could find some one who would let me have it for one or two years, and not being accustomed to borrow money, it did not occur to me that an indorser would be necessary, until the cashier of the bank informed me that it was their invariable custom to require security. Capt. Cole, who happened to be in at the time, overheard the conversation and came forward with a pleasant 'Good morning,' saying, 'I shall be only too happy to indorse for my friend, Mr. Day.' I felt both grateful and flattered, and when a few months later I happened to be in the bank when he wanted an indorser, I was glad to return the favor.

"We had two years of prosperity, and I paid the debt on my house. I now determined to build a fine barn, and as I had always paid my debts easily and could not well get along with my old barn until I had saved the money to build the new one, I determined to borrow one thousand dollars, and happening to meet Capt. Cole, I asked him if he knew where I could get that amount for three years. He told me he did, and offered to become my security. The money was borrowed and my barn begun.

"A few weeks later Capt. Cole called to see me. Like 'Squire Black to-day, he seemed delighted with everything he saw. His flattery put me in the best possible humor, and when he asked me to indorse a note of $5,000 for sixty days, and assured me that he could meet it (or even twice as much) promptly, to the day, I consented against my better judgment, and affixed my signature to the note. That act ruined me. Before the sixty days expired I learned that he was bankrupt. My farm was sold at a sacrifice, under the hammer, and when I paid the thousand dollars which I had borrowed to build the barn with, I was left penniless.

"With my history in your possession, do you wonder that I was alarmed to-day when I saw you about to fall into the same trap? I tell you I have a right to feel deeply on this subject. Would that I could make my voice heard by every young man in the land. I would say to him, shun as you would a serpent this evil which has brought ruin to so many families. I realize fully what it means to put my name on another man's paper, and it is just this—that I assume all the risks of his business, without any voice in its management or any possible chance of profit if he is successful; but with a fearful certainty that if from any cause he makes a failure, my earnings must make it good, even though it reduces my family to beggary. Since my own misfortune I have made this a matter of study, and I find that a very large per cent. of the business failures, of the country (and nearly all among farmers) are due to this practice."

The remainder of my story is soon told. My father was deeply impressed by Mr. Day's story, and before night I was dispatched to 'Squire Black's with a note from father stating that after carefully considering the matter he had decided not to sign the note. In less than a year after this 'Squire Black was declared a bankrupt, and in the final settlement of his business it did not pay ten cents on the dollar.

Father felt that he owed a debt of gratitude to Mr. Day, and he presented him with a good team and helped him to rent a farm. This encouraged him, and he worked so industriously and managed so prudently that in a few years he was able to buy a small farm and has since been able to support his family comfortably.

Many years have passed since these events occurred, and I am now past middle life, but I have never ceased to be thankful for the lesson taught me by Mr. Day, and in fulfilling his wish I would repeat the lesson which the story teaches—never indorse.

## WATCH YOUR WORDS.

KEEP a watch on your words, my darling,
　For words are wonderful things;
They are sweet like the bee's fresh honey—
　Like the bees, they have terrible stings;
They can bless, like the warm, glad sunshine,
　And brighten a lonely life;
They can cut in the strife of anger,
　Like an open two-edged knife.

Let them pass through your lips unchallenged,
　If their errand is true and kind—
If they come to support the weary,
　To comfort and help the blind;
If a bitter, revengeful spirit
　Prompt the words, let them be unsaid;
They may flash through a brain like lightning,
　Or fall on a heart like lead.

Keep them back, if they are cold and cruel,
　Under bar and lock and seal;
The wounds they make, my darling,
　Are always slow to heal.
May peace guard your life, and ever,
　From the time of your early youth,
May the words that you daily utter
　Be the words of beautiful truth.

# A·LIFE LESSON

**A**LBERT MOORE, at the age of twenty-five, took Alice Warren for his wife. He had been in the army—fought through from Bull's Bluff to Richmond—had come out with a captain's commission. He had come from the army with but little money; but he had a good trade, a stout pair of hands, and had borrowed no trouble for the future. Alice had saved up a few hundred dollars from her wages as a teacher, and when the twain had become husband and wife they found, upon a careful inventory, that they had enough to furnish a small house comfortably. Albert proposed that they should hire a tenement in the city; but Alice thought they had better secure a pretty cottage in the suburbs—a cottage which they might, perhaps, in time, make their own.

Albert had no disposition to argue the question, so the cottage was found and secured. It was a pleasant, rural location, and so connected with the city by rail, that Albert found no difficulty in going to and from his workshop.

During her five years' experience in school-teaching

Alice had learned many things, and having been an orphan from an early age, she had made the problems of real life one of her chief studies ; and what she had learned in this latter department served her well in her new station. After marriage she found Albert to be just the man she had known him to be in other years. He was kind to a fault ; free-hearted and generous ; ready always to answer the call of friendship ; and prone to pluck the flowers that bloom to-day, regardless of what may be nurtured to bloom to-morrow.

They had been married but a few months when Alice found he was cutting his garments according to his daily supply of cloth. Not a shred was he likely to save up from the cuttings for an extra garment for a rainy day to come.

"Albert," she said to him one evening, " do you know we ought to be laying up a little something ? "

Albert looked up from his paper and waited for his wife to explain.

"I think I heard you tell Mr. Greenough that you had no money—that you had paid out your last dollar this very afternoon ? "

"Exactly, my dear ; but you know to-morrow is pay-day."

"And you have spent your last month's earnings ? "

" Yes."

A brief silence ensued, which Albert broke.

" Come, Alice, you've got something on your mind. Out with it—I'll listen."

And then Alice, in a smiling, pleasant way, went on to tell her husband that they ought to be laying up something.

Albert smiled in turn, and asked how such a thing could be done when it cost all he earned to live.

"You earn three dollars and a half a day," said Alice.

"Yes."

"George Summers earns only three dollars a day."

"You are right."

"And yet he lives and does not run in debt."

"But he is forced to deny himself many little comforts which we enjoy."

"And the one great comfort which we might enjoy we are throwing away."

"How is that, Alice."

"The comfort of a little sum in the bank, which we should see growing toward the answering of future wants."

Albert could not see how it was to be done; and Alice feared that a lesson of empty words might be wasted. She knew that his ambition needed a substantial prop. Never, of his own accord, would he commence to save by littles. He did not estimate money in that way. Had some kind fairy dropped into his hand a five-twenty bond for five hundred dollars, he would have put it away gladly; and with such a nest-egg in the start, he might have sought to add to the store. But he could see no hope in a dollar bill, and much less could he discover the nucleus of a grand saving in a fifty-cent piece.

With Alice it was different. From her meager earnings as school-teacher she had in less than five years, saved up three hundred dollars; and the first saving she had put by was a silver dime. She knew what little by little could do, and she was determined to show it to her husband.

She must be patient and persevering, and these qualities she possessed in an eminent degree. It was to be the grand undertaking of the first years of her married life, and to do it she would bend every available energy. She planned that if possible she would get hold of that fifty cents every day; or, if she could not do that she would do the best she could.

Generous, frank, loyal, and loving, Albert was an easy prey to the wiles of a wife loyal and loving as himself. He gave her money when she asked for it; and she asked for it when she thought he had any to give.

And here let me say that Alice knew her husband would not run in debt. That was an evil they both arrayed themselves against in the outset. When Albert's purse was empty he bought nothing; but when it was full he was apt to buy more than he needed. Alice knew all this and governed herself accordingly.

"I think," said Alice, one evening, "that I must fix over my old brown cashmere for winter, I should like a new one, but I do n't suppose you can afford it."

Albert looked grieved. The idea that he could not afford his wife a new dress!

But such a one as she wanted would cost twenty-five or thirty dollars.

"If you want it, get it," said Albert emphatically. "I will let you have twenty dollars from this month's pay, and the balance you shall have next month."

Alice got the thirty dollars, but she did not get the new dress. By the outlay of five dollars for new trimmings she contrived to fix over the brown cashmere so that it looked every bit as good as new.

And so Alice worked. Sometimes she asked her husband for ten cents, sometimes for fifty cents, sometimes for a dollar, and sometimes for more, and at the end of a year, upon carefully reckoning up, she found that she had managed to get hold of rather more than fifty cents a day; but she had done it by denying herself of many things, some of which seemed really needful.

The result of the first year's effort inspired Alice with new life and vigor. She had saved one hundred and fifty dollars, and had invested it in government funds. Through the influence of a dear friend who was in a banking establishment, and to whom she had confided her secret, she was enabled to get the bonds at their face value.

It was only a little at a time—sometimes a very little—but those littles multiplied by other littles, grew amazingly. The husbandman who would sit himself down by a hill of corn, and wait to see the tender blades put forth would be disheartened; but he knows if he plants the tiny seed, and cultivates it as he ought, the harvest of golden grain will come at length.

Albert and Alice were married in the spring of 1865. It was on an evening of August, 1870, that Albert came home. He had been notified that they must leave the cottage. They must give up the pleasant home, and lose the little garden they had cultivated with so much fondness and care

"The owner wishes to sell," he exclaimed; "and has an offer. He asks two thousand dollars, and must have five hundred down."

Alice's eyes gleamed with radiant delight.

She had been thinking for some time that she must let
her husband into her secret.   It had begun to wear upon
her.   And now the time had come as by providential in-
terposition.

She got up and went away to her cabinet, and when
she came back she brought a little book in her hand.

" Albert ! "  said she, " lets you and I buy the cottage."

Albert looked at her in amazement;  and directly it
flashed upon him that there was too much solemnity in her
look and  tone for badinage.   Something that he had
noticed during the past few months came back to him, and he
trembled with the weight of suspense that fell upon him.

Alice then  showed her book—that she had more than
eight hundred  dollars in the bank.   The  ice was broken—
she told her  story  in  glowing words.   She  told how she
had saved up  little by little, and  how she had at length
found herself able to purchase a fifty-dollar bond.   And
then she told how her uncle in the banking-house had taken
charge of her investment ; and how, under his management,
the interest had accrued in amazing volume.

But the grand result was not the chief thing.   The
chief thing was the beginning—was the very little which
had been religiously saved until the second little could be
added to it.

And now, as a result of his wife's careful and tireless
working, Albert found something upon which his ambition
could take a fair start.   He never could himself, from so
small a commencement, have reared the pile ; but with the
structure started, and its proportions all blocked out, he
could help on the work.   He could see how it was done—

and not only that, but the demonstration was before him that the thing could be done.

One year has elapsed since Albert Moore received the lesson from his wife, and joining hands with her, and bending his energies in the same direction, he has accomplished during the twelve months what would have seemed to him a marvel in the earlier time. He has laid by more than fifty cents a day; and the cigars, and the beer, and the other condiments of life which he has surrendered to the work, are not missed—rather, he holds they are so many enemies conquered. And Albert can improve his home with cheerful heart, and he can set out new trees and vines in his garden with bright promises, because he sees, day by day, the pretty cottage growing more and more his own. The end approaches a little at a time—little by little it approaches, but surely, nevertheless; and there is a great and satisfying joy even in the labor and in the anticipation.

O DEEM not they are blest alone
    Whose lives a peaceful tenor keep;
For God, who pities man, hath shown
    A blessing for the eyes that weep.

The light of smiles shall fill again
    The lids that overflow with tears,
And weary hours of woe and pain
    Are promises of happier years.

For God has marked each sorrowing day,
    And numbered every secret tear,
And heaven's long age of bliss shall pay
    For all his children suffer here.
                    —*William Cullen Bryant.*

# Hard Times Conquered.

BOUT seventy years ago, a physician with a young family springing up about him, consulting his wife, as all good husbands find it prudent to do, bought a large farm in one of our New England States, where every farmer truly earns his living by the sweat of his brow. Both felt that nowhere could their children be trained to industry and frugality so thoroughly as on a good farm.

The doctor was obliged to " run in debt" for this property, and he gave a mortgage on the place. The payments were to be made quarterly, and promptly, or the whole would be forfeited and revert to the original owner. In those days physicians were not likely to become millionaires, and though Dr. Mason's practice was large, the pay was small, and not always sure. He therefore looked to the farm for the means to release him from the bondage of debt; and the children, even to the youngest, were taught to labor for, and look forward eagerly to, the time "when we have paid for the farm!"

The creditor was the doctor's father-in-law, through his first wife, and while the good old gentleman lived, if by any mishap or overpress of business the quarterly payment had been delayed, it would have been kindly excused. But for the ten or fifteen years that he lived after the sale of the farm, there had not been one delay in payment, though

now and then there would come a time when it was very
hard to secure the needed sum in time, for even in the
olden days "hard times" were often experienced, to the
terror of our hard-working New England farmers. But
little by little, the heavy debt was diminishing, and the
doctor's family were looking forward hopefully to the year
of jubilee, when they could sit under their own vine and
fig-tree with none to molest and make them afraid.

At this period the father-in-law died. He had but two
children,—daughters. The younger, the doctor's wife, died
childless. The elder married a hard, close, scheming man
who lost no opportunity of remarking that he would, no
doubt, soon come in possession of Dr. Mason's farm, as the
latter, with his large family, must fail by and by.

The financial troubles which the war of 1812 had
caused, as all wars are sure to do, were not yet adjusted.
Money was scarce, and payments very difficult. Ten children now filled the old house with merriment and gladness;
but they were to be clothed and educated.

Let us see how successfully they had been taught to
make their high spirits and resolute wills cheerful auxiliaries
in lifting the burden, which, since their grandfather's death,
was pressing upon their parents.

At the time of which we write, among other crops, rye
was extensively raised. It was used for food among the
farmers quite as much as wheat, and was also valuable for
other purposes. When full-grown, but still in the milk,
large quantities were cut to be used for "braiding." The
heads were used for "fodder;" the stalks, after being
soaked in strong hot soap-suds, were spread on the grass

for the sun to whiten. When sufficiently bleached and ready for use, they were cut at each joint, and the husk stripped off, and the straw thus prepared was then tied in pound bundles for sale.

Bonnets, then, meant something more than a small bit of silk or velvet with a flower or feather attached, and the "straw braid" for making them was in great demand. Boys and girls were alike taught to braid, and the long winter evenings were not spent idly. Dr. Mason raised large crops of rye, and each child, almost as soon as he could walk, was taught to braid, and was soon able to do much by it toward clothing himself. At six years of age a dollar a week was easily earned; at eight, three dollars; and in something of that proportion up to the eldest.

Does any one think that such a life, with such an object in view, was hard or cruel? Never was there a greater mistake. It was of great value to those young spirits. They had something real, that they could understand, to labor for. There was life and courage and true heroism in it. It was an education—with here and there, to be sure, some rough places to pass over—which was worth more to them than all the money millionaires bequeath their sons and daughters; an education which prepared them in after-life to be courageous and self-helpful.

It is this kind of training that has made New England's sons and daughters strong and self-reliant, and the lack of it which makes these hard times such a horror that we hear of many who seek death by their own hands as preferable to the struggle for better times.

In the long winter evenings, when the labor of the day

was over, the children home from school, and the "chores" all finished, the candles were lighted and the evening work began.   The mother in her corner was busy making and mending for her large family.   The doctor, if not with the sick, read and studied opposite her.   The children gathered around the long table in the middle of the room, where lay the school-books and straw previously prepared for braiding, while the old fireplace, heaped with blazing logs of hickory, oak, and fragrant birch, made the room warm and cheerful.   Here, with their books before them and fastened open to the next day's lessons, the children with nimble fingers plaited the straw and studied at the same time.   For children taught to be industrious, usually carry into the schoolroom the principles thus developed, and are ambitious to keep as near the head of the class as possible.

Such a family as this was well equipped to meet and conquer adversity.   For several days Dr. Mason had been unusually grave and silent.   All noticed it, but no remarks were made until evening, when he came to supper, so unmistakably worried and despondent that his wife inquired if he were not well.

"Yes, well enough.   But, Lucy, I have so far been unable to collect money for our quarterly payment.   So much is due me that I had no fears but that enough would be promptly paid to save me any trouble."

"How much is there lacking?"

"Not quite a hundred dollars; but it might as well be thousands for any chance I now see of getting it in season. There is now so much sickness about, that, as you know, I have had no rest, and little time to collect money.   If not

ready before midnight to-morrow, we are ruined.  I have
kept it from you as long as I dared, still hoping that those
who ought to pay me would do so."

"Have you told them how very important it is that you
should have the money ? "

"No ; I did not wish to speak of it.  Mr. H. is watching greedily for a 'slip,' and we need expect no mercy at
his hands.  Under our hard labor and good care, this farm
has risen greatly in value—too much so for him to spare us
an hour, if he can once get hold of it.  I am about discouraged.  It is the darkest time we have seen yet.  But I
must be off, and will probably be kept out all night.  To
think there are not forty-eight hours between us and ruin !
And my hands are so tied by several severe cases, that I
may not find one hour to make up the little that is needed."

For a few minutes after the doctor left, the children
stood silent and sad, watching their mother.  At last she
said,—

"Children, we can help father through this, and save
our home, if you are willing to submit to some little self-
denial.  No ; I should have said to *great* self-denial.  Each
of you has worked diligently to buy new garments for winter.  You need them and deserve them, and I should be
happy and proud to see you all neat and comfortable.  But
to help father, are you willing to let me try to clean, mend,
or make over your old clothes, and use what you have
earned to help brighten this dark day?  The braid you
have on hand, and what is now due at the store, is all your
own, or to be expended for your own clothes, and if each
one of you is not *perfectly willing*, I do n't wish you to give
it up."

It was a beautiful sight to see those eager faces watching their mother, ready to answer the moment she had finished; for in the olden time children were taught that it was disrespectful to interrupt any one when speaking, even when, as in this case, it was difficult to keep silent. But the reply, when given, was prompt, enthusiastic, as she had confidently looked for it to be.

"Thanks, dear children? Now, then, hasten. First bring me all your braid, and let us see how much it will come to."

The braid, in ten-yard rolls, was brought, and its value estimated.

"With that which is now due us at the store, we have nearly sixty dollars! Well done, for all these little fingers! But now we must devise a way to make up the remainder. Your father spoke last night of a large quantity of straw, which, if cut, would bring in something. He will be away all night. If you work well, we can cut many pounds before midnight. Now, girls, help me wash the dishes, while your brothers bring, before dark, the straw we can cut to-night."

By the time the candles were lighted, all was ready to begin.

The younger children were excused at their usual bed-time, but the others worked with their mother till the tall clock in the corner struck one. Then all retired for a few hours' rest.

Dr. Mason returned home in season for breakfast, and his wife inquired if the eldest son could drive her over to the neighboring town to dispose of some braid for the children. He replied that he must be gone again nearly all day, and neither son nor team could well be spared from important work at home. But a strange thing followed this implied refusal. Mrs. Mason, who never allowed her plans or wishes to interfere with her husband's, now repeated her request, and urged it till he yielded, apparently from sheer surprise that his wife could be so persistent.

The doctor went his usual round, and the mother and her son departed on their mysterious errand. Their business accomplished, they returned well satisfied and ready for supper when the father arrived.

A deeper gloom was on his face when he entered; but no word was spoken till all were seated at the table. Then in a slightly agitated voice his wife inquired,—

"Have you been successful in obtaining the money?"

He shook his head, but remained silent. Each young quivering face was turned first toward him, then with earnest, questioning glance to the mother.

"Be not discouraged, dear, even at this late hour."

"Are you wild, Lucy? There are but six hours between us and ruin. Can you talk of hope now? I have none."

With a warning gesture to the children, she rose, stepped to her husband's chair, and passing her arm round his neck, said, gently,—

"Yet still hope on, my husband; God will not forsake us."

He moved impatiently from under her arm; but as he did so, she dropped a roll into his bosom and turned toward her chair.

"Lucy! Lucy! what is this? Where did you get it?"

All was wild with excitement. Each child laughing, sobbing, shouting, but one glance from that strong but gentle mother quelled the confusion, and she replied,—

"It is our children's offering, and is sufficient to make up the needed sum. I persisted in going away this morning against your wish, because I saw no escape. We cut the straw last night—many willing hands made quick work; I sold it, and their braid added to it, with what was already due them, completed the sum."

Those who witnessed that scene will never forget it; Dr. Mason with his arm around his wife, and both in tears, calling her all happy names, the children clinging about their parents, so joyful that home was saved, and they had helped to save it.

"Put Charlie into the wagon, quick. If he fails me not, the six miles between here and M—— will be the shortest I ever rode. I shall be home before bedtime to thank you all. I cannot now. I hope we shall never come so near ruin again."

And they never did. In two years the last dollar was paid, and then Dr. Mason resolved he would never again owe any one a cent. He kept his resolution.

> It is easy enough to be pleasant
>   When life flows by like a song,
> But the man worth while is the one who will smile
>   When everything goes dead wrong.

# A GOOD LESSON SPOILED

A DARKENED room, spacious and handsomely furnished—being, in fact, the chamber of Mrs. Wilcox, the mother of the little fellow who occupied the wide bed. He lay there in lugubrious state, the rosy face stained with much crying, just showing above the edge of the counterpane; his tangle of yellow curls crushed upon the bolster. Below these was a white mound, stretched along the middle of the bed, just the length of Robby, aged seven and a half, the youngling of the Wilcox family. Two big blue eyes, glazed with tears, wandered from one to another of the two faces gazing at him from opposite sides of the horizontal pillory. Both were kindly, both loving, both sad. They belonged to the parents of Robby, and he had been convicted, sentenced, and punished for telling a lie.

His mother had sent him to the fruit-store with twenty-five cents and an order for two lemons. The tempter, in the form of a " street-boy," waylaid him at the corner with a challenge to a competitive show for tops. The silver " quarter" was in the same pocket with Robby's new air top and card, the pride of his soul. He may have drawn it out with his handkerchief when he wiped his face after the game. The tempter may have known more about it than the tempted suspected. At any rate, the money was not to be found, and he was close by and ready with his proposition when Robby discovered the loss.

" Mamma will certainly scold me this time," he subjoined, turning every pocket inside out, and staring distractedly up and down the street. " I lost ten cents last week, and she told me to be more careful.".

" Do n't tell her! And do n't pay for the lemons. When the bill comes in, your mamma will have forgotten all about sending you for them, or she will think the lemonfeller made a mistake. I know lots of real gamey fellers who get out of scrapes that way. It's only milk-sops who run to mammy with every little bother."

The experiment thus suggested and urged, was a success until mamma demanded the change.

" He said there was n't any!" faltered the errand-boy.

" No change! out of twenty-five cents!" Then with a searching look at the scarlet face painfully averted— " *Robby!*"

The " milk-sop " bethought himself of the " gamey fellers."

" Honest-true, mamma!" he plucked up courage to say.

" Put on your hat, my son, and go with me to the store where you bought the lemons. There is something wrong when my boy cannot look me in the eyes!"

13

Thus came about the tragedy that darkened the June day for the whole Wilcox household. It was at nine o'clock on Saturday morning that the falsehood was detected. At two P. M. Mrs. Wilcox brought up the prisoner's dinner. Only bread and water! He had smelled the savory soup and roast lamb, and the cook had hinted at strawberry short-cake when he passed, whistling, through the kitchen, turning the silver quarter over in his pocket. That was almost five hours ago, and he was to lie here until supper-time, *alone!* When he had eaten the bread of affliction, seasoned with tears of self-pity and remorse, mamma re-appeared with papa.

"My son!" said the latter, "I would rather have you die in your innocent boyhood than grow up a *liar!* Tell the straight, simple truth always and everywhere. No brave man will lie. Papa does not want his boy to be a coward. No honest man will deceive or tell a falsehood. Papa does not want his boy to be a cheat!"

Mrs. Wilcox sat down on the bed when her husband had gone. All the mother-heart in her was crying out and tearing itself with longing and pity ineffable. Arms and heart ached to enfold the precious little sinner so grievously worsted in the battle with temptation. "Mamma is very sorry that her darling has been so naughty!" she said, bowing her head upon the pillow beside the mat of curls dampened by the rain from the culprit's eyes.

"Mamma! Indeed, I will *never* tell another lie—not the leastest fib!" he sobbed.

"God help you to keep your word, my son. Every falsehood is like a drop of ink upon snow to your soul!"

She stroked back his hair and comforted herself by giving him, one after another, the passionate kisses withheld through all these miserable hours. Holding the chubby fingers in hers, she talked to him a few minutes longer of his sin, and to whom he should look for forgiveness ; then bending over him, she prayed in simple words and few for the little one who had stumbled to his own hurt. " Lie still and think it all over, dear ! " was her parting injunction.

At the tea-table, Robby was not disposed to talk. He noted and understood the grave gentleness of his father's countenance and demeanor ; the chastened loveliness of his mother's look ; the quiet tone caught by the other children from the grown-up sister who sat next to him. His transgression had affected the spirits of the whole party. The very avoidance of all direct reference to it was significant and impressive. It was something too disgraceful for table-talk. A blackened soul ! soiled lips ! These were the figures most distinct to his imagination as he crept after supper into the library, and sat down at the alcoved window looking upon a side street. The boys were playing noisily in the warm twilight. Robby watched them, curled up on the window bench, one foot tucked under him, his face more sober each minute. He was sure his mother would shake her head sadly were he to request permission to join the joyous group of his fellows. Nor did he care—very much—to go out. The recollection of sin and consequent suffering was too fresh.

Nettie, the grown-up sister, had a visitor, and mamma had joined the girls, and was chatting cheerfully with them

—not at all as she looked at the cowering little liar under the counterpane up-stairs.

"Mamma," suddenly exclaimed the daughter, "there are old Mr. and Mrs. Bartol! I do believe you are to be honored by a call from them."

"I sincerely hope not," was the answer. "Papa and I had planned a walk on this lovely evening, and our friends the Bartols are given to long sittings."

"Besides being insufferably prosy," interpolated plain-spoken Nettie. "They *are* coming in. Milly, you and I can run away!" and they fluttered through the back-parlor door.

Mamma's face was overcast with genuine vexation. Her sigh, "How provoking!" reached the alcoved auditor. Then she advanced to meet a fat old lady, and a fatter, bald old gentleman.

"Is this really you, Mr. Bartol? It is an age since I have met you. I am happy to see you both. Pray be seated."

"Oh, *good* gracious!" said Robby, under his breath, sinking back into his corner, actually sick and trembling.

When he could listen and think again, papa had been sent for, and Mr. Bartol was apologizing for mingling business with a friendly visit. He wanted to buy a house owned by Mr. Wilcox, situated near his—Mr. Bartol's—home. The play of negotiation, of parry and thrust, was courteous, as befitted actors and scene, but Mr. Bartol's intention to buy cheap, and his host's desire to sell dear, were palpable to the unworldly eavesdropper.

"I am sorry you hold the property at so high a figure!" finally remarked Mr. Bartol, rising to take leave. "I must consult the friend who commissioned me to make inquiries, before I can say anything definite."

Mr. Wilcox was the impersonation of smiling indifference. "The truth is, my dear sir, I do not care to sell at all. The property is rising in value, and I may remove to that part of the city myself next year. I should lose on it were I to take less than the price I have named."

When the guests had gone, Mr. Wilcox turned laughingly to his wife:

"Well, my love, you have lost your walk, but your husband has made four thousand dollars—clear!"

"You think he will buy the place, then?"

"I know he will! He wants to settle his daughter there. She is to be married next month. I had a hint to that effect some days since. I had the game in my hands from the first. I bought the property, three years ago, at a low figure. The rent has covered interest, taxes, etc. I shall never live there myself. It would not be convenient for my business. I have been anxious this great while to sell. I am already carrying more real estate than I ought to hold."

"I am afraid Robby is less impressed by the lesson of to-day than we could desire," observed Mrs. Wilcox sorrowfully to her husband at bedtime. "He strode off to bed without saying 'Good night' to any one, and pretended to be asleep when I looked into his room just now, answering gruffly after I told him I knew he was awake. What shall I do if my child becomes an habitual deceiver?"

"We must watch his associations narrowly," replied the judicious father. "Everything depends upon the examples and impressions of early life."

# Benevolent Society.

IN the snug, cozy barroom of the "Farmers' Inn," at Madisonville, sat six young men. It was a cold, bleak evening in December; and the wind that howled and drove without, drifting the snow and rattling the shutters, gave to the blazing fire and steaming kettle additional charms and comforts. There was Peter Hobbs, a youth of five and twenty, who seemed to be the leader, *par excellence*, of the party. He was a good-natured, intelligent, frank-looking man, and was really a noble-hearted citizen. Then there was John Fulton, a youth of the same age, who worked with Hobbs, both being journeyman carpenters. Samuel Green was a machinist; Walter Mason, a tin worker; Lyman Drake, a cabinet maker; and William Robinson, a clerk. They ranged, in age, from twenty-three to twenty-eight, and were really industrious youths, receiving good wages, and maintaining good characters for honesty, sobriety, and general good behavior. Yet they were looked upon by some as ungodly youths, and given over to perdition. True, they belonged to no church; and, amid the various conflicting creeds by which they were surrounded, they had not yet settled down upon any one in particular, believing that there was good in all of them, and evil among the members of each.

On the present occasion, they were all of them smoking. and the empty mugs which stood upon the table near them, showed pretty conclusively that they had been drinking something besides water. The subject of the cold winter had been disposed of; the quality of the warm ale and cigars had been thoroughly discussed, and at length the conversation turned upon the missionary meeting, which had been held in the town on the previous Sabbath.

"I don't know but this missionary business is all right," said Sam Green, knocking the ashes from his cigar with his little finger, "but at the same time, I don't believe in it. Them Hindoos and South Sea Islanders may be savage and ignorant, by our scale of measuring folks; but that is no reason why we folks should send all our money off there, while our own folks are starving at home."

"Did you put anything into the box?" asked Lyman Drake.

"No, I didn't. When they shoved it into my face, I told 'em I'd left all my money at home—and so I had."

"You're about right, Sam," said Bill Robinson. "But I did more than you did. When the box was handed to me, I spoke right out, so that everybody around me heard. I told the old deacon if he'd take up a subscription to help the poor in our town, I'd put in something."

"What did he say to that?"

"Why—he said, 'Souls are of more consequence than bodies.' So I just said back that I guessed he'd find it hard work to save a soul out of a starving body. But you see that isn't the thing. They won't try to save the souls, or the bodies either, of their own townfolks. Now when Squire Truman came here to settle, they tried quick enough to save his soul. Ye see his body was already salted down

with ten thousand dollars, so his soul was worth something
to 'em.   Why don't they try to save poor old Israel Trask's
soul, and his wife's too? "

"Wasn't there a committee of the church that visited
old Israel last month?" queried Drake.

"Yes—there was," answered Sam, giving his cigar an
indignant shake; "and what did they do?   They went
there—four on 'em—and found the old folks suffering for
want of food and clothing.   They tried to make the old
man believe their religion was the only true one in the
world, but he would not.   So they gave him three tracts
and a little cheap book, and then went away.   That's what
they did.   Afore I'd give a cent to such chaps to send off
to feed their missionaries in  Baugwang and  Slapflam
Islands, I'd throw it into the fire."

"But these missionaries are honest people, and do some
good," remarked Peter Hobbs, who had not before spoken
on the subject.

"Of course they do," responded Sam.   "But wouldn't
it look better of 'em to begin some of their charities at
home?   I judge of a man's order by the way his own shop
looks, and not by the way he may fuss around on another
man's premises.   And just so with those philanthropists.
I'd rather see how much their religion does toward keeping
the Gentiles of their own town, than to go away off to the
other end of the earth to look for the fruits of their Christianity.   Them's my sentiments."

"And mine too," uttered Walter Mason, who had just
thrown away the stump of one cigar, and was about lighting
another.   "Just think; they collected, last Sunday, to send

off to the Hindoos, over two hundred dollars. Now, that would have made half the poor families in this town—and I do n't know but all—comfortable for the winter. There was Mr. Netherly—worth forty thousand dollars—he put in a ten-dollar bill. It was a great, new bill, and he opened it, and held it up, and even turned it round, so 't everybody could see it before he let it drop. Then at the end, when the box was carried up into the pulpit, the deacon whispered to the minister; and the minister got up, and, said, taking hold of the corner of the rich man's bill: 'Here is ten dollars from one brother. Let that brother be assured that his deed is remembered of him in heaven.' Yes, that's what was said; and Mr. Netherly held up his head, bowed very low, and then looked around at the rest of the congregation, as much as to say, '*that's me.*' Now I know of another thing that I guess 'll be remembered in heaven, alongside of this one. Last week, poor old Trask—Uncle Israel —called at Netherly's with some baskets. You know the old man gets out stuff in the summer, and then in the winter makes it up. Well, he went there, and asked Netherly if he would n't buy a basket. No; he did n't want one. Then the old man told him how he and his poor old wife were suffering, and he asked him if he could n't help him in some way; and what do you think Netherly said ?—Why, he said that he had to pay taxes to help support a poorhouse, and told Uncle Israel that he'd find help there, if he'd only apply to the selectmen! Now what d'ye think of that, eh?"

"Why," returned Sam, "I think if he's got an account in heaven, he'll find a balance against him, when he comes to settle up."

"So he will," responded three or four of the others.

For some moments after this, the party smoked in silence. Peter Hobbs had been pondering very deeply upon something, and at length he spoke:

"Now look here, boys," he said, throwing his half-smoked cigar into the fire, "there's a good deal of truth in what's been said—in fact, it's all true; but, before we blame others, we ought to do something ourselves. Now I'm ready to form a regular benevolent society. Let us six go at the work, and see what we can do toward alleviating some of the distress about us. What say you?"

The other five looked on in wonder.

"But," said Sam, "how are we to do it? We arn't among the favored ones. We weren't born with silver spoons in our mouths."

"I should like to do it," added Drake, "but what's the use? We couldn't do much any way—not enough to amount to anything."

And so the others expressed their opinions in like manner. They all "would like," but "where was the money to come from?"

"Listen," said Peter; and they all turned toward him with real deference, for they knew he never wore a cloak over his heart, and that when he spoke in earnest, his meaning had depth to it. "Now I have formed a plan. There is old Uncle Israel and his wife; then there is the widow Manley, with four little children, suffering for want of the actual necessaries of life; and then there is Mrs. Williams—she is very poor. Her son Philip, who is her mainstay, was sick all the summer and fall, and is sick now; so the woman got nothing from her little patch of land, and is now absolutely reduced to beggary, with herself and sick son to support. Now let us take these three cases in hand, and support them."

"But how?" asked three or four voices, anxiously, for they really and fully sympathized with the noble plan.

"I'll tell you," resumed Peter. "Here, Tim," he called, turning to the bar-keeper, "what's our bill?"

"Let's see," responded the worthy, coming up. "There's two cigars apiece, three cents each—that's thirty-six. Then the ale—three pints—eighteen cents; and wine —three gills—that's eighteen more—makes just thirty-six more; and twice thirty-six is—is—seventy-two—seventy-two cents in all."

"Come, boys," said Peter, "let s pay an equal share to-night. Let's give him ninepence apiece."

So the "boys" paid up, and after Tim had gone, Peter resumed:

"Now see what we've spent to-night for nothing. I'll begin with you, Sam. How much do you suppose you spend each day for cigars and ale? Now reckon fairly."

"Let's see," was Sam's response after gazing into the face of his interlocutor until he had fairly got hold of the idea. "I certainly average four—no, five cigars a day, and I suppose they average three cents apiece. Then comes my ale—but I could not tell how much that amounts to, for I do n't drink it regularly, but perhaps six cents a day."

"That's just twenty-one cents a day, utterly wasted," said Peter; and I'll own up to wasting twenty-five cents a day. How is it with you, John?"

"I'll say twenty-five."

"And you, Walter?"

"Just about the same."

"Lyman?"

"The same."

"Bill?"

"The same."

"Now look at it. Here we are, a little worse than wasting about a dollar and a half a day. But let us put our loss at a shilling each—"

"No, no," cried Sam, who saw through the whole plan. "Let's give honest measure. I'll own up to the twenty-five. Let's go the whole, if any."

"Very well," returned Peter; "then let us commence and pledge ourselves not to smoke, or drink ale, for one month from this date. Every night we will lay away a quarter of a dollar, and at the end of the week we'll put our savings all together, and then go on our mission. What say you?"

With one voice the other five joined in the plan. The novelty of the thing may have pleased them; but the real incentives lay deeper down in the natural goodness of their hearts. There was no written pledge, but they took a more speedy method. Peter laid his hand upon the table, and said:

"Here's my hand, pledged to the work."

"And mine too," cried Sam, laying his broad palm atop of Peter's.

"And mine," "and mine," "and mine," chimed the rest, placing their hands atop of the other until the six right hands lay upon the table in a pyramid.

"This is Tuesday," resumed Peter. "Will we meet next Saturday?"

"Yes," answered Sam, and call it a week. Let's throw in two days."

And so the week was begun.

On the next day, as Sam Green sat atop of his bench after dinner, he felt rather lost without his cigar, and for awhile he argued the question with himself, whether it wouldn't be just as well for him to put an extra quarter into his box and have his cigars as usual. But he remembered his pledge. He looked forward to Saturday, when he should find himself an ambassador of mercy to the sick and needy—and his resolution grew strong again. That was his last real hesitation, though it must be confessed he had some trials and hankerings.

And so with the rest, they had some moments of doubt and mental warfare with appetite and habit, but conquered, and were true.

Saturday came, and the six youths left their work at noon, having done more than enough overwork to make up for the loss of the half day.

"Must have a time once in awhile, eh?" said Sam's boss, as the young man pointed to the work he had done, and informed him that he should not work the rest of the day.

"Some sort of a time," replied Sam.

"Very well, but you're too good a fellow to go very deep into dissipation."

"I'll be up bright in the morning, sir;" and with this he left.

The new Benevolent Society met at Walter Mason's tin-shop.  Each took out his money and they had in all nine dollars, it being in thirty-six silver quarters.

"Now," says Peter, "let's visit the three families we have taken under our charge.  We'll go together, and expend the money as we see it is most needed.  Let us go to Uncle Israel's first."

So off they went to Uncle Israel Trask's.  The old couple lived in a small hut at the edge of the village, which was reached by a narrow lane, and here the six philanthrophists found the old lady, who was now in her eightieth year, suffering with a severe attack of the rheumatism, while the old man sat crouched over the fire, shivering with cold.

"Good day, good day, Uncle Israel."

"Aha, good day, boys, good day," cried the old man, trying to smile.  "Can ye find seats?  Sit down somewhere and make yourselves at home.  But ye see it's a poor home that old Israel can offer ye to-day."

"But how are you getting along?" asked Peter, after the party had found seats.

"Ah, God a'mercy, I won't complain, for he is taking meself and Molly home fast.  Only cold and hunger are not kind helpmates, Mr. Hobbs, ye ken that, eh?"

"Right weil, Uncle Israel.  And we have come to help you.  Do you want any medicine?"

"Nay, nay, the old 'ooman's got a' the medicine laid up we want.  It's only the food an' heat we need.  I can't wade through the drifting snow as I could once."

"Suppose we send you a dollar's worth of other things,

PURE RELIGION IS VISITING THE FATHERLESS AND WIDOWS IN THEIR
AFFLICTION.

such as butter, flour, potatoes and the like—could you live a week on it?"

"Ah, yes, yes, boys, meself and Molly'd live a long, long while on that.   But ye'll not do it for us."

"Yes, we will."

"Ah, it's too much."

"No, no," cried Sam, "we've got to do it, Uncle Israel, for we six have sworn to help you through the winter.   So spunk up."

"D'ye mean that?" uttered the old man, clasping his thin, tremulous hands.

"We do," they all answered, and then Sam added, "and while one of us lives, you shall not suffer the want of what one of us can give."

A moment the old man bowed his snow-white head, and then while the big tears streamed down his face, he raised his eyes and murmured:—

"Oh! God's blessin' be on ye, ye noble boys.   If me heart was gold, an' I could take it out an' give it ye—for it's yours all, all your own!"

In a little while the six went away, promising to send or come back soon, and even after they had reached the yard they could hear the voices of Israel and his wife, both raised to God in blessings upon their heads.

"I say, Sam," said Peter, "this is better than cigars and ale."

"Don't say a word now," replied Sam, "for my heart's full, and I can't bear any more."

Next, they drove through the biting wind and snow to the humble cot of Widow Manley.   They found her in the only habitable room of her dwelling, sitting by a fire of chips and fagots, with a babe asleep in her lap, and engaged in sewing a coarse frock. Three other children were crouched by the fire, the eldest not yet eight years old.

Mr. Manley had been one of the many unfortunates who are swept off by rum, and in the prime of early manhood he had gone, leaving a young wife with four children in absolute penury.

"Ah, good day, Mrs. Manley."

The woman would have arisen, but Sam Green placed his hand upon her shoulders to keep her down.

"We have come," said Peter, seeing that she was anxious and fearful, "to see how you get along, and see if we can help you."

"Help me, sir?" uttered the widow with amazement.

"Yes; now tell us plainly how you are situated."

The woman was silent for a few moments, but at length she seemed to regain her self-control, and replied:—

"Ah, gentlemen, it is all comprised in three short words: Hunger, cold, and nakedness!"

"And if we will supply you with food and fuel for a week, can you manage to get along until that time without more clothing?"

"Oh—h—yes—sirs. But what is it? Who can help us? Who can care for the—"

"We can, we will," cried the energetic Sam, not so good to plan as Peter, but good at execution. "We six have pledged ourselves to see you safe through the winter So cheer up and take hope, for neither you nor your children shall suffer while we can help it."

The widow's hands were clasped and her eyes wandered vacantly from one to the other of her strange visitors. She saw tears of goodness in their eyes, and her own soul's flood burst forth

" O God bless you—bless you always."

" And we shall have something good to eat, mamma, and something to make us warm?" asked the eldest girl, clasping her mother's knees.

" Yes, yes, you shall," exclaimed Drake, catching the child and kissing her clean, pale face. "You shall have it before supper time, too."

The widow gradually realized the whole object of her visitors, and she tried to express her gratitude in words, but they failed her, and streaming tears had to tell the tale of thanks.

After this our society went to see Widow Williams. Her's was a neat cot, but they found suffering painful enough inside. Philip, a youth of about their own age, sat in a large stuffed chair, looking pale and thin, and wasted away almost to a skeleton, and his great blue eyes peered at them wonderingly as they entered. The mother, too, looked careworn and sick, and the dry, hacking cough that sounded in her throat told how much she needed proper food and care.

The youths made their business known as before, and with about the same result. The widow and her son could hardly realize that such a blessing had dawned upon them, but when they did realize it their joy and gratitude knew no bounds.

" Look here," said Sam Green, as soon as they had

14

reached the road, " it strikes me that we are just about a week behind hand. We ought to have commenced this work just one week earlier than we did, for our nine dollars won't quite bring matters all up square to the present time. But if they were square now, they'd keep so with our weekly allowance."

"You're right, Sam," said Fulton, gleefully.

"Then let's commence back two weeks, eh?"

"I think so," said Peter.

And all the rest said so, too. So they had eighteen dollars instead of nine.

First, our party went and bought three half cords of wood, which they sent at once to their respective destinations, and they agreed that when the other matters were attended to they would go and work it up. Then they went to the stores and purchased such articles of provisions and comfort as they could agree were best adapted to meet the wants of their charges, and, having done this, they separated into three parties of two each, so as to have each family provided for with as little delay as possible. Besides carrying provisions enough to last a week, they left with each about a dollar in change.

When the poor people saw the promised blessing—when they thus met the fruition of their newly raised hopes, their joy was almost painful. The noble youths were blessed over and over again.

The wood was sawed and split, and put under cover, and then the society returned to the village, as happy as happy could be. On the next day, they went to the church and heard how many heathen had been converted to the peculiar *isms* of the preachers; and on the day following that, they commenced another week of their newly found *Christianity*.

"Sam," said the owner of the machine-shop, "what were you and the rest of your party doing last Saturday afternoon?"

"Converting the *heathen*," answered Sam.

His employer was a church member, and in for foreign missions, and moreover had often tried to induce Sam into the mysteries.

It was some time before Sam would tell the secret, but his boss became so earnest that he at length told the whole story. For awhile the employer gazed upon his journeyman with wonder, but gradually, as a sense of the fact came over him, he hung his head.

"Sam," he said at length, earnestly, and with a tear in his eye, "let me join your society."

"But how'll you raise the money?" inquired Sam.

"Money?" echoed the boss. "Look at my bank-book."

"Ah, but that won't answer. You must save the money by depriving yourself of some superfluity, or luxury you now enjoy."

"Is that the rule?"

"It is most rigidly. Our cigars and ale furnish us."

"And won't you smoke again?"

"Never, while within the reach of my influence there's a human being in want!"

"Then I'll throw away my tobacco and beer; may I join at that?"

"I'll propose you."

And the master machinist was proposed and admitted.

Another week passed away, and the new Christians went again on their mission, and there were more tears of joy, more prayers, and more blessings. Mr. Boothby, the machinist, had gained a new ray of light on the subject of Christian missions.

At length it became known that the poor families of Madisonville had found friends. People were wonder-struck when they discovered how happy and joyous these once miserable wretches had become; and more still when, one Sunday they saw Uncle Israel and his wife, and Mrs. Manley with her two elder children, enter the church.

Of course the truth leaked out, and we can imagine where the public eye of sympathy and appreciation was turned. Before a month was out, more than fifty people had engaged indirectly in the work, by placing money, food, and clothing in the hands of the original six, for them to distribute as they deemed proper.

But there was one rule to which the "society" adhered. They would not receive a cent in money which was not the result of a cutting off of some superfluity, and thus they showed to the people how simple and easy in its work is true charity, and also how many professed Christians not only lose sight of duty, but really lose the greatest joy of Christian life.

It was a glorious day for Madisonville when those six young mechanics met in the village barroom and concocted the plan for their society. And the good has worked in two ways. The members find themselves happier, healthier, and stronger, for having given up their pipes and cups; and the poor unfortunate ones of the town are once again basking in the sunlight of peace, content, and plenty.

How very many professed Christian churches there are in our land which would be benefited by following the example of the six noble youths who still stand at the head of the *Madisonville Benevolent Society.*

### LIFE THAT LASTS.

THEY err who measure life by years
  With false or thoughtless tongue.
Some hearts grow old before their time;
  Others are always young.
'T is not the number of the lines
  On life's fast-filling page,
'T is not the pulse's added throbs
  Which constitute their age.

Some souls are serfs among the free,
  While others nobly thrive;
They stand just where their fathers stood,
  Dead, even while they live.
Others, all spirit, heart, and sense,
  Theirs the mysterious power
To live in thrills of joy or woe
  A twelve-month in an hour.

He liveth long who liveth well!
  All other life is short and vain;
He liveth longest who can tell
  Of living most for heavenly gain.
He liveth long who liveth well!
  All else is being flung away;
He liveth longest who can tell
  Of true things truly done each day.

# AN INSTRUCTIVE ANECDOTE

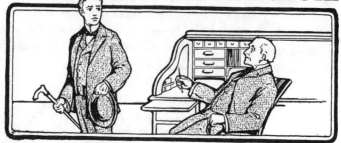

**M**OST young people are very fond of display in dress. Rings, breastpins, and similar superfluities, are in great demand among them. We have known a girl to spend a month's wages for a single article of this kind, and a young man to run in debt for a cane when he had scarcely clothing enough to appear respectable. The following story of a successful merchant will show to such how these things look to sensible people. Said he:

"I was seventeen years old when I left the country store where I had 'tended' for three years, and came to Boston in search of a place. Anxious, of course, to appear to the best advantage, I spent an unusual amount of time and solicitude upon my toilet, and when it was completed, I surveyed my reflection in the glass with no little satisfaction, glancing lastly and approvingly upon a seal ring which embellished my little finger, and my cane, a very pretty affair, which I had purchased with direct reference to this occasion. My first day's experience was not encouraging.

I traveled street after street, up one side and down the other, without success. I fancied, toward the last, that the clerks all knew my business the moment I opened the door, and that they winked ill-naturedly at my discomfiture as I passed out. But nature endowed me with a good degree of persistency, and the next day I started again. Toward noon I entered a store where an elderly gentleman was talking with a lady near by the door. I waited until the visitor had left and then stated my errand.

"'No sir,' was the answer, given in a crisp and decided manner. Possibly I looked the discouragement I was beginning to feel, for he added in a kindlier tone, 'Are you good at taking a hint?'

"'I do n't know,' I answered, and my face flushed painfully.

"'What I wished to say is this,' said he, looking me in the face and smiling at my embarrassment, 'If I were in want of a clerk, I would not engage a young man who came seeking employment with a flashy ring upon his finger, and swinging a cane.'

"For a moment, mortified vanity struggled against common sense, but sense got the victory, and I replied, with rather shaky voice, 'I'm very much obliged to you,' and then beat a hasty retreat. As soon as I got out of sight, I slipped the ring into my pocket, and walking rapidly to the Worcester depot. I left the cane in charge of the baggage-master 'until called for.' It is there now, for aught I know. At any rate, I never called for it. That afternoon I obtained a situation with the firm of which I am now a partner. How much my unfortunate finery had injured my prospects on the previous day I shall never know, but I never think of the old gentleman and his plain-dealing with me, without always feeling, as I told him at the time, 'very much obliged to him.'"

### REAPING.

WHILE the years are swiftly passing,
　　As we watch them come and go,
Do we realize the maxim,
　　We must reap whate'er we sow?

When the past comes up before us,
　　All our thoughts, our acts and deeds,
Shall they glean for us fair roses,
　　Or a harvest bear of weeds?

Are we sowing seeds to blossom?
　　We shall reap some day,—somewhere,
Just what here we have been sowing,
　　Worthless weeds or roses fair.

All around us whispering ever,
　　Hear the voice of Nature speak,
Teaching all the self-same lesson,
　　"As you sow so shall you reap."

Though there's pardon for each sinner
　　In God's mercy vast and mild,
Yet the law that governs Nature,
　　Governs e'en fair Nature's child.

# Why He Didn't Smoke.

THE son of Mr. Jeremy Lord, aged fourteen, was spending the afternoon with one of his young friends, and his stay was prolonged into the evening, during which some male friends of the family dropped in. The boys withdrew into the recess of the bay window, at the end of the room, and the men went on chatting about the most important matters of the day, politics, etc. Still apparently entertaining each other, the two boys yet kept their ears open, as boys will, and, taking their cue from the sentiments expressed by their elders, indorsed one or the other as they happened to agree with them.

"Gentlemen, will you smoke?" asked Mr. Benedict, the host. A simultaneous "Thank you," went round, and a smile of satisfaction lighted all faces but one. Not that he was gloomy, or a drawback on the rest, but his smile was not one of assent. A box of cigars was soon forthcoming, costly and fragrant, as the word goes.

"Fine cigar," said one, as he held it to his nose, before lighting. "What, Linton, you don't smoke?" "I'm happy to say I do not," was the firm rejoinder.

"Well, now, you look like a smoking man, jolly, care free, and all that. I'm quite surprised," said another.

"We are hardly doing right, are we," asked a rubicund-visaged man, who puffed away heartily "to smoke in the

217

parlor? I condone that much to my wife's dislike of the weed. She makes a great ado about the curtains, you know."

"For my part, that's a matter I don't trouble myself about," said the host, broadly. "There's no room in this house too good for me and my friends to smoke in. My wife has always understood that, and she yields, of course."

"But you don't know how it chokes her," said young Hal Benedict. "Yes, indeed, it gets all through the house, you know, and she almost always goes into Aunt Nellie's when there are two or three smoking. There she goes now," he added, as the front door closed.

"Why, it's absolutely driving her out of the house, isn't it?" asked Johnny. "Too bad!"

"Why don't you smoke, Dalton?" queried one of the party. "'Fraid of it? Given it up lately? It don't agree with some constitutions."

"Well, if you want to know why I don't smoke, friend Jay," was the answer, "I will tell you, I respect my wife too much."

"Why, you don't mean—" stammered his questioner.

"I mean simply what I said. When I was married I was addicted to the use of cigars. I saw that the smoke annoyed her, though she behaved with the utmost good taste and forbearance, and cut down my cigars so as to smoke only when going and returning from business. I then considered what my presence must be to a delicate and sensitive woman, with breath and clothes saturated with the odor, and I began to be disgusted with myself, so that I finally dropped the habit, and I can't say I'm sorry."

"I should n't be, I know," said another, admiringly. "I'm candid enough to own it, and I think your wife ought to be very much obliged to you."

"On the contrary, it is I who ought to be obliged to my wife," said Mr. Dalton, while the host smoked on in silence, very red in the face, and evidently wincing under the reproof that was not meant.

"I say that Dalton is a brick," whispered young Benedict.

"He's splendid!" supplemented Johnny, who was thinking his own thoughts while the smoke was really getting too much for him, and presently he took his leave.

The next day Johnny was thoughtful, so quiet, indeed, that everybody noticed it, and in the evening, when his father lighted his pipe with its strong tobacco, Johnny seemed on thorns.

"I can't think that you do n't respect mother," he blurted out, and then his face grew scarlet.

"What do you mean?" asked his father, in a severe voice. "I say, what do you mean, sir?"

"Because mother hates the smoke so; because it gets into the curtains and carpet—and—and because I heard Mr. Dalton last night give as a reason that he did not smoke that he respected his wife too much."

"Pshaw! Your mother do n't mind my smoking—do you, mother?" he asked, jocularly, as his wife entered just then.

"Well—I—I used to rather more than I do now. One can get accustomed to anything, I suppose, so I go on the principle that what can't be cured must be endured."

"Nonsense! you know I could stop to-morrow if I wanted to," he laughed.

"But you won't want to," she said, softly.

I don't know whether Johnny's father gave up the weed. Most likely not; but if you want to see what really came of it, I will give you a peep at the following paper, written some years ago, and which happens to be in my possession.

"I, John Lord, of sound mind, do make, this first day of January, 1861, the following resolutions, which I pray God I may keep:—

"*First.* I will not get married till I own a house, for I expect my uncle will give me one, one of these days; mother says he will.

"*Second.* I will never swear, because it is silly, as well as wicked.

"*Third.* I will never smoke and so make myself disagreeable to everybody who comes near me, and I will always keep these words as my motto after I am married:

"'I don't smoke, because I respect my wife.' Mr. Dalton said that, and I will never forget it.

"(Signed) JOHN LORD."

And Johnny kept his word like a hero.

THE world will never adjust itself
  To suit your whims to the letter.
Some things must go wrong your whole life long,
  And the sooner you know it the better.
        —*Ella Wheeler Wilcox.*

# STORY OF SCHOOL LIFE

OH, girls! I shall just die, I know I shall!" exclaimed Belle Burnette, going off into a hysterical fit of laughter, which she vainly tried to smother behind an elegant lace-edged handkerchief.

"What is it, you provoking thing? Why do n't you tell us, so we can laugh too?"

"Well—you—see," she gasped out at last, "we've got a new pupil—the queerest looking thing you ever saw. I happened to be in Madam's room when she arrived. She came in the stage, and had a mite of an old-fashioned hair trunk, not much bigger than a bandbox, and she came into Madam's room with a funny little basket in her hand, and sat down as if she had come to stay forever. She said, 'Are you Madam Gazin?' 'Yes,' she replied, 'that is my name.' 'Well, I've come to stay a year at your school.' And then she pulled a handkerchief out of her basket, and unrolled it till she found an old leather wallet, and actually took out $250 and laid it in Madam's hand, saying, 'That is just the amount, I believe; will you please give me a receipt for it?' You never saw Madam look so surprised. She actually did n't know what to say for a minute, but she gave her the receipt, asked a few questions, and had her taken to No. 10, and there she is now, this very minute."

"Well, what was there so funny about all that?"

"Why this: she has red hair, tucked into a black net, and looks just like a fright, every way. She had on a brown delaine dress, without a sign of a ruffle, or trimming of any kind, and the shabbiest hat and shawl you ever saw. You'll laugh, too, when you see her."

Belle Burnette was an only child, and her wealthy father was pleased to gratify her every whim. So, besides being far too elegantly dressed for a schoolgirl, she was supplied with plenty of pocket-money, and being very generous, and full of life and fun, she was the acknowledged leader among Madam's pupils.

When the tea-bell rang, the new-comer was escorted to the dining-room, and introduced to her schoolmates as Miss Fannie Comstock. She had exchanged her brown delaine for a plain calico dress, with a bit of white edging about the neck. She did look rather queer, with her small, thin, freckled face, and her red hair brushed straight back from her face, and hidden as much as possible under a large black net, and but for the presence of Madam her first reception would have been exceedingly unpleasant. She was shy and awkward, and evidently ill at ease among so many strangers. As soon as possible she hastened back to the seclusion of her own room. The next day she was examined, and assigned to her place in the different classes, and to the surprise of all she was far in advance of those of her age. But this did not awaken the respect of her schoolmates as it should have done. On the contrary, Belle Burnette and her special friends were highly incensed about it, and at once commenced a series of petty annoyances, whenever it was safe to do so, which kept poor Fannie miserable, indeed, although she seemed to take no notice of it. A few weeks passed by. Her lessons were always perfectly recited. She made no complaint of the slights and sneers of her companions, but kept out of their way as much as possible. Her thin face grew paler, however, and there were dark rings about her eyes. A watchful friend would have seen that all these things were wearing cruelly upon her young life. One Saturday the very spirit of wickedness seemed let loose among them. Madam was away, and the other teachers were busy in their rooms. Fannie had been out for a walk and was near the door of her room when a dozen or more of the girls surrounded her, clasping hands together so she was a prisoner in their midst. For a moment she begged piteously to be released, but they only laughed the more, and began going around, singing something which Belle had composed—cruel, miserable, insulting words. She stood for an instant pale and still, then, with a piercing cry, she burst through the ring, and rushed into her room, closed and locked the door. Through their wild peals of laughter the girls heard a strange moan and a heavy fall.

"I believe she has fainted," said Belle.

"What shall we do?" said another.

For a moment they stood there sober enough; then one of them ran for the matron and told her that Fannie Comstock had fainted in her room and the door was locked.

She had a long ladder put to the window, and sent the janitor to see if it was true. Fortunately the window was open, and in a few moments he had unlocked the door from the inside. The girls were huddled together in a frightened group, while Madam lifted the poor girl and laid her upon her bed. She was in violent spasms. The doctor was sent for, but when the spasms ceased, alarming symptoms set in, and he pronounced it a serious case of brain fever. It is impossible to tell the shame and remorse of the conscience stricken girls. They were not brave enough to confess their guilt, but hung around the sick room, offering their services, vainly wishing that they might atone for it in some way. But their presence only excited the poor sufferer, so that they were all sent away. Day after day passed, and still she raved in violent delirium. The little hair trunk was searched to find some clue to her friends, but there was nothing found in it but the plainest, scantiest supply of clothes. Day after day the doctor came, looking grave and anxious, and at last the crisis came. For many hours she lay as if dead, and not a noise was permitted to disturb the awful silence while they waited to see if she would live or die. At last she opened her eyes ; and the suspense was relieved by an assuring word from the doctor, that with careful nursing she would soon be well again. But her convalescence was slow and tedious.

Her former tormentors dared not speak of what they had done, but they sent daily little bouquets of fragrant flowers and other delicacies to tempt her returning appetite. Her eyes would light up with surprise and pleasure at the little gifts. And amidst all her wild ravings not a word of complaint at the ill treatment she had received ever escaped her lips.

One day Madam was sitting by her side, and as Fannie seemed to be much stronger, she ventured to ask after her friends.

"I have no friends, Madam, only Cousin John, who has a large family of his own, and has never cared for me. Mother died when I was born. I had a step-mother, but father died five years after, and I've taken care of myself ever since."

"And you are only fifteen now?"

"Yes, ma'am."

"How did you get money enough to pay for a year's board and tuition here?"

"I earned it all, Madam, every cent of it. As soon as I was big enough I went into a factory, and earned two dollars a week at first, and finally $3.50; and I worked for my board nights and mornings."

"Poor child!"

"Oh no, ma'am, I was very glad to do it."

"But how did you keep along so well with your studies?"

"I used to fix a book open on my loom, where I could catch a sentence now and then, and the overseer did not object, because I always did my work well. You see, Madam, I wanted to be a teacher some time, and I'd have a better chance to learn here than anywhere else, so I determined to do it."

"What are your plans for the long vacation?"

"I must go back to the factory and earn enough to get some warmer clothes for the winter. You see, Madam, why I can't afford to dress better."

15

Madam's heart was full. She bent over the white, thin little face, and kissed it reverently.

That evening, when the girls gathered in the chapel for worship, she told Fannie's story. There was not a dry eye in the room. The moment Madam finished, Belle Burnette sprang up with the tears pouring down her cheeks, and said:

"Oh, Madam! We have been awfully cruel and wicked to that poor girl. We have made fun of her from the first, and she would not have been sick as she was if we had not tormented her almost to death. I was the most to blame. It was I that led on the rest, and we have suffered terribly all these weeks, fearing she might die. You may expel me, or punish me in any way you please; for I deserve it; and I shall go down on my knees to ask her pardon, as soon as you will let me see her."

"My child, I am shocked to hear this. I can scarcely believe that any of my pupils would ill-treat a companion because she was so unfortunate as to be plain and poor. But you have made a noble confession, and I forgive you as freely as I believe she will, when she knows how truly you have repented of your unkindness." By degrees, as she was able to bear it, one after another went to Fannie and begged her forgiveness, which was freely granted. She said, "I do n't wonder you made fun of me. I know I was poorly dressed, *and awful homely*. I would have pulled every hair out of my head long ago, only I knew it would grow out as red as ever. But, oh! if I could have felt that I had just one friend among you all, I could have borne it; but somehow it just broke my heart to have you all turn against me."

After this she gained rapidly, and one fine morning the doctor said she might join the girls in the drawing-room for an hour before tea. There had been a vast deal of whispering and hurrying to and fro of late, among the girls, of which Fannie had been totally unconscious in the quiet seclusion of her room.

At the appointed time, Madam herself came to assist her, and leaning upon her strong arms, the young girl walked feebly through the long hall and down the stairs.

"My dear, the girls have planned a little surprise for you, to make the hour as pleasant as possible."

She opened the door and seated Fannie in an easy chair, and the girls came gliding in, with smiling faces, singing a beautiful song of welcome. At its close Belle Burnette approached and placed a beautiful wreath of flowers upon her head, saying: "Dear Fannie, we crown you our queen to-day, knowing well how far above us all you are in His sight, who looketh upon the heart instead of the outward appearance. You have taught us a lesson we shall never forget, and we beg you to accept a token of sincere love and repentance for our treatment of you in the past, which you will find in your room on your return."

Fannie's eyes were full of tears, and she tried to say a word in reply, but Madam spoke for her, and after another song they followed their newly crowned queen to the dining-room, where a most tempting feast was laid in honor of the occasion. Fannie was quietly, tearfully happy through it all, yet so wearied with the unusual excitement that Madam said she must not see the girls' "peace-offering" that night. The first thing she saw the next morning was a fine large trunk, and lying upon it a card, "For Miss Fannie Comstock, from her teacher and schoolmates." Having opened it, she saw it was packed full of newly folded garments, but she had no time to examine the contents, until after breakfast, when they left her alone with her wonderful gifts. There were pretty dresses and sacques, a fine new parasol, gloves and ribbons, cuffs and collars in abundance—indeed, everything that a young schoolgirl could possibly need. Every one of Madam's two hundred and ten pupils had contributed from their choicest and best, to furnish a complete outfit for their less favored mate. At the bottom was a well-filled writing-desk, an album containing all their pictures, and a pretty purse containing five dollars, and the following note from Madam:

"MY DEAR CHILD: This shall be a receipt in full for all expenses, during whatever time you may choose to remain in the seminary, which I present to you as a sincere token of my love and respect.

"JEANNETTE GAZIN."

They found her at dinner time on the floor, surrounded by her new treasures, crying like a baby; but it did her good. She was soon able to resume her studies, and was ever afterward treated with kindness and consideration, even though all her hair came out and left her head bald as her face, so she had to wear a queer, cap-like wig for many weeks.

When the long vacation arrived, Belle carried her off to her beautiful home on the Hudson, where for the first time in her life she was surrounded with beauty and luxury on every side, and was treated as a loved and honored guest.

It was not long before the hateful wig was cast aside, and Fannie's head was covered with a profusion of dark auburn curls, which were indeed a crown of glory that made her plain face almost beautiful.

Gentle, loving, and beloved by all, she remained in the seminary until she graduated with honor, after which Madam offered her the position of head teacher, with a most liberal salary, which she gratefully accepted.

THERE are loyal hearts, there are spirits brave,
   There are souls that are pure and true,
Then give to the world the best you have,
   And the best will come back to you.

Give love, and love to your life will flow,
   A strength in your utmost need.
Have faith, and a score of hearts will show
   Their faith in your word and deed.

Give truth, and your gift will be paid in kind,
   And honor will honor meet,
And a smile that is sweet
   Will surely find a smile that is just as sweet.

For life is the mirror of old king slave;
   'T is just what we say or do,
Then give to the world the best you have,
   And the best will come back to you.

# Grandmother's Room.

OHN LYMAN was what his neighbors and townsfolk called a "hard-fisted" man; and he had earned the name by dint of persevering stinginess from boyhood up. He and his good wife Phœbe had accumulated a snug little property, besides the many-acred farm which was to be his when "grandmother" should relinquish her claim to all earthly possessions. So he was really able to live in comfort; but, instead of that, the old red farmhouse, which was his father's before him, was a model of angularity, unadorned and unattractive, both inside and out, only preserving a decent aspect through Phœbe's thrift and neatness.

Six little ones made music in the old house, save when their father was there. His presence always seemed to send a chill to their little warm hearts; for he made them feel that they were "bills of expense," and whenever they clamored for pretty things he told them that they "cost money," and sent them away with a reproof for their desires.

And yet John Lyman claimed that he was *just*. "Don't I pay the minister two dollars every single year?" he would say when the puzzled collectors came to him, bankbook in hand. Of course he did; and, if the reverend gentleman was a smart preacher, he added a peck of beans to his annual subscription, although this came a little hard when the harvest was poor. Not being a church member,

he did n't feel called to give to the "heathen," as he was
wont to style all benevolent objects of whatever character;
and it was generally understood that the two dollars were
given on grandmother's account.

Dear Grandmother Lyman! Known and loved by
everybody in Peltonville, she was peacemaker, adviser, and,
in fact, condensed sunshine in John's household from January to December. She was a *Christian*, too; and John
was glad of that, for he believed that she and the Bible
were good in case of sickness or death; and, to tell the
truth, he had a vague idea that she would see that he had a
place in heaven sometime, after he had grown old and tired
of this world. But Grandmother Lyman knew better than
this; and morning, noon, and night, her prayers ascended
for him, her only remaining child, and his family.

One would suppose that such a mother would have
every want supplied, even by a *penurious* son. But Oh!
the love of gain had so eaten into John's best affections
that it sometimes seemed as if he had forgotten all claims
upon him! So it was very trying to ask a favor of him,
and his mother denied herself many a necessity before doing it.

Something more than usually important troubled her
mind, however, on one bright spring morning as she sat by
the kitchen fire. All the funny little wrinkles in her dear
old face, which were generally only telegraph lines for
smiles to run over, were sobered by some weighty consideration. Her knitting-work lay idle in her lap; and she did
not even notice that little Tillie had pulled two of the
needles out, nor that mischievous Nick was sawing away on

the back of her chair with his antiquated pocket-knife. Whatever the problem was, it troubled her all the forenoon; but after dinner she followed John to the door, and, said she, "I've been thinking, John, couldn't I have a little room somewhere all to myself? I'm going on seventy-eight now, you know, and the children get pretty noisy some-times; and I thought, maybe, if it wouldn't be too much trouble—" "Hem! Well, really, grandma'm," taking off his hat and scratching his head dubiously, "the children do make a precious hubbub here, that's a fact. But I declare! Well, I'll see." And John went to the field.

As result of the "seeing," on the next rainy day there was heard the noise of hammer and saw in a chamber over the kitchen. This chamber had never been finished or used save as a place in which to store old rubbish of all kinds, and was a gloomy, out-of-the-way room at best. Grand-mother Lyman looked rather sober over the prospect; and Phœbe wanted to interfere, but as that was against the rules of the house, John worked on in his own way, until, at the end of two days, and after Phœbe had made several journeys up and down the back-stairs, grandmother was told that her room was ready. The dear old lady dragged herself up to the little chamber, while two little tots came scrambling after, bearing her Bible, hymn-book, Wesley's Sermons, and knitting-work. But it was no "palace of beauty" which she found awaiting her. The room was low, slanting on one side, unpapered, uncarpeted, and only lighted by two little dormer-windows, which did their best to admit pure daylight in spite of the dark gingham curtains so trimly hung before them. A bed stood in one corner, before which was a braided rug, while a stove with two good legs occupied the center of the room.

Grandmother looked out at the windows, but the view was not pleasant; two barns, the watering trough, and the fashionable summer resort of the ducks and geese, that was all. She was not one to complain; but she sadly missed the grand sweep of mountain and valley which had greeted her eyes from the " fore-door " ever since she was brought there a happy bride. Turning to arrange her books on the little table, she sang, in her wavering way,

"Thus far the Lord hath led me on;"

and, before the verse was finished, her heart was at peace again. " Doin to stay up here all 'lone, g'anma? " said wee Tillie in pitying accents. "O no! I guess you and Nick will come up real often, won't you?" "I dess so; but 'taint very pitty," said the little one, as she trotted downstairs again.

Meanwhile, John, as he followed the plow, was thinking of the five dollars expended in repairing the room, and trying to persuade himself that he was indeed a worthy son. " Five dollars! It aint every one that would do as much for his mother as I do for mine," he soliloquized. " Too old to go up-stairs! Oh well, when she once gets up she is more out of the way; and she wants quiet, you know."

Be it known that John sometimes found it necessary to reason with himself in order to assure his conscience that everything was as it should be in her domain; and sometimes, as on this occasion, she asked so many questions that he was obliged to talk the livelong afternoon.

He retired that night thinking, "Five dollars for grandma'm's room and the mare lame in both forefeet!" But while these dismal thoughts filled his mind, his body seemed to be very suddenly transported to the kitchen below. He was not alone, however, for a woman was there before him, walking the floor with a child in her arms. Back and forth she paced, carefully holding the pale-faced boy in the same position while he slept.

"Ruth," said a voice from an adjoining room, "that little chap will wear you all out. Can't I take him a little while?" "O no," was the reply. "He likes to have me carry him so, poor little fellow." "Ah," said John to himself, "that's the way mother carried me six nights, when I got scalded so terribly." The scene changed, and he saw himself again. A crushed foot this time, demanding his mother's untiring care. Again and again incidents of his life were re-enacted before him, but always with his mother there, comforting, working, watching, or praying. Whether sick in body or in mind, he saw how, all through his life, a mother's tender love had surrounded him. And then he stood once more beside his father's death-bed, and heard again the solemn charge: "Be kind to your mother, John, and make her old age pleasant. She is all you've got now." With these words ringing in his ears John Lyman awoke to find the perspiration standing on his forehead, and a strange, wierd sensation resting on him like a spell, which he tried in vain to throw aside. He tried to compose his mind, and again to sleep; but though nothing peculiarly frightful had troubled his slumber, he trembled from head to foot. In fact, Conscience so long soothed and stifled, had with a terrible effort freed herself, and determined to make one more effort for John's soul.  She lashed him unmercifully. She showed him how his soul was growing smaller and meaner every day—how he was just a plague-spot on God's fair earth.  He saw himself in a mirror that reflected the inmost recesses of his heart, and he was horrified at sight of the foulness so long concealed.

As the hours wore slowly on toward the day, John grew to hate himself more and more, until, almost stifled in-doors, he rose and went out.  Everything wore that unreal look that the first faint twilight gives.  Mysterious and still the mists lay along the foot of the mountain, while the stars twinkled in the sky that seemed very, very far away.

From force of habit John Lyman strode into the yard where the cattle were; but they only stared at him sleepily, as they lay tranquilly chewing the cud; so he wandered out and down the path that led into the little maple grove, which had been a playground for three generations.  As he passed slowly along under the solemn trees, his boyhood days came back to him so fresh that the twoscore years of hard, grinding toil, flew away as by magic.  Oh, that happy, careless boyhood!  How had its golden promises been fulfilled!  A blush of shame rose to the man's cheek as he thought how hard and cold his heart had grown.  Hundreds of times he had stood beside the little stream which he had now reached, without noticing a trace of beauty; but now, as the sun lighted the distant mountain-top with a glow that crept over its sides, a gladdening, awakening glow, seen only in the spring, it seemed as though he had never looked upon the scene before.  So new, so beautiful!  And a wonderful sense of God's nearness stole over him, such as he had not felt before for years, and, at the same time, a new love for his mother, who had so long been the only Bible he read, filled his heart, like a fresh revelation from the Father. The lowing of the cattle recalled him to himself, and he turned homeward, passed up the lane into the barn, and was soon throwing hay into the mangers below. Suddenly he stopped, thrust his pitchfork deep into the hay, and said: "My mother *shall* have a better room than that if it costs *five hundred dollars!* Now that's so! Hurrah!" Good once more had triumphed over evil, as the experience of the morning culminated in this worthy resolution.

Soon the patter of childish feet was heard, and Tillie cried, "Pa, pa, mother wants to know where you be, 'cause she's been worryin' about you, fear you's sick, and breakses is all gettin' cold this minute. Boiled eggs, too, aint it, Ruth?"

"I'll be in directly," came the answer from the high mow; so happy, chattering, Tillie and quiet Ruth climbed down the high steps and started toward the house. Their father overtook them as they stopped to look at the ducks taking their morning bath, and catching Tillie up, he put her on his shoulder, then drew down the little face and kissed the fresh, sweet lips. "How natural!" one may say. No, not natural for John Lyman, whose children feared far more than they loved him.

Tillie was astonished and half frightened, and as she began to wriggle uneasily, her father set her gently down.

In a trice she was beside Ruth, and pulling her head

down she whispered in her ear, "Pa just kissed me all his own self, Ruth." "Did he?" said Ruth, opening her eyes very wide. Then she hurried on and walked close by her father's side, while at her little heart fluttered the hope that she too might receive a kiss. But she was not noticed; and very much grieved she shrank away wondering if he loved Tillie best.

"I dreamed of your father last night, John," said grandmother while they were at breakfast, "and you can't think how good and natural he looked." John did n't say anything. During the forenoon John had a long conference with his wife which seemed to be satisfactory, for as he left her he said, "Well, then, you take the things out this afternoon, and Johnson shall come over to do the painting to-morrow." Before night the cheerful little spare room which adjoined the parlor was empty, and the old-fashioned paper, with its ever-recurring pictures of a shepherdess, a hunter, and Rebecca at the well, stripped from the walls.

Silence was imposed upon the children, for "grandma'm must n't know," and the little things went round the house fairly aching with the importance of their secret, and holding on to themselves for fear they might tell. Mysterious trips were taken in the old market-wagon, and a suspicious smell of new things filled the air; but when grandmother inquired what was going on down-stairs, Ruth clapped both hands over her mouth and Tillie screamed, "O nuffin, grandma, on'y—O Ruthie, come down, quick!"

One bright May afternoon, however, the work was finished, and John, jealous of the privilege, donned his Sunday coat and stumbled up to his mother's room in the most awkward manner to break the news. "Mother, can you come down below a few minutes now?" said he, trying to appear unconcerned.

"Why, la me!" smoothing her "front" and refolding her neckerchief, "has the minister come? I aint fixed up one bit."

"No, no, mother, there's no occasion for fixin' up. It aint much of anything, only me—that is,—well, perhaps you'd better come now."

"John," said the old lady solemnly, laying her hand on his arm, "if it's bad news, just tell me right away. The Lord will give me strength to bear it, just as he has the dispensations all along."

Poor John! how to acquaint the old lady with this "dispensation" he did n't know; but Tillie came to the rescue.

"O g'anma," said she, seizing one of the wrinkled hands, "we can't wait another minute. It's all splendid; and Nick, and Ruth, and baby, and I have all got our clean aprons on, and Wesley, he's in, so come straight down," and timing her impatient hops to the tottering footsteps she guided, Tillie soon had grandmother in the midst of a smiling group, while the relieved father brought up the rear.

"Now, g'anma," said Ruth, seizing the free hand, "shut up your eyes tight till we say open 'em," and then the delighted children, followed by the rest of the family, drew her into the old spare room. "Now, now, g'anma, open, open! and what do you see?" they cried, dancing and clapping their hands. Grandmother looked around her in perfect amazement. Truly a wondrous change had been wrought! Beautiful light paper covered the walls, and a

bright, soft carpet the floor, while pretty shades hung before the four great windows, whose tassels swung back and
forth in the sweet May air like bells, dumb for joy.

"John, John, what does this mean?"

"It's your room, g'anma," shouted a chorus of voices.

"Why, this is good enough for a queen! You can't
mean it all for a poor old creature like me," and the darling
old lady's eyes began to run over with happy tears, while
John tried in vain to find voice to answer, and dear, patient
Phœbe sobbed outright.

"Why, g'anma," shouted little Nick at the top of his
voice, "I shouldn't think you'd cry, 'cause this is the cutest
room in the house; and when me and Wes comes in, we've
got to take off our boots and talk real soft. And Oh, just
look at this table-cloth and this rug! It feels like velvet!
and this stool—do you see?—it's got a cat's foot on every
one of its legs. That's to put you foot on, you know; and,
O say, can't we play puss in the corner sometimes if we're
easy?" "G'anma, I can almost smell the roses," said
Ruth, patting the paper.

So with the help of the children the room was chris-
tened, everything examined and praised, and at last the
noisy little troop withdrew. Then Grandmother Lyman,
with a sense of exquisite comfort, sank into the nice, new
arm-chair close to the window.

"Like it pretty well, do you?" queried John, as he took
another chair near her.

"Like it? It seems too good to be real. I've thought
sometimes that perhaps in my mansion—heavenly, you
know—I should find everything soft, and bright, and cozy

like; but to have a room like this here on earth, why, John, I can't tell you how thankful I feel. 'T was lonesome up garret there, and yesterday I dragged in the old cradle and the little wheel to make it seem more social like; but the cradle was empty and broken, and the wheel brought back the old days when I used to sit and spin, while your father husked corn; so they didn't cheer me up much. But I never mistrusted what you was doing down here for me. John, I believe nothing but the Spirit of God could have coaxed you into this. Don't you think I'll see you a Christian yet before I die?" and the anxious mother laid her trembling hand on her son's big brown one.

"Well, mother, I don't know;" then came a long pause, for the farmer, almost as silent habitually as the fields he tilled, could find no words to express his feelings.

"I've been feelin' kind of queer lately, and seems as if everything has changed wonderfully. 'T was a shabby trick, my putting you up in that old room, and it troubled me considerably one night, and then other things kept coming up, till—well—I believe I'm the worst man on earth. Speaking of being a Christian, I guess likely I might fly about as easy. I wish I was an out-and-out one; but I tell you what, mother, there aint a man in town but that would think I pretended it all so's to make a dollar out of somebody;" and John drew his hand across his eyes, as though there were tears starting somewhere which must be warned to keep away from the windows.

Grandmother didn't care if the tears did come in her eyes, for they were joyful ones.

"Well, the Lord would know better," said she comfort-

CHRIST THE CONSOLER.

ingly, "and by and by others would.  It'll be your works, as well as your words, that will tell if you're in earnest."

"That's so, mother, that's so ; the minister said that very thing last Sabbath.  He's been preaching right at me this two months, and it made me mad at first.  I thought I would n't give him a cent this year, but I guess he told the truth."

" Yes, of course he did.  That's what he's made for. But now, John, you won't give up seeking until you get the blessing, will you?  Promise me this and one thing more. Do n't let the love of this world, and the deceitfulness of riches, tempt you to give way to Satan for one minute."

" Well, I'll see what I can do, but it looks like a great task before me."  And John really felt as though he was preparing for a stern conflict.  He went out to his work again, while Grandmother Lyman knelt down on the soft, bright carpet, the sunset light falling around her, and sent a prayer up to the Father's throne so full of thanksgiving and love that the answer was not delayed, but came, bringing peace and joy to her trusting heart.

Pretty soon Phœbe came stealing in with a look of apprehension resting upon her countenance.

" Mother," said she, sinking into the first chair she reached, " I'm afraid John's going to die."

" My child, what do you mean?" queried the old lady, pushing her spectacles to the top of her head.

"Because he's changed so lately.  Fixing up this room, you know, and being so gentle like—what can it mean unless he's going to die?"

" Do n't worry, Phœbe, John's just getting ready to live. I tell you, daughter, he's experiencing religion."

16

A flash of joy lighted up Phœbe's worn face as she spoke.

"Do you think so, mother? Oh, if it only could be true!"

A cry from the kitchen called her thither again, but her heart was light, and old hymns sprang unbidden to her lips, all tuned to the upgushing happiness within. The little ones caught the infection, and capered up and down the old kitchen, until wearied out they dropped off to sleep and to bed.

That day saw the beginning of true happiness in the old red farmhouse. Not but that John passed through many fierce struggles, for the world acquires a strong hold in forty-five years, but with God's help he gained the victory; and humble and happy, one week later he called his little family together, and told them of his new hopes and purposes. We can not describe that scene, but surely the angels saw and rejoiced over it. Then once more, before his friends and neighbors in prayer-meeting, with trembling voice he related his experience. Tears and "amens" greeted it, all testifying to the spirit of true brotherly love. Some, to be sure, there were who said, "Can the leopard change his spots?" But when, Sabbath after Sabbath, they saw that the head of the "Lyman pew" neither pretended to be asleep, nor to have forgotten his wallet when the much-abused green contribution bag swung along, but instead deposited therein the freshest scrip, they said, "Truly, this is the Lord's doings, and is marvelous in our eyes."

Perhaps the story of the change at home is about as

Tillie whispered it in the ear of a confidential friend. "You see pa asks a blessin' now 'fore we eats; and then we read the Bible; and he prays the Lord to keep us good all the day long; and so we grow gooder and gooder. Pa bought mother a new black silk dress the other day, and Oh, he's so much lovinger than he ever was before!" Yes, he was "lovinger," as Tillie called him, for truly he had passed from death unto life.

The old homestead, too, soon began to change visibly. The shades of ugliness that had so long hung over it vanished away. Its very angles seemed to grow less acute, and never, in its palmiest days, had it rejoiced in such bright coats of paint. But, with all the brightening up without and within, there was one most cozy place of all where the family was wont to assemble each Sabbath evening. "Seem's though it's always full of rainbows," Nick said; but that must have been owing to the blessed influence of her who sat there, for this dearest of all nooks was "grandmother's room."

> GOD has not promised skies ever blue,
> Flower-strewn pathways always to you·
> God has not promised sun without rain,
> Joy without sorrow, peace without pain;
> But God has promised strength from above,
> Unfailing sympathy, undying love.

# THE YOUNG MUSICIAN

JONAS JOHNSON was the youngest son of an
organ-builder in New England. He was a
small, quiet boy, in no way remarkable except
in his passion for harmonies. So great was
his love for music, that from his most tender years he
could not listen unmoved to the singing of his sisters as
they went about their homely work; and if the voices happened to be discordant he ran shuddering from the sound.
The choir of untutored singers in church services made
tears fall from his eyes upon his hymn-book while he
joined his small voice with theirs.

Although Jonas let his tears fall unwittingly, the organ-
builder saw them and treasured them in his heart. When
the boy had reached his eleventh year the family left the
country town and came to live in New York. Here the
father determined to let his son learn the organ.

"Remember, Jonas," said he, "I am a poor man, and
can ill afford to go into this expense unless you do the

work before you manfully and patiently. I give you this profession instead of a trade because I believe it to be your wish."

Jonas was entirely satisfied, and his slim fingers quivered in the anticipation of one day being able to move those mysterious white and black keys to the sound and measure of *Te 'Deums* and chants. A teacher was selected whose manner of educating was thorough and profound. At the first lesson Jonas became unequivocally assured that the business was a serious one, when after a third time striking G instead of G-sharp, the heavy, quick blow of the master's stick hummed and stung across his hands as they hovered over the organ keys. Poor little fingers! they could work no more that day—they were stiffened and red. He wept so profusely that he was requested to retire and to return in two days.

All the way home he sobbed, and held his hands suspended from the wrists, a most pitiable object. "Ah! you old ruffian!" soliloquized the tearful pupil, "won't my father give it to you for this?"

He found his father in the workshop.

"Well," cried the organ-builder, "how went the lesson?" He saw there had been trouble.

Jonas with fresh tears showed his chafed fingers and told the event. The father listened with darkened brow, and when the sad tale was ended he solemnly led his son into a back room, and after inflicting a thorough corporal punishment, warned him in a terrible voice never again to complain of his master.

Our hero felt for a while that this was almost beyond

human endurance, and for several hours he lay upon a pile of shavings plotting vengeance upon those he considered his worst enemies, when a sudden thrill shot through him at the sound of the rich organ tones. They came from his father's wareroom. Evidently a master hand was there. Jonas sat up and listened. It was the portion of a prelude by Sebastian Bach, and the marvelous harmonies seemed to speak to Jonas as the voice of a spirit. He rose upon his feet, and his whole soul trembled with the wonderful words it spoke to him, though as yet he hardly understood their meaning. He went to the door and gently opened it. The back of the high organ stood opposite to him. He did not wish to be observed, and he passed quietly along at the end of the large room until he saw the musician. Could it be the master? Yes, Jonas recognized the long curling beard, and even the *baton* as it lay upon a chair. Amidst the glowing chords the boy contrived to pass on unnoticed. He remembered that in two days he must again present himself. Could that terrible personage be confronted with an imperfect scale? The very thought was a shudder. Besides, Jonas felt an inspiration now. He again burned to be a musician. The revengeful spirit had left him—he thought only of Sebastian Bach.

A small organ had been placed in the little garret where Jonas slept. Thither he repaired, and commenced the work that ever since he has performed so well.

The dreaded master found no fault with the next lesson, and as Jonas advanced and he perceived that he studied with a zeal, an earnestness quite unusual in a boy, his stern manner relaxed, and he dared allow all the warmth of his heart to cheer his now beloved pupil.

At the end of five months Jonas met with a great misfortune. His master, after a short and sudden illness, died—which so cut him down that the organ-builder feared for his son's health. The boy stoutly refused to work under any other teacher, assuring the family that he felt able now to go on alone. Early morning and late evening found the young musician at his organ in the garret. Those who read this biography will scarcely believe how great was his progress. But I state facts.

Just after he had entered his twelfth year he happened to overhear two men, in a music store, conversing about a church in the upper part of the city, where the organist was to leave in a few weeks. Jonas listened.

" He plays in too operatic a style to suit the congregation," said one.

" Yes," said the other, "the simpler the playing the better they are pleased."

" Where is the church ? " asked Jonas.

" It is Saint C——'s, in —— Street."

Jonas returned to his organ, swelling with a new and great idea. The following Sabbath morning he went very early to the church. No person had arrived except the organist who was arranging music in the loft. Jonas stepped up the stairway and came round in front where he could see the selections. The organist turned at the intrusion.

" What do you want here, Sir ? " said he.

" I heard there was to be a vacancy, Sir."

" And do you know of one who wishes to occupy it ? "

" I should like it."

"You?"

"Yes, I am an organist."

This simple reply brought a smile to the lips of the questioner. He pointed to a page in the service, and said "Play that." And giving up his seat to Jonas, he went to the side to blow the bellows. Feeling nervous and anxious, Jonas began—at first tremulously, but gaining courage with every chord, he successfully accomplished the task, while the organist ran from the bellows to the music, and from the music to the bellows again in surprise. At the conclusion they both drew a long breath.

"Well, that is remarkable!" said the organist. "And you want the vacancy?"

"Very much," replied Jonas, trembling with pleasure.

"Then come here this afternoon, just before church, and I will take you to the minister. He makes all these arrangements."

The boy went home overflowing with great anticipations. He said nothing to his father on the subject. He dared not trust himself yet. Never did hours pass so slowly as those between dinner and church that afternoon. But the good time came and Jonas was true to his appointment, as was the organist, who took him into the vestry-room, and introduced him as an applicant for the vacancy.

Tall, white-haired, and benign the minister stood as Jonas told him his desire.

"Yes, my boy, the present organist will leave in three weeks. Will that give you time to become acquainted with our service?"

"Yes, Sir."

"Then I have only to hear you play before deciding. Will you take the organist's place this afternoon? He will show you the forms."

The proposal was sudden and unexpected, and made Jonas' heart quake; but he felt that all depended on his courage, and he accepted.

He took his seat before the great organ with a brave but serious spirit. The bell ceased tolling; the minister entered; and Jonas pressed his slight fingers upon the first chord of the voluntary, which, extemporaneous as it was, may be considered the corner-stone of his life.

The music that afternoon was simple and pure as the heart from which it flowed. Again Jonas presented himself before the minister, who received him in a most affectionate manner.

"Keep to this simple style," said he, "and we shall never wish to change. How much salary have you fixed upon?"

"Indeed, Sir, I never thought of it. I only wished to play in a church."

The minister sat down at a table, and taking pen and paper, went on: "You shall receive what we have always paid—the sum of one hundred and fifty dollars a year. I will draw the agreement. Come now, and sign your name."

"Your chirography is not equal to your organ-playing," continued the minister, smiling, as he saw the childlike, uneven signature of Jonas Johnson: "but one cannot expect everything of such a little fellow. Here, then, is the contract. Take care of it."

Jonas took leave of his friend and hurried home. When the family of the organ-builder gathered about the hearth-stone that evening, the youngest came to the father and drew forth his contract.

"What is this, my son?"

"Jonas made no answer, but waited while the spectacles were adjusted on the respective noses of both parents—waited till they had read the agreement, and his father had taken two turns across the floor, and said, "He's going to be a great master, wife. God bless him!" And then he could wait no longer, but ran up to his little garret, and throwing himself upon the cot, gave vent to his welling heart in sobs of joy, and hope, and ambition.

The organ-builder's prophecy came true. The world is now indebted to Jonas for some of its best church music. As a composer and teacher he is "great." Those who are as fortunate as the writer of this sketch in having him as a teacher to their children can truly say they know a "great master" of music.

Jonas' perseverance to become a musician, notwithstanding the severe discipline to which he was subjected, was rewarded by success. And not only was his perseverance commendable in accomplishing a musical education, but in securing a position in which to be useful. And every boy and girl should take this as a lesson, that by their own energy and perseverance may be laid the foundation of their success in life.

# Lyman Dean's Testimonials.

I DO not believe two more worthy, excellent people could be found than Gideon Randal and his wife. To lift the fallen, and minister to the destitute was their constant habit and delight, so that often they shortened their own comforts for the good of others. Mr. Randal's friends urged him to reduce his charities, as such generous giving might mar his fortune and bring him to want; but his unfailing reply was:—

"I think there's enough left to carry Martha and me through life, and some over. What we give to the poor, we lend to the Lord, and if a dark day comes, He will provide."

A dark day did come, but it was not till after he had reached threescore and ten years. As old age advanced, his little farm had become less productive, and debts accumulated. Being forced to raise money, he had borrowed a thousand dollars of Eugene Harrington, giving him a mortgage on his house for security. The interest was regularly paid, and with this Esquire Harrington was well satisfied; but he died suddenly, and his son, a merciless, grasping man, wrote to Mr. Randal, demanding payment of the mortgage. The old man asked for an extension of the time, but he pressed the demand, and threatened if it was not settled within a given time, to deprive him of his home. Mr. Randal was greatly distressed.

251

"Martha," he said to his wife, "young Harrington is a hard man. He has me in his power now, and I fear he will not scruple to ruin me. I think I had better go and talk with him, and tell him how little I have. It may be he'll pity two old people, and allow us better terms."

"But husband, you are not used to traveling, and Harrowtown is a hundred miles away, and you are old and feeble, too."

"True, wife, but I can say to him a great deal more than I can write, and besides, Luke Conway lives there. I took an interest in him when he was a poor boy. Perhaps he'll advise and help me, now that I'm in trouble."

At last, seeing he felt that he must go, Martha reluctantly consented, and fitted him out with wifely care.

The next morning was warm and sunny for November, and Mr. Randal started for Harrowtown.

"Gideon," called Mrs. Randal, as he walked slowly down the road, "be sure and take tight hold of the railing when you get in and out of the cars."

"I'll be careful. You take good care of yourself, Martha;" and, with a parting look, the old man hastened on to take the stage, which was to convey him to the railroad station. But misfortune met him at the very outset of his journey. The stage was heavily loaded, and on the way, one of the wheels broke down, which caused such a detention that Mr. Randal missed the morning train, and the next did not come for several hours.

It was afternoon when he finally started. He was anxious and weary from long waiting; and after three stations were passed, he began to ask questions.

"How long before we get to Harrowtown?" he inquired, stopping the busy conductor.

"We get there at half past eight"

Another question was upon Mr. Randal's lips, but the conductor had hurried on. He looked around as if to appeal to some one else, but turned back, talking to himself. "Not get there till into the evening," he said, "and pitch dark, for there's no moon now. I shan't know where to go." The poor old man was sorely troubled.

Presently the conductor came back, and as he passed his seat, he stopped him again.

"Mr. Conductor, how shall I know when to get out? I've never been to Harrowtown, and I don't want to get out at the wrong place."

"Give yourself no concern," was the polite reply. "I'll tell you when we come to Harrowtown. I won't forget you."

Soothed by this assurance, Mr. Randal's mind grew tranquil, and he finally went to sleep.

In the seat behind him sat a tall, handsome boy. His name was Albert Gregory. He was bright and intelligent, but his well-featured face was spoiled by a wicked-looking eye and a hard, cruel mouth.

He saw the aged passenger fall asleep, and nudged his seat-fellow.

"Look there, John. By and by, I'll play a joke on that old country greeny, and you'll see fun."

On rushed the swift express; mile after mile was passed; daylight faded and the lamps were lit in the cars, and still the aged man slept, watched by his purposed tormentor, and the other boy who waited to "see fun."

At length the speed of the train began to slacken, coming near a stopping-place. Albert sprang up and shook Mr. Randal violently.

"Wake up! Wake up!" he called, sharply, putting his mouth close to his ear. "This is Harrowtown. You must get off here."

The old man, thus roughly roused, started from his seat and gazed around him, bewildered. The change from day to night, the unaccustomed waking on a moving train, the glare of the lights, added tenfold to his confusion.

"Wh—what did you say boy?" he asked helplessly.

"This is Harrowtown. The place where you want to stop. You must get off. Be quick or you'll be carried by."

The noise of the brakes, and the distracted attention of the passengers on reaching a new station, possibly ignorance of the real locality on the part of those near enough to have heard him, prevented any correction of the boy's cruel falsehood. Mr. Randal knew it was not the conductor who had aroused him; but, supposing Albert to be some employee of the road, he hurried to the car door with tottering steps. The name of the station was called at the other end, as unlike as possible to the name of "Harrowtown," but his dull ears did not notice it. He got off upon the platform, and before he could recover himself or knew his error, the train was in motion again.

Albert was in ecstasies over the success of his "joke," and shook all over with laughter, in which, of course, his companion joined. "Oh dear! that's too good for anything!" he cried, "aint it, John?"

John assented that it was very funny indeed.

Neither of the boys noticed that the seat lately occupied by poor, deceived Mr. Randal had just been taken by a fine-looking middle-aged man, wrapped in a heavy cloak, who appeared to be absorbed in his own thoughts, but really heard every word they said.

They kept up a brisk conversation, Albert speaking in quite a loud tone, for he was feeling very merry. "Ha, ha, ha!—but I did think the old fool would hear the brakeman call the station, though. I didn't suppose I could get him any further than the door. To think of his clambering clear out on the platform, and getting left! He believed every word I told him. What a delicious old simpleton!"

And having exhausted that edifying subject for the moment, he presently began to brag of his plans and prospects.

"I don't believe you stand much of a chance there; they say Luke Conway is awful particular," the middle-aged stranger heard John remark.

"Pooh! shut up!" cried Albert. "Particular! That's just it, and makes my chance all the better. I've brought the kind of recommendation that a particular man wants, you see."

"But there'll be lots of other fellows trying for the place."

"Don't care if there's fifty," said Albert, "I'd come in ahead of 'em all. I've got testimonials of character and qualifications from Professor Howe, Rev. Joseph Lee, Dr. Henshaw, and Esquire Jenks, the great railroad contractor. His name alone is enough to secure me the situation."

At this juncture, the strange gentleman turned around and gave Albert a quick, searching glance. But the con-ceited boy was too much occupied with himself to notice the movement, and kept on talking. Now and then the thought of the victim whom he had fooled seemed to come back and tickle him amazingly. "Wonder where the old man is now. Ha, ha! Do you suppose he has found out where Harrowtown is? Oh, but wasn't it rich to see how scared he was when I waked him up? And how he jumped and scrambled out of the car! 'Pon my word, I never saw anything so comical."

Here the stranger turned again and shot another quick glance, this time from indignant eyes, and his lips parted as if about to utter a stern reproof. But he did not speak. Some hidden motive withheld him.

We will now leave Albert and his fellow travelers, and follow good Gideon Randal.

It was quite dark when he stepped from the cars, and he inquired of a man at the station, " Can you tell me where I can find Mr. Aaron Harrington ? "

"There's no such man living here, to my knowledge," was the reply.

"What, isn't this Harrowtown?" asked Mr. Randal in great consternation.

"No, it is Whipple Village."

"Then I got out at the wrong station. What shall I do?" in a voice of deep distress.

"Go right to the hotel and stay till the train goes in the morning," said the man, pleasantly.

There was no alternative, Mr. Randal passed a restless

night at the hotel, and at an early hour he was again at the station, waiting for the train.   His face was pale, and his eye wild and anxious.   "The stage broke down, and I missed the first train," thought he, "and then that boy told me to get out here.   I've made a bad beginning, and I'm afraid this trip will have a bad ending."

There were other passengers walking to and fro on the platform, waiting for the cars to come.

One was a plain-featured, honest-looking boy, who had been accompanied to the station by his mother.   Just before his mother bade him good by, she said, "Lyman, look at that pale, sad, old man.   I do n't believe he is used to traveling.   Perhaps you can help him along."

Soon a loud, prolonged whistle was heard.   The cars were coming.

"Allow me to assist you, sir," said Lyman Dean to Mr. Randal, as the train stopped ; and he took hold of his arm, and guided him into a car to a seat.

"Thank you, my boy.   I'm getting old and clumsy, and a little help from a young hand comes timely.   Where are you going, if I may ask ? "

"To Harrowtown, sir.   I saw an advertisement for a boy in a store, and I'm going to try to get the situation. My name is Lyman Dean."

"Ah ?   I'm sure I wish you success, Lyman, for I believe you're a good boy.   You are going to the same place I am.   I want to find Aaron Harrington, but I've had two mishaps.   I do n't know what's coming next."

"I'll show you right where his office is.   I've been in Harrowtown a good many times."

17

Half an hour later, the brakeman shouted the name of the station where they must stop. Lyman assisted Mr. Randal off the train, and walked with him to the principal street. "Here's Mr Harrington's office," said he.

"Oh, yes, thank you kindly. And now could you tell me where Mr. Luke Conway's place of business is?"

"Why, that's the very gentleman I'm going to see," said Lyman. "His place is just round the corner, only two blocks off."

Mr. Randal looked deeply interested. He turned and shook the boy's hand warmly. "Lyman," he said, "Mr. Conway knows me. I am coming to see him by and by. I am really obliged to you for your politeness, and wish I could do something for you. I hope Mr. Conway will give you the situation, for you deserve it. If you apply before I get there, tell him Gideon Randal is your friend. Good by."

Fifteen minutes after found Lyman waiting in the counting-room of Luke Conway's store. Albert Gregory had just preceded him. The merchant was writing, and he had requested the boys to be seated a short time, till he was at leisure. Before he finished his work, a slow, feeble step was heard approaching, and an old man stood in the doorway.

"Luke, don't you remember me?" The merchant looked up at the sound of the voice. Then he sprang up from his chair and grasped the old man's hands in both his own. "Mr. Randal! Welcome, a thousand times welcome, my benefactor!" he exclaimed. And seating his guest on the office lounge beside him, Mr. Conway in-

quired after his health and comfort, and talked with him as
a loving son. It was evident to the quick perception of
the merchant that the good old man's circumstances had
changed, and he soon made it easy for him to unburden
his mind.

"Yes, Luke, I am in trouble. Aaron Harrington
owns a mortgage on my farm, and I can't pay him, and he
threatens to take my home," said Mr. Randal, with a quivering lip. "I went to his office, but did n't find him, and
I thought may be you'd advise me what to do."

"Mr. Randal," answered the merchant, laying his hand
on the old man's shoulder, "almost thirty years ago when
I was cold, and hungry, and friendless, you took me in
and fed me. Your good wife—God bless her!—made me
a suit of clothes with her own hands. You found me
work, and you gave me money when I begun the world
alone. Much if not all that I am in life I owe to your
sympathy and help, my kind old friend. Now I am rich,
and you must let me cancel my debt. I shall pay your
mortgage to-day. You shall have your home free again."

"Mr. Randal wiped great hot tears from his cheeks,
and said in a husky voice, "It is just as I told Martha. I
knew if we lent our money to the Lord, when a dark day
came, he would provide."

The reader can imagine the different feelings of the two
boys, as they sat witnesses of the scene. The look of
derision, that changed to an expression of sickly dismay,
on Albert's face, when the old man came in and was so
warmly greeted by the merchant, was curiously suggestive.
But his usual assurance soon returned. He thought it un-

likely that Mr. Randal would recognize him in the day-light, and he determined to put on a bold front.

For a minute the two men continued in conversation. Mr. Conway called up pleasant reminiscences of "Aunt Martha," his boy-life on the farm, and the peace and still-ness of the country town. He thought a railway ride of a hundred miles must be a hardship for a quiet old man. "It was a long way for you," he said, "Did you have a comfortable journey?"

"Well, I can't quite say that. First, the stage broke down and delayed me. Then I slept in the cars, and a boy played a trick on me, and waked me up, and made me get out at the wrong station, so I had to stay over night in Whipple Village. To tell the truth I had a good deal of worriment with one thing and another, getting here; but it's all bright now," he added with a radiant face.

"You shall go with me to my house and rest, as soon as I have dismissed these boys," said Mr Conway, ear-nestly; and turning to Albert and Lyman, who anxiously waited, he spoke to them about their errand.

"I suppose you came because you saw my advertise-ment?"

"Yes, sir," replied both, simultaneously.

"Very well. I believe you came in first. What is your name?"

"I am Albert Gregory, sir. I think I can suit you. I've brought testimonials of ability and character from some of the first men—Esquire Jenkins, Rev. Joseph Lee, Dr. Henshaw, and others. Here are my letters of recom-mendation," holding them out for Mr. Conway to take.

"I don't want to see them," returned the merchant, coldly. "I have seen you before, I understand your character well enough for the present."

He then addressed a few words to Lyman Dean.

"I should be very glad of work," said Lyman. "My mother is poor, and I want to earn my living, but I hav'n't any testimonials."

"Yes, you have," said old Mr. Randal, who was waiting for an opportunity to say that very thing. And then he told the merchant how polite and helpful Lyman had been to him.

Mr. Conway fixed his eyes severely upon the other boy. The contrast between him and young Dean was certainly worth a lesson.

"Albert Gregory," said the merchant, "I occupied the seat in the car in front of you last evening. I heard you exulting and wickedly boasting how you had deceived a distressed old man. Mr. Randal, is this the boy who lied to you, and caused you to get out at the wrong station?"

Mr. Randal looked earnestly at Albert. "I declare! Now I remember him. It is! I'm sure it is."

It was useless for Albert to attempt any vindication of himself. His stammered excuses stuck in his throat, and he was glad to hide his mortification by an early escape. Crestfallen, he slunk away, taking all his "testimonials" with him.

"Lyman," said Mr. Conway, kindly, "I shall be very glad to employ you in my store. You shall have good pay if you do well, and I am sure you will. You may begin work at once."

Lyman's eyes danced with joy as he left the counting-room to receive his instructions from the head clerk.

Mr. Conway paid to Mr. Harrington the money owed him by Mr. Randal, and a heavy load was lifted from the good old farmer's heart. He remained a visitor two or three days in Mr. Conway's house, where he was treated with the utmost deference and attention. Mr. Conway also purchased for him a suit of warm clothes, and an overcoat, and sent his confidential clerk with him on his return journey to see him safely home. Nor was good Mrs. Randal forgotten. She received a handsome present in money from Mr. Conway, and a message full of grateful affection. Nothing ever after occurred to disturb the lives of the aged and worthy pair.

Albert Gregory obtained an excellent situation in New York, but his false character, and his wanton disregard of others' feelings and rights, made him as hateful to his employers as to all his associates, and he soon found it desirable to seek another place.

He has changed places many times since, and his career has been an unhappy one—another example of the penalty of frivolous habits and a heartless nature.

Lyman Dean is now a successful merchant, a partner of Mr. Conway, and occupies a high position in society, as an honorable, enterprising man.

> WHAT is it that gives to the plainest face
> The charm of the noblest beauty?
> Not the thought of the duty of happiness,
> But the happiness of duty.

# UNFORGOTTEN WORDS

HAVE you examined that bill, James?"

"Yes, sir."

"Anything wrong?"

"I find two errors."

"Ah, let me see."

The lad handed his employer a long bill that had been placed on his desk for examination.

"Here is an error in the calculation of ten dollars, which they have made against themselves; and another of ten dollars in the footing."

"Also against themselves?"

"Yes, sir."

The merchant smiled in a way that struck the lad as peculiar.

"Twenty dollars against themselves," he remarked in a kind of pleasant surprise. "Trusty clerks they must have!"

"Shall I correct the figures?" asked the lad.

"No, let them correct their own mistakes. We don't examine bills for other people's benefit," replied the merchant. "It will be time to rectify those errors when they find them out. All so much gain as it now stands."

The boy's delicate moral sense was shocked at so unexpected a remark. He was the son of a poor widow, who had given him to understand that to be just was the duty of man.

Mr. Carman, the merchant in whose employment he had been for only a few months, was an old friend of his father, and a person in whom he reposed the highest confidence. In fact, James had always looked upon him as a kind of model man; and when Mr Carman agreed to take him into his store, he felt that great good fortune was in his way.

"Let them correct their own mistakes." These words made a strong impression on the mind of James Lewis. When first spoken by Mr. Carman, and with the meaning then involved, he felt, as we have said, shocked; but as he turned them over again in his thoughts, and connected their utterance with a person who stood so high in his mother's estimation, he began to think that perhaps the thing was fair enough in business. Mr. Carman was hardly the man to do wrong. A few days after James had examined the bill, a clerk from the house by which it had been rendered, called for settlement. The lad, who was present, waited with interest to see whether Mr. Carman would speak of the error. But he made no remark. A check for the amount of the bill rendered, was filled up, and a receipt taken.

"Is that right?" James asked himself this question. His moral sense said no; but the fact that Mr. Carman had so acted, bewildered his mind.

"It may be the way in business"—so he thought to himself—"but it don't look honest. I wouldn't have believed it of him."

Mr. Carman had a kind of way with him that won the boy's heart, and naturally tended to make him judge of whatever he might do in a most favorable manner.

"I wish he had corrected that error," he said to himself a great many times when thinking in a pleased way of Mr. Carman, and his own good fortune in having been received into his employment. "It don't look right, but it may be in the way of business."

One day he went to the bank and drew the money for a check. In counting it over he found that the teller had paid him fifty dollars too much, so he went back to the counter and told him of his mistake. The teller thanked him, and he returned to the store with the consciousness in his mind of having done right.

"The teller overpaid me by fifty dollars," he said to Mr. Carman, as he handed him the money.

"Indeed," replied the latter, a light breaking over his countenance ; and he hastily counted the bank bills.

The light faded as the last bill left his fingers.

"There's no mistake, James." A tone of disappointment was in his voice.

"Oh, I gave him back the fifty dollars. Wasn't that right?"

"You simpleton!" exclaimed Mr. Carman. "Don't you know that bank mistakes are never corrected? If the teller had paid you fifty dollars short he would not have made it right."

The warm blood mantled the cheek of James under this reproof.   It is often the case that more shame is felt for a blunder than a crime.   In this instance the lad felt a sort of mortification at having done what Mr. Carman was pleased to call a silly thing, and he made up his mind that if they should ever overpay him a thousand dollars at the bank, he should bring the amount to his employer, and let him do as he pleased with the money.

"Let people look after their own mistakes," said Mr. Carman.

James Lewis pondered these things in his heart.   The impression they made was too strong ever to be forgotten. "It may be right," he said, but he did not feel altogether satisfied.

A month or two after the occurrence of that bad mistake, as James counted over his weekly wages, just received from Mr. Carman, he discovered that he was paid half a dollar too much.

The first impulse of his mind was to return the half-dollar to his employer, and it was on his lips to say, "You have given me half a dollar too much, sir," when the unforgotten words, "Let people look after their own mistakes," flashing upon his thoughts, made him hesitate.   To hold a parley with evil is to be overcome.

"I must think about this," said James, as he put the money in his pocket.   "If it is true in one case, it is true in another.   Mr. Carman don't correct mistakes that people make in his favor, and he can't complain when the rule works against him."

But the boy was very far from being in a comfortable

state. He felt that to keep half a dollar would be a dishonest act. Still he could not make up his mind to return it, at least not then.

James did not return the half-dollar, but spent it to his own gratification. After he had done this it came suddenly into his head that Mr. Carman had only been trying him, and he was filled with anxiety and alarm.

Not long after Mr. Carman repeated the same mistake. James kept the half-dollar with less hesitation.

"Let him correct his own mistakes," said he resolutely; "that's the doctrine he acts on with other people, and he can't complain if he gets paid in the same coin he puts in circulation. I just wanted half a dollar."

From this time the fine moral sense of James Lewis was blunted. He had taken an evil counselor into his heart, stimulated a spirit of covetousness—latent in almost every mind—which caused him to desire the possession of things beyond his ability to obtain.

James had good business qualifications, and so pleased Mr. Carman by his intelligence, industry, and tact with customers, that he advanced him rapidly, and gave him, before he was eighteen years of age, the most reliable position in the store. But James had learned something more from his employer than how to do business well. He had learned to be dishonest. He had never forgotten the first lesson he had received in this bad science; he had acted upon it, not only in two instances, but in a hundred, and almost always to the injury of Mr. Carman. He had long since given up waiting for mistakes to be made in his favor, but originated them in the varied and complicated transactions of a large business in which he was trusted implicitly.

James grew sharp, cunning, and skilful; always on the alert; always bright, and ready to meet any approaches towards a discovery of his wrong-doing by his employer, who held him in the highest regard.

Thus it went on until James Lewis was in his twentieth year, when the merchant had his suspicions aroused by a letter that spoke of the young man as not keeping the most respectable company, and as spending money too freely for a clerk on a moderate salary.

Before this time James had removed his mother into a pleasant house, for which he paid a rent of four hundred dollars; his salary was eight hundred, but he deceived his mother by telling her it was fifteen hundred. Every comfort that she needed was fully supplied, and she was beginning to feel that, after a long and painful struggle with the world, her happier days had come.

James was at his desk when the letter was received by Mr. Carman. He looked at his employer and saw him change countenance suddenly. He read it over twice, and James saw that the contents produced disturbance. Mr. Carman glanced towards the desk, and their eyes met; it was only for a moment, but the look that James received made his heart stop beating.

There was something about the movements of Mr. Carman for the rest of the day that troubled the young man. It was plain to him that suspicion had been aroused by that letter. Oh, how bitterly now did he repent, in dread of discovery and punishment, the evil of which he had been guilty! Exposure would disgrace and ruin him, and bow the head of his widowed mother even to the grave.

" You are not well this evening," said Mrs. Lewis, as she looked at her son's changed face across the table, and noticed that he did not eat.

" My head aches."

" Perhaps a rest will make you feel better."

" I'll lie down on the sofa in the parlor for a short time."

Mrs. Lewis followed him into the parlor in a little while, and, sitting down on the sofa on which he was lying, placed her hand upon his head. Ah, it would take more than the loving pressure of a mother's hand to ease the pain from which he was suffering. The touch of that pure hand increased the pain to agony.

" Do you feel better?" asked Mrs. Lewis. She had remained some time with her hand on his forehead.

" Not much," he replied, and rising as he spoke, he added, " I think a walk in the open air will do me good."

" Don't go out, James," said Mrs. Lewis, a troubled feeling coming into her heart.

" I'll walk only a few squares." And James went from the parlor and passed into the street.

" There is something more than headache the matter with him," thought Mrs. Lewis.

For half an hour James walked without any purpose in his mind beyond the escape from the presence of his mother. At last his walk brought him near Mr. Carman's store, and at passing he was surprised at seeing a light within.

" What can this mean?" he asked himself, a new fear creeping, with its shuddering impulse, into his heart.

He listened by the door and windows, but he could hear no sound within.

"There's something wrong," he said, "what can it be?
If this is discovered what will be the end of it? Ruin!
ruin! My poor mother!"

The wretched young man hastened on, walked the
streets for two hours, when he returned home. His mother
met him when he entered, and with unconcealed anxiety,
asked him if he were better. He said yes, but in a manner
that only increased the trouble she felt, and passed up
hastily to his own room.

In the morning the strangely altered face of James, as
he met his mother at the breakfast table, struck alarm into
her heart. He was silent, and evaded all her questions.
While they sat at the table the door-bell rang loudly. The
sound startled James, and he turned his head to listen, in a
nervous way.

"Who is it?" asked Mrs. Lewis.

"A gentleman who wishes to see Mr. James," replied
the girl.

James rose instantly and went out into the hall, shutting
the dining-room door as he did so. Mrs. Lewis sat waiting
her son's return. She heard him coming back in a few
moments; but he did not enter the dining-room. Then he
returned along the hall to the street door and she heard it
shut. All was silent. Starting up, she ran into the passage, but James was not there. He had gone away with the
person who called.

Ah, that was a sad going away. Mr. Carman had spent
half the night in examining the accounts of James, and discovered frauds of over six thousand dollars. Blindly indignant, he sent an officer to arrest him early in the morning;

and it was with this officer that he went away from his mother, *never* to *return.*

"The young villain shall lie in the bed he has made for himself!" exclaimed Mr. Carman, in his bitter indignation. And he made the exposure completely. At the trial he showed an eager desire to have him convicted, and presented such an array of evidence that the jury could not give any other verdict than guilty.

The poor mother was in court, and audibly in the silence that followed came her convulsed sobs upon the air. The presiding judge addressed the culprit, and asked if he had anything to say why the sentence should not be pronounced against him. All eyes were turned upon the pale, agitated young man, who rose with an effort, and leaned against the railing by which he stood, as if needing the support.

"Will it please your honors," he said, "to direct my prosecutor to come a little nearer, so that I can look at him and your honors at the same time?"

Mr. Carman was directed to come forward to where the boy stood. James looked at him steadily for a few moments, and turned to the judges.

"What I have to say to your honors is this [he spoke calmly and distinctly], and it may in a degree extenuate, though it cannot excuse, my crime. I went into that man's store an innocent boy, and if he had been an honest man I would not have stood before you to-day as a criminal!"

Mr. Carman appealed to the court for protection against an allegation of such an outrageous character; but he was peremptorily ordered to be silent. James went on in a firm voice,—

"Only a few weeks after I went into his employment I examined a bill by his direction, and discovered an error of twenty dollars."

The face of Mr. Carman crimsoned.

"You remember it, I see," remarked James, "and I shall have cause to remember it as long as I live. The error was in favor of Mr. Carman. I asked if I should correct the figures, and he answered 'No; let them correct their own mistakes. We do n't examine bills for other people's benefit.' It was my first lesson in dishonesty. I saw the bill settled, and Mr. Carman take twenty dollars that was not his own. I felt shocked at first; it seemed such a wrong thing. But soon after he called me a simpleton for handing back a fifty-dollar bill to the teller of a bank, which he had overpaid me on a check, and then—"

"May I ask the protection of the court" said Mr. Carman.

"Is it true what the lad says?" asked the presiding judge.

Mr. Carman hesitated and looked confused. All eyes were on his face; and judges and jury, lawyers and spectators, felt certain that he was guilty of leading the unhappy young man astray.

"Not long afterward," resumed Lewis, "in receiving my wages I found that Mr. Carman had paid me fifty cents too much. I was about to give it back to him, when I remembered his remark about letting people correct their own mistakes, and said to myself, 'Let him correct his own errors,' and dishonestly kept the money. Again the same thing happened, and I kept the money that did not of right belong to me. This was the beginning of evil, and here I am. If he had shown any mercy, I might have kept silent and made no defense."

The young man covered his face with his hands, and sat down overpowered with his feelings. His mother who was near him sobbed aloud, and bending over, laid her hands on his head, saying:—

"My poor boy! my poor boy!"

There were few eyes in the court-room undimmed. In the silence that followed Mr. Carman spoke out:—

"Is my character to be thus blasted on the word of a criminal, your honors? Is this right?"

"Your solemn oath that this charge is untrue," said the judge, "will place you in the right." It was the unhappy boy's only opportunity, and the court felt bound in humanity to hear him.

James Lewis stood up again instantly, and turned his white face and dark, piercing eyes upon Mr. Carman.

"Let him take his oath if he dare!" he exclaimed.

Mr. Carman consulted with his counsel, and withdrew.

After a brief conference with his associates, the presiding judge said, addressing the criminal:—

"In consideration of your youth, and the temptation to which in tender years you were unhappily subject, the court gives you the slightest sentence, one year's imprisonment. But let me solemnly warn you against any further steps in the way you have taken. Crime can have no valid excuse. It is evil in the sight of God and man, and leads only to suffering. When you come forth again after your brief incarceration, may it be with the resolution to die rather than commit crime!"

18

And the curtain fell on that sad scene in the boy's life. When it was lifted again, and he came forth from prison a year afterwards, his mother was dead. From the day her pale face faded from his vision as he passed from the court-room, he never looked upon her again.

Ten years afterward a man was reading a newspaper in a far western town. He had a calm, serious face, and looked like one who had known suffering and trial.

"Brought to justice at last!" he said to himself, as the blood came to his face; "convicted on the charge of open insolvency, and sent to State prison. So much for the man who gave me in tender years the first lessons in ill-doing. But, thank God! the other lessons have been remembered. 'When you come forth again,' said the judge, 'may it be with the resolution to die rather than commit a crime!' and I have kept this injunction in my heart when there seemed no way of escape except through crime; and God helping me, I will keep it to the end."

## YOUR CALL.

THE world is dark, but you are called to brighten
　　Some little corner, some secluded glen;
Somewhere a burden rests that you may lighten,
　　And thus reflect the Master's love for men.

Is there a brother drifting on life's ocean,
　　Who might be saved if you but speak a word?
Speak it to-day. The testing of devotion
　　Is our response when duty's call is heard.

# Herrings for Nothing.

THE darkness was coming on rapidly, as a man with a basket on his head turned the corner of a street in London. He cried loudly as he went, "Herrings! three a penny, red herrings, good and cheap, at three a penny!"

Soon he came close to me and commenced conversation.

"Governor, why can't I sell these herrings? I have walked two miles along this dismal place, offering them; and nobody will buy."

"The people have no work at all to do, and they are starving; there are plenty of houses round here that have not had a penny in them for many a day," was my reply.

"Ah! then, governor," he rejoined, "if they have n't the half-pence, they can't spend 'em, sure enough; so there's nothing for me but to carry 'em elsewhere."

"How much will you take for the lot?" I inquired.

"I'll be glad to get four shillin'."

I put my hand in my pocket, produced that amount and transferred it to him.

"Right! governor, thank'ee! what'll I do with 'em?" he said, as he quickly transferred the coins to his own pocket.

"Go round this corner into the middle of the street, shout with all your might,—

'HERRINGS FOR NOTHING!'

and give three to every man, woman, and child, that comes
to you, till the basket is emptied."

So he proceeded into the middle of the street, and went
along shouting, "Herrings for nothing! good red herrings
for nothing!"

I stood at the corner to watch his progress; and soon
he neared the house where a tall woman stood at the first
floor window looking out upon him.

"Here you are missus," he cried, "herrings for nothing!
come an' take 'em."

The woman shook her head unbelievingly, and left the
window.

"Vot a fool!" said he; "but they won't all be so.
Herrings for nothing!" A little child came out to look at
him, and he called to her, "Here, my dear, take these in to
your mother, and tell her how cheap they are—herrings for
nothing." But the child was afraid of him and them, and
ran in-doors. So, down the street, in the snow, slush, and
mud, went the cheap fish, the vender crying loudly as he
went, "Herrings for nothing!" and then adding savagely,
"Oh, you fools." Thus he reached the end of the street;
and then turning to retrace his steps, he continued his
double cry as he came.

"Well," I said to him calmly, as he reached me at the
corner.

"Well!" he repeated, "if yer think so! When yer
gave me the money for herrings as yer did n't want, I
thought you was training for a lunatic 'sylum! Now I
thinks all the people round here are fit company for yer.
But what'll I do with the herrings if yer do n't want 'em,
and they won't have 'em?"

"We'll try again together," I replied; "I will go with you and we'll both shout."

Into the road we both went, and he shouted once more, "Herrings for nothing!"

"Then I called out loudly also, "Will any one have some herrings for tea?"

They heard my voice, and they knew it well; and they came out at once, in twos and threes and sixes, men and women and children, all striving to reach the welcome food. As fast as I could take them from the basket, I handed three to each eager applicant, until all were speedily disposed of. When the basket was empty, the hungry crowd that had none was far greater than that which had been supplied; but they were too late, there were no more "herrings for nothing!"

Foremost among the disappointed was a tall woman of a bitter tongue, who began vehemently, "Why haven't I got any? aint I as good as they? aint my children as hungry as theirs?"

Before I had time to reply, the vender stretched out his arm toward her, saying, "Why, governor, that's the very woman as I offered 'em to first, and she turned up her nose at 'em."

"I didn't," she rejoined passionately, "I didn't believe you meant it!"

"Yer goes without for yer unbelief!" he replied. "Good-night, and thank'ee, governor!"

I told this story upon the sea-beach, to a great crowd gathered there on a summer Sabbath day. They looked at each other; first smiled, then laughed outright, and at length shouted with laughter.

It was my time then; and I said, "You cannot help laughing at the quaint story, which is strictly true. But are you sure you would not have done as they did, and been as unbelieving as they? Their unbelief cost them only a hungry stomach a little longer; but what may your unbelief cost you? God has sent his messengers to you for many years to offer

PARDON FOR NOTHING!

peace for nothing! salvation for nothing! He has sent to you the most loving and tender offers that even an almighty God could frame; and what have you replied? Have you taken the trouble to reply at all? Have you not turned away in utter scornful unbelief, like the woman? or ran away in fear, like the child? You are still without a hope on earth, or a hope in heaven, because you will not believe God's messengers when they offer you all that you need for time and eternity—FOR NOTHING.

"Take warning by that disappointed crowd of hungry applicants. When they were convinced that the offer was in good faith, and would gladly have shared with their fellows, they were too late!

"Let it not be so with you! Do not be in that awfully large crowd of disappointed ones, who will be obliged to believe when belief will not help them; whose knowledge, when it comes, will only increase the sorrow that they put off believing until it was *too late*."

As I looked earnestly upon that vast crowd, the laughter was entirely gone, and an air of uneasy conviction was plainly traceable upon many faces.

"Will you not come to Jesus now?" I entreated.

COME UNTO ME.

" He is waiting, pleading with you! Here is salvation, full, free, and eternal; help, guidance, and blessing,—all for nothing! without money and without price."

## DID YOU EVER THINK?

DID you ever think what this world would be
If Christ had n't come to save it?
His hands and feet were nailed to the tree,
And his precious life—he gave it.
But countless hearts would break with grief,
At the hopeless life they were given,
If God had not sent the world relief,
If Jesus had stayed in heaven.

Did you ever think what this world would be
With never a life hereafter?
Despair in the faces of all we'd see,
And sobbing instead of laughter.
In vain is beauty, and flowers' bloom,
To remove the heart's dejection,
Since all would drift to a yawning tomb,
With never a resurrection.

Did you ever think what this world would be,
How weary of all endeavor,
If the dead unnumbered, in land and sea,
Would just sleep on forever?
Only a pall over hill and plain!
And the brightest hours are dreary,
Where the heart is sad, and hopes are vain,
And life is sad and weary.

Did you ever think what this world would be
If Christ had stayed in heaven,—
No home in bliss, no soul set free,
No life, or sins forgiven?
But he came with a heart of tenderest love,
And now from on high he sees us,
And mercy comes from the throne on high;
Thank God for the gift of Jesus!

# BREAD UPON THE WATERS

AH! Jacob, now you see how all your hopes are gone. Here we are worn out with age—all our children removed from us by the hand of death, and ere long we must be the inmates of the poorhouse. Where now is all the bread you have cast upon the waters?"

The old, white-haired man looked up at his wife. He was, indeed, bent down with years, and age sat tremblingly upon him. Jacob Manfred had been a comparatively wealthy man, and while fortune had smiled upon him he had ever been among the first to lend a listening ear and a helping hand to the call of distress. But now misfortune was his. Of his four boys not one was left. Sickness and failing strength found him with but little, and had left him penniless. An oppressive embargo upon the shipping business had been the first weight upon his head, and other misfortunes came in painful succession. Jacob and his wife were all alone, and gaunt poverty looked them coldly in the face.

"Do n't repine, Susan," said the old man. "True we are poor, but we are not yet forsaken."

"Not forsaken, Jacob? Who is there to help us now?"

Jacob Manfred raised his trembling finger toward heaven.

"Ah! Jacob, I know God is our friend, but we should have friends here. Look back and see how many you have befriended in days long past. You cast your bread upon the waters with a free hand, but it has not returned to you."

"Hush, Susan, you forget what you say. To be sure I may have hoped that some kind hand of earth would lift me from the cold depths of utter want; but I do not expect it as a reward for anything I may have done. If I have helped the unfortunate in days gone by, I have had my full reward in knowing that I have done my duty to my fellows. Oh! of all the kind deeds I have done to my suffering fellows, I would not for gold have one of them blotted from my memory. Ah! my fond wife, 'tis the memory of the good done in life that makes old age happy. Even now, I can hear again the warm thanks of those whom I have befriended, and again I can see their smiles."

"Yes, Jacob," returned the wife, in a lower tone, "I know you have been good, and in your memory you can be happy; but, alas! there is a present upon which we must look—there is a reality upon which we must dwell. We must beg for food or starve!"

The old man started, and a deep mark of pain was drawn across his features.

"*Beg!*" he replied, with a quick shudder. "No, Susan, we are—"

He hesitated, and a big tear rolled down his furrowed cheek.

"We are what, Jacob?"

"We are going to the poorhouse!"

"O God! I thought so!" fell from the poor wife's lips, as she covered her face with her hands. "I have thought so, and I have tried to school myself to the thought; but my poor heart will not bear it!"

"Do not give up," softly urged the old man, laying his hand upon her arm. "It makes but little difference to us now. We have not long to remain on earth, and let us not wear out our last days in useless repinings. Come, come."

"But when—when—shall we go?"

"Now—to-day."

"Then God have mercy on us!"

"He will," murmured Jacob.

That old couple sat for a while in silence. When they were aroused from their painful thoughts it was by the stopping of a wagon in front of the door. A man entered the room where they sat. He was the keeper of the poor-house.

"Come, Mr. Manfred," he said, "the selectmen have managed to crowd you into the poorhouse. The wagon is at the door, and you can get ready as soon as possible."

Jacob Manfred had not calculated the strength he should need for this ordeal. There was a coldness in the very tone and manner of the man who had come for him that went like an ice-bolt to his heart, and with a deep groan he sank back in his seat.

"Come, be in a hurry," impatiently urged the keeper.

At that moment a heavy covered carriage drove up to the door.

"Is this the house of Jacob Manfred?"

This question was asked by a man who entered from the carriage. He was a kind-looking man, about forty years of age.

"That is my name," said Jacob.

"Then they told me truly, uttered the new-comer. "Are you from the almshouse?" he continued, turning toward the keeper.

"Yes."

"Then you may return. Jacob Manfred goes to no poorhouse while I live."

The keeper gazed inquisitively into the face of the stranger, and left the house.

"Don't you remember me?" exclaimed the new-comer, grasping the old man by the hand.

"I can not call you to my memory now."

"Do you remember Lucius Williams?"

"Williams?" repeated Jacob, starting up and gazing earnestly into the stranger's face. "Yes, Jacob Manfred —Lucius Williams, that little boy whom, thirty years ago, you saved from the house of correction; that poor boy whom you kindly took from the bonds of the law, and placed on board your own vessels."

"And are you—"

"Yes—yes, I am the man you made. You found me

a rough stone from the hand of poverty and bad example. It was you who brushed off the evil, and who first led me to the sweet waters of moral life and happiness. I have profited by the lesson you gave me in early youth, and the warm spark which your kindness lighted up in my bosom has grown brighter and brighter ever since. With an affluence for life I have settled down to enjoy the remainder of my days in peace and quietness. I heard of your losses and bereavements. Come, I have a home and a heart, and your presence will make them both warmer, brighter, and happier. Come, my more than father — and you my mother, come. You made my youth all bright, and I will not see your old age doomed to darkness."

Jacob Manfred tottered forward and sank upon the bosom of his preserver. He could not speak his thanks, for they were too heavy for words. When he looked up again he sought his wife.

"Susan," he said, in a choking, trembling tone, "my bread has come back to me!"

"Forgive me, Jacob."

"No, no, Susan. It is not I who must forgive—God holds us in his hand."

"Ah!" murmured the wife, as she raised her streaming eyes to heaven, "I will never doubt him again."

> All my griefs by Him are ordered
> Needful is each one for me,
> Every tear by Him is counted,
> One too much there cannot be;
> And if when they fall so thickly.
> I can own His way is right,
> Then each bitter tear of anguish
> Precious is in Jesus' sight.

Far too well my Saviour loved me
   To allow my life to be
One long, calm, unbroken summer,
   One unruffled, stormless sea;
He would have me fondly nestling
   Closer to His loving breast,
He would have that world seem brighter
   Where alone is perfect rest.

Though His wise and loving purpose,
   Once I could not clearly see,
I believe with faith unshaken,
   All will work for good to me;
Therefore when my way is gloomy,
   And my eyes with tears are dim,
I will go to God, my Father,
   And will tell my griefs to Him.

## THE FATHER IS NEAR.

A WEE little child in its dreaming one night
Was startled by some awful ogre of fright,
And called for its father, who quickly arose
And hastened to quiet the little one's woes.
" Dear child, what's the matter ? " he lovingly said,
And smoothed back the curls from the fair little head;
" Do n't cry any more, there is nothing to fear,
Do n't cry any more, for your papa is here."

Ah, well ! and how often we cry in the dark,
Though God in His love is so near to us !   Hark !
How His loving words, solacing, float to the ear,
Saying, " Lo ! I am with you : 'tis I, do not fear."
God is here in the world as thy Father and mine,
Ever watching and ready with love-words divine.
And while erring oft, through the darkness I hear
In my soul the sweet message : " Thy Father is near."

# A Rift in the Cloud.

ANDREW LEE came home at evening from the shop where he had worked all day, tired and out of spirits; came home to his wife, who was also tired, and dispirited.

"A smiling wife, and a cheerful home—what a paradise it would be!" said Andrew to himself as he turned his eyes from the clouded face of Mrs. Lee, and sat down with knitted brow, and a moody aspect.

Not a word was spoken by either. Mrs. Lee was getting supper, and she moved about with a weary step.

"Come," she said at last, with a side glance at her husband.

There was invitation in the word only, none in the voice of Mrs. Lee.

Andrew arose and went to the table. He was tempted to speak an angry word, but controlled himself, and kept silence. He could find no fault with the chop, nor the sweet home-made bread, and fresh butter. They would have cheered the inward man if there had only been a gleam of sunshine on the face of his wife. He noticed that she did not eat. "Are you not well Mary?" The words were on his lips, but he did not utter them, for the face of his wife looked so repellant, that he feared an irritating reply. And so in moody silence, the twain sat together until Andrew had finished his supper. As he pushed his chair back, his wife arose, and commenced clearing off the table.

"This is purgatory!" said Lee to himself, as he commenced walking the floor of their little breakfast-room, with his hands clasped behind him, and his chin almost touching his breast.

After removing all the dishes and taking them into the kitchen, Mrs. Lee spread a green cover on the table, and placing a fresh trimmed lamp thereon, went out and shut the door, leaving her husband alone with his unpleasant feelings. He took a long, deep breath as she did so, paused in his walk, stood still for some moments, and then drawing a paper from his pocket, sat down by the table, opened the sheet and commenced reading. Singularly enough the words upon which his eyes rested were, " Praise your wife." They rather tended to increase the disturbance of mind from which he was suffering.

" I should like to find some occasion for praising mine." How quickly his thoughts expressed the ill-natured sentiment. But his eyes were on the page before him, and he read on.

"Praise your wife, man, for pity's sake, give her a little encouragement ; it wont hurt her."

Andrew Lee raised his eyes from the paper and muttered, "Oh, yes. That's all very well. Praise is cheap enough. But praise her for what? For being sullen, and making your home the most disagreeable place in the world?" His eyes fell again to the paper.

" She has made your home comfortable, your hearth bright and shining, your food agreeable ; for pity's sake, tell her you thank her, if nothing more. She do n't expect it; it will make her eyes open wider than they have for ten years; but it will do her good for all that, and you, too."

It seemed to Andrew as if these sentences were written just for him, and just for the occasion. It was the complete answer to his question, "Praise her for what?" and he felt it also as a rebuke. He read no farther, for thought came too busy, and in a new direction. Memory was convicting him of injustice toward his wife. She had always made his home as comfortable as hands could make it, and had he offered the light return of praise or commendation? Had he ever told her of the satisfaction he had known, or the comfort experienced? He was not able to recall the time or the occasion. As he thought thus, Mrs. Lee came in from the kitchen, and taking her work-basket from the closet, placed it on the table, and sitting down without speaking, began to sew. Mr. Lee glanced almost stealthily at the work in her hands, and saw it was the bosom of a shirt, which she was stitching neatly. He knew it was for him that she was at work.

"Praise your wife" The words were before the eyes of his mind, and he could not look away from them. But he was not ready for this yet. He still felt moody and unforgiving. The expression on his wife's face he interpreted to mean ill-nature, and with ill-nature he had no patience. His eyes fell on the newspaper that spread out before him, and he read the sentence :—

"A kind cheerful word, spoken in a gloomy home, is like the rift in the cloud that lets the sunshine through."

Lee struggled with himself a while longer. His own

ill-nature had to be conquered first; his moody, accusing spirit had to be subdued. But he was coming right, and at last got right, as to will. Next came the question as to how he should begin. He thought of many things to say, yet feared to say them, lest his wife should meet his advances with a cold rebuff. At last, leaning towards her, and taking hold of the linen bosom upon which she was at work, he said, in a voice carefully modulated with kindness:—

"You are doing the work very beautifully, Mary."

Mrs. Lee made no reply. But her husband did not fail to observe that she lost, almost instantly, that rigid erectness with which she had been sitting, nor that the motion of her needle had ceased. "My shirts are better made, and whiter than those of any other man in our shop," said Lee, encouraged to go on.

"Are they?" Mrs. Lee's voice was low, and had in it a slight huskiness. She did not turn her face, but her husband saw that she leaned a little toward him. He had broken through the ice of reserve, and all was easy now. His hand was among the clouds, and a few feeble rays were already struggling through the rift it had made.

"Yes, Mary," he answered softly, "and I've heard it said more than once, what a good wife Andrew Lee must have."

Mrs. Lee turned her face towards her husband. There was light it it, and light in her eye. But there was something in the expression of the countenance that puzzled him a little.

"Do you think so?" she asked quite soberly.

19

"What a question!" ejaculated Andrew Lee, starting up and going around to the side of the table where his wife was sitting.—"What a question, Mary!" he repeated, as he stood before her.

"Do you?" It was all she said.

"Yes, darling," was the warmly-spoken answer, and he stooped down and kissed her.—"How strange that you should ask me such a question!"

"If you would only tell me so now and then, Andrew, it would do me good." And Mrs. Lee arose, and leaning against the manly breast of her husband, stood and wept.

What a strong light broke in upon the mind of Andrew Lee. He had never given to his faithful wife even the small reward of praise for all the loving interest she had manifested daily, until doubt of his love had entered her soul, and made the light thick darkness. No wonder that her face grew clouded, nor that what he considered moodiness and ill-nature took possession of her spirit.

"You are good and true, Mary. My own dear wife. I am proud of you—I love you—and my first desire is for your happiness. Oh, if I could always see your face in sunshine, my home would be the dearest place on earth."

"How precious to me are your words of love and praise, Andrew," said Mrs. Lee, smiling up through her tears into his face. "With them in my ears, my heart can never lie in shadow."

How easy had been the work for Andrew Lee. He had swept his hand across the cloudy horizon of his home, and now the bright sunshine was streaming down, and flooding that home with joy and beauty.

# SUCCESS IS THE REWARD

*of* PERSEVERANCE

IF a person has ambition to engage in any enterprise, he desires to succeed in his undertaking. It is generally right that he should prosper in all that is truly good or great; and the fact that success is attainable by continued effort, we have all verified so many times in our pursuit of different objects, that we feel sure we can accomplish almost any purpose if we with patient perseverance bend all our energies in the right direction. If there is much to be gained, we may make apparently slow progress; but if we apply ourselves closely, and do not let little things discourage us we shall eventually succeed. There are always plenty of little things in the way of the accomplishment of any good or great thing. These must be gotten out of the way; and if, in our first attempt, we fail to win the prize, we must make another effort, varying the manner of our labor as circumstances shall suggest.

It takes only a little at a time to accomplish a great deal if we work long enough. Perhaps most of you have read of the little girl whose mother was presented with a ton of coal by a charitable neighbor. She took her little fire-shovel, and began to take up the coal, a shovelful at a time, and carry it into the cellar. A friend, who was passing by, said to the child, "Do you expect to get all that coal in with that little shovel?" "Yes, sir," said the little girl, dipping her shovel again into the heap, "I'll do it if I work long enough." She possessed the right spirit.

The true spirit of success is not to look at obstacles, but to keep the eye on the many ways in which to surmount them. This may be illustrated by the incident of the little factory girl who had one of her fingers so badly mangled in the machinery that she was obliged to have it cut off. Looking at the wounded hand, she said, "That is my thimble finger; but I must learn to sew with my left hand." She did not think of her loss, but of what she still possessed with which to work.

We may prosper in the several schemes in which it is lawful for Christians to take part, but, if we fail to win the strife for eternal life, we shall have lived in vain. To make life a success, the glory of God must be the ruling motive to actuate us in all the walks of life. If we do really glorify him in our lives, success will surely crown our efforts—everlasting life will be our reward.

Another instance of perseverance, against apparently insurmountable difficulties, is given in an anecdote, not generally known out of Russia, connected with a church spire of St. Petersburg, which place is remarkable for its spires. The loftiest is the church of St. Peter and St. Paul.

The spire, which is properly represented in an engraving as fading away almost into a point in the sky, is in reality terminated by a globe of considerable dimensions, on which an angel stands supporting a large cross. This angel fell into disrepair; and some suspicions were entertained that he designed visiting, uninvoked, the surface of the earth. The affair caused some uneasiness, and the government at length became greatly perplexed. To raise a scaffolding to such a height would cost more money than all the angels of this description were worth; and in meditating fruitlessly on these circumstances, without being able to resolve how to act, a considerable time was suffered to elapse.

Among the crowd of gazers below, who daily turned their eyes and their thoughts toward the angel, was a mujik called Telouchkine. This man was a roofer of houses (a slater, as he would be called in countries where slates are used), and his speculations by degrees assumed a more practical character than the idle wonders and conjectures of the rest of the crowd. The spire was entirely covered with sheets of gilded copper, and presented to the eye a surface as smooth as if it had been one mass of burnished gold. But Telouchkine knew that the sheets of copper were not even uniformly closed upon each other; and, above all, that there were large nails used to fasten them, which projected from the side of the spire.

Having meditated upon these circumstances till his mind was made up, the mujik went to the government and offered to repair the angel without scaffolding, and without assistance, on condition of being reasonably paid for the time expended in the labor. The offer was accepted; for it was made in Russia, and by a Russian.

On the day fixed for the adventure, Telouchkine, provided with nothing more than a coil of ropes, ascended the
spire in the interior to the last window.   Here he looked
down at the concourse of people below, and up at the glittering "needle," as it is called, tapering far above his head.
But his heart did not fail him, and stepping gravely out
upon the window, he set about his task.

He cut a portion of the cord in the form of two large
stirrups, with a loop at each end.   The upper loops he
fastened upon two of the projecting nails above his head,
and placed his feet in the other.   Then digging the fingers
of one hand into the interstices of the sheets of copper, he
raised up one of the stirrups with the other hand, so as to
make it catch a nail higher up.   The same operation he
performed on behalf of the other leg, and so on alternately.
And thus he climbed, nail by nail, step by step, and stirrup
by stirrup, till his starting-point was undistinguished from
the golden surface, and the spire had dwindled in his embrace till he could clasp it all around.

But Telouchkine was not dismayed.   He was prepared
for the difficulty, and the means by which he essayed to
surmount it exhibited the same astonishing simplicity as the
rest of the feat.

Suspending himself in his stirrups, he girded the needle
with a cord, the ends of which he fastened around his waist;
and, so supported, he leaned gradually back, till the soles
of his feet were planted against the spire.   In this position,
he threw, by a strong effort, a coil of cord over the ball;
and so coolly and accurately was the aim taken, that at the
first trial it fell in the required direction, and he saw the
end hang down on the opposite side.

To draw himself into his original position, to fasten the cord firmly around the globe, and with the assistance of his auxiliary to climb to the summit, were now easy portions of his task; and in a few moments more Telouchkine stood by the side of the angel, and listened to the shout that burst like sudden thunder from the concourse below, yet came to his ear only like a faint and hollow murmur.

The cord, which he had an opportunity of fastening properly, enabled him to descend with comparative facility; and the next day he carried up with him a ladder of ropes, by means of which he found it easy to effect the necessary repairs.

This person must have put forth all the energies of his being to accomplish what he did. If we will strive as hard for the society of good angels as he did to reach the artificial one, we shall be sure of their society and a place in the new earth.

THE golden sun shone brightly down the world,
　Soft shadows gathered on the twilight track;
The day is gone; with all our sighs and tears
　We can not call one little moment back.

Ah, soul, what loss is thine! awaken now!
　Let not the moments slip unheeded by;
For just such moments make the golden hours
　That bring us nearer to eternity.

# Richest Man in the Parish.

THE richest man in our parish was the squire. He dwelt in a great house on the hill that overlooked, with its broad white face, the whole of the village below, with its clustering cottages and neat farmers' houses, and seemed to say proudly, as it looked down, " I have my eyes on you all, and intend to keep you in order." And in truth, a great many eyes it had, with its rows of high windows brightly reflecting the summer sun, from early morning till evening, when not unfrequently the last flush in the west left them glowing as with red fire. When strangers looked up at the great house, and inquired about it, the people of our parish used to tell them with some awe what treasures of grand furniture, and pictures, and choice specimens of art, the squire had collected in its many handsome rooms; what was the worth of one picture alone, that he had refused thousands of pounds for, and the number of others that were beautiful enough, and valuable enough, to have adorned a palace.

They were very proud to be able to say that so rich a man belonged to them, and lived among them, and to point out his crimson-lined and curtained pew at church, and the great tombstone that stood behind the pathway in the churchyard, recording the virtues of his ancestors, and testifying, as well as it could, to his own riches.

I suppose the squire knew the homage that was paid to

him, and liked it, and was proud in his turn, not of his
neighbors, but of himself, and of the wealth he possessed.
Whenever he rode abroad, he met with bows and smiles
from rich and poor, everybody made way for him, everybody courted him.    A man with so much money, and so
much land, and such fine furniture, and pictures, and
statues, and gardens, was not to be pushed in a corner and
thought little of, and he knew it, as he went along the lanes
and roads on his thorough-breds, and nodded to this man,
and "good-morninged" that, with some degree of conde-
scension.    He knew that he was courted, and admired, and
deferred to, because of his riches, and was quite satisfied
that it should be so.    He did not wish to be thought ill-
natured, so he gave, every year, a treat to his workpeople,
and sent money, and coal, and blankets to the poor at
Christmas, but he thought little more about them.    They
were poor, and he was rich; those two words, "poor" and
"rich," indicated a great difference, and he was quite well
pleased there should be such a difference.

One summer morning, he was taking a ride through the
woods that skirted one side of his estate.    It was very hot,
and in the lanes the sun and the flies teased both him
and his horse, so when they turned in beneath the shadows
of the oaks and beeches, it was a great relief to both.    The
squire gave Dandy the rein, and went along softly.    He
was soon thinking of other things than oaks and beeches.
Perhaps the glitter of the sunshine here and there, as it lay
upon a cluster of trembling leaves, or turned to richer red
the tall heads of the willow herb beside his path, suggested
the crimson draperies and gilded ornaments of his home,

for he was thinking of a sight he had seen there only the day before; when there had been at the birthday of his eldest son a grand gathering of friends, and a feast such as a rich man makes to the rich, with dainties, and spices, and wines, served in gold, and silver, and rarest china, in the utmost profusion, and with the greatest display. He remembered the hilarity of the guests, the healths drank, the speeches made, the compliments so freely given and taken; and with some pride he remembered, too, it had been said, that within the memory of man, no one had given so grand a feast in the parish as he had done that day.

Dandy's feet fell softly, and made little noise on the soft carpet of grass and last year's leaves, that covered and hid the stout roots of the oaks. It was no wonder, then, that presently the squire heard a gentle sound not far away. He became aware that some other human being than himself was in the wood, and checking his horse, he listened a moment, as words, half prayer, half praise, met his ears. "Who can be praying here?" he asked himself, and as the voice was near, he pushed aside a bough or two, and stretched his head, till he could see into a little shady hollow not far from the roadside, and discovered the strange wood-guest.

Ah! it was only an old man, a pauper, or next door to one, whom he had frequently seen before, breaking stones by the highway.

But what was the deaf old man about? *"Praying!"* With his eyes shut, and his head uplifted, and his hat just taken off, held in his toil-swollen fingers, while before him was spread out his dinner—a piece of dry bread, part of a small loaf, and a can of water by his side—bread and water, nothing else ; but the old man was thanking God for it, and was content. *More than content.*   An expression of happy praise was on his uplifted face.   Such an expression the squire had not seen on any face at his own loaded table for many years.   And he was thanking God for bread and water, and was happy !   The old man was a sincere Christian.

The richest man in the parish did not understand how, when the soul loves God, the least mercies from his hands are felt to be priceless blessings ; how bread and water, with a thankful heart, are sweeter to the taste than any food without it ; and he felt humiliated.   What right had that old man to thank God for bread and water, when *he* never thanked him for all his great possessions ?

The woods closed in on him again, he left the stone-breaker behind, and his face soon assumed its usual self-satisfied expression.   But during that morning's ride, again and again returned to him the picture he had seen in the green hollow, of the man who had thanked God for bread and water, and the thought of his own great riches did not give him quite its usual satisfaction.   Had those riches ever made him as happy as that old man looked to be over his poor meal ?   He was obliged to confess to himself that they had not, and it was to him a sad confession.   His pride was sorely touched, and his heart disquieted, and the farther he rode, the more he felt a sense of discomfort and discontent, that was strangely new to him.

Presently the bright sun became overcast, great clouds gathered, and the woods looked dark and gloomy.   Dandy walked along untroubled by nervous fears and fancies, but an influence came over the squire for which he could not account. A strange sinking was at his heart, and an impression of coming calamity. Then a voice struck his inward ear, a voice not of this world, one of those voices God sends sometimes to be heard for our good and guidance, and the words it uttered were terrible to him. That voice spoke to him clearly and distinctly, "This night the richest man in the parish will die." Strange and fearful were these words. He did not look round to know whence they proceeded; he knew it was an inward and spiritual voice that spoke, and he believed what it said. With a shudder he remembered the parable of the rich man in the Gospel, to whom had come the same terrible warning— "This night thy soul shall be required of thee."

"What shall it profit a man if he gain the whole world, and lose his own soul? and what shall a man give in exchange for his soul?" were words that haunted him now, and a cold perspiration covered him from head to foot. He felt that he had been an unwise merchant, who had exchanged his soul for very little. Unable at length to bear his own reflections, he galloped home.

There he arrived in a state of great agitation, and alarmed his wife and family by sending at once for a physician. To all inquiries he gave the answer that he was about to die, and must prepare for it. In vain they tried to persuade him that his health was as good as ever, that he was only the subject of a nervous fancy. The physician arrived, and laughed at his fears, but he heeded neither ridicule nor entreaties. Death was not a thing to be

CHRIST IN THE HOME OF MARY AND MARTHA.

laughed or entreated away, and to death he was doomed.
What did it signify what the world said about it? He
must make ready for it. His solicitor was called in, and
his worldly affairs settled. Wife and children were all provided for, houses and lands were portioned out to his
beloved ones, then he had nothing to do but prepare himself for the great change ; that, however, he found impossible. In great perturbation of mind he awaited the coming
of his great enemy, Death. When night drew on, his fears
increased; every time the great hall clock sounded the
hour he shuddered, not knowing if he might ever hear it
again. The physician and lawyer remained with him at his
request, but they could not bring calm to his agitated
mind. They could only listen to what he said, as to the
ravings of a madman, for mad they judged him to be.

Hour after hour went by, and the richest man in the
parish, lying in his splendid bed, expecting Death every
moment, found how poor he had become, and of how little
real use all his vast possessions were to him now. Midnight passed away, early morning came, light dawned upon
the hills. A faint color came into the sky, and with it
color once more stole back into the cheeks of the squire,
and hope returned to his heart. Death had not arrived as
he had feared; he was still living. The night was passed,
the morning was come, and the prophecy of the mysterious
voice was not accomplished. His family gathered about
him, and with smiles congratulated him, advising him to
take his rest, now the danger was past. But how could he
rest after such a night, such an upturning of all the cherished thoughts and aims of his life, such a revelation of the

poverty of riches? He chose rather to walk abroad, and with thoughtful face and slow steps proceeded towards the village. There he heard that Death had indeed been a visitor in one house during the night, but instead of appearing in his own grand mansion, he had entered the poorest cottage in the place—the old stone-breaker had died during the night. With a still more thoughtful face he returned home, for his heart smote him. He remembered the old man's simple dinner; he saw again the uplifted face, on which God's sunshine rested in a double sense; he heard again the words of his thankful prayer, and his own laugh of derision, and he was again humiliated, but this time to better purpose.

His wife met him at the threshold of his house, with a smiling face, glad to see him once more, "clothed and in his right mind," for she, too, had feared for his reason. She accompanied him in, and then, when seated at his side, gently chided him for his last night's fears, and what she called "superstitious fancies." "I hope now," she added, "you are quite satisfied that there was no truth in what that mysterious voice told you. The night is past, and you are alive, and as well as ever."

"True, my dear," he replied, "the night is past, and I am alive and well. But nevertheless the richest man in the parish *has* died. If you will take the trouble to inquire in the village, you will find it is so."

"How is that?" she asked, and as she spoke she looked round somewhat proudly, as though a rival to her grandeur had appeared. "Who can be richer here than you?"

"The man who can say to God, 'Whom have I in

heaven but thee, and there is none upon earth that I desire beside thee.' I cannot say that, for I have desired many things and persons besides God, and almost all things more than God. But there was a poor stone-breaker alive yesterday, who in possessing God possessed all things. I call him poor after the manner of the world, but he was really rich—an heir of the kingdom of heaven. Last night I was shown his riches and my poverty. People will tell you he is dead, and I dare say that he did not leave a shilling to pay for his burial; but *he* was '*the richest man in the parish.*'"

## WALKING WITH GOD.

WALKING with God in sorrow's dark hour,
Calm and serene in his infinite power;
Walking with him, I am free from all dread,
Filled with his Spirit, O! softly I tread.

Walking with God, O! fellowship sweet,
Thus to know God, and in him be complete;
Walking with him whom the world can not know,
O! it is sweet through life thus to go.

Walking with God in sorrow's dark hour,
Soothed and sustained by his infinite power;
O! it is sweet to my soul thus to live,
Filled with a peace which the world can not give.

Walking with God, O! may my life be
Such that my Lord can walk always with me;
Walking with him, I shall know, day by day,
That he is my Father, and leads all the way.

# OVER THE CROSSING

O PLEASE sir, take me over the crossing," said a little faint voice, as I was leisurely taking my morning walk.

The strange request roused me from my reverie; and looking imploringly in my face stood a thinly-clad, shivering little girl, who carried a small bundle, which she held in her hand with a singular tenacity. I gave a searching look into the child's face, while she imploringly repeated :—

" Will you take me over the crossing quick, I'm in such a hurry."

Tossing her in my arms I bounded over the muddy pathway; and just as I set down my little charge, the bundle slipped from her grasp, or rather its contents, leaving the empty paper in her hands, and an embroidered vest on the sidewalk. I picked up the vest, and in doing so unrolled the same, when lining, sewing-silk and padding were all disengaged, so that the nimble fingers of the poor child picked up, and brushed, and packed them together again with scrupulous care ; and tying them firmly, she gave me a sweet smile and bounded along. She would soon have passed from my sight had I not again called after her, and interrogated her why she made such haste.

"O sir," she replied, "because my mother must have expected me an hour ago. I have been waiting for the young gentleman at the tailor's to decide which color he preferred, and then the tailor told me to stop while he cut it, and then he gave me such a beautiful pattern for my mother to embroider it by—but it is a sight of work to do it, sir, and I'm afraid she will set up all the long nights to sew, while I am sleeping, for the man said he must have it completed by next Thursday ; the young gentleman is to be married then, and will want it—and if it isn't done, maybe he would never give mother another stitch of work, and then what would become of us ?"

And as the child hurried on I caught the same hurried footsteps, and followed on until we came to another crossing, when again came the beseeching tone:—

"Will you take me over this crossing too, sir ?"

It was done in a trice, and my interest in the child increased as her prattle continued :—

"Mamma is to have a dollar for this work, and she means to buy me a new frock with part of the money, and then we shall have a great loaf of bread and a cup of milk, and mother will find time to eat with me—if there is any money left, I shall have a little open-work straw bonnet, and go to Sabbath-school with Susy Niles."

And her little feet scarcely touched the walk, so light and fairy-like was her tread.

20

"And does your mother work for one man all the time, little girl?" I inquired.

"Oh, no, sir; it is only now and then she gets such a nice job. Most of the time she has to sew for shops where she earns about twenty-five cents a day, and then she has hardly enough to pay her rent, and it is n't all the time we get enough to eat—but then mother always gives me the big slice when there is one big and one little one; sometimes she cries and do n't eat her's at all."

A coach was passing—the child looked toward it and remarked:—

"I know the lady in that pretty carriage; she is the very one that is going to marry the young gentleman who is to wear this embroidered vest. She came to my home yesterday to get my mother to spangle the wreath round her white satin dress; and it's just the same pattern that is to be put on this vest; but she could not do it, 'cause her eyesight is so poor, and the spangles shined so."

My tongue was silent. Could it be that these were to be the very articles that were to be worn at my Ellen's wedding? For did I not pay for spangles yesterday, and what was it that vexed Ellen but because she could not find anybody to sew them on when she returned? She said Mrs. Taggard was almost blind.

"My little girl," said I, "Is your name Taggard?"

"Yes, sir—'Gusta Taggard, and we live down in Sullivan court. Are you going home with me?"

It was a sensible conjecture; for why else should I follow on?

"I am going to see you safely at the door, and to help you over all the crossings."

"There's only one more, sir, and here it is; we live down there at No. 3, on the third floor back."

The child looked kindly, and as she sweetly bade me "good by, sir," I thrust my hand in my pocket and drew from it all the change it contained, which was a bright fifty cent piece, and placed it in her little palm. 'Gusta Taggard gave me her heartfelt thanks, and was soon out of my sight.

An hour before, I had started from my home an invalid. I had long deliberated whether an exposure to a chilly east wind would not injure rather than improve me. I was melancholy, too; my only daughter was about to be married—there was confusion all over the house—the event was to be celebrated in fashionable style. Ellen's dress had cost what would have been a fortune to this poor seamstress, and I moralized. But I had forgotten myself; the cough which had troubled me was no longer oppressive. I breathed quite freely, and yet I had walked more briskly than I had done for months, without so much fatigue as slow motion caused, so that when I returned, my wife rallied me upon looking ten years younger than when I left her in the morning; and when I told her the specific lay in my walk with a little prattler, and the satisfaction of having left her happier than I found her, she took the occasion to press the purchase of a diamond brooch for Ellen, affirming if the gift of half a dollar made me so much happier, and that, too, to a little errand street girl, what would fifty times that amount confer upon one's only daughter, upon the eve before her marriage?

I gave the diamond brooch—I paid the most extrava-

gant bills to upholster's, dry goods establishments, confec-
tioners and musicians, with which to enliven the great
occasion, and yet I found more real satisfaction in provid-
ing for the real wants of little 'Gusta Taggard and her
mother than in all the splendid outlay of the wedding
ceremony ; and it was not that it cost less which made the
satisfaction, but it was that all extravagant outlays, in the
very nature of things, are unsatisfactory, while ministering
to the necessities of the truly needy and industrious con-
fers its own reward.

I had seen the glittering spangled dress—but it was
made ready by some poor, emaciated sufferer, who toiled
on in patient trust, and the embroidered vest as finished by
the strained vision and aching head of another, who was
emphatically one of "God's poor," upon whom blight or
disgrace had not fallen, save by his appointment; and the
diamond brooch was borne off by admiring throngs but to
be envied and coveted, while the simple coin bestowed
upon my little street acquaintance had introduced me to a
new species of enjoyment that never cloys in the retrospective.   I had learned to do good in small ways—my
morning walks have now an object and aim.   I pass by
splendid palaces to hasten to Sullivan court, and thence on
to yet other sources of enjoyment, so that my invalidism is
fast leaving me by the new direction which is given to my
thoughts.

I am free to acknowledge that while I cheerfully pay
for flannel robes, and silverware, and servants, and all the
requirements which fashion imposes, I derive far less
pleasure from surveying them, than in sitting beside some

worthy recipient of charity, who tells me that "the little sum you gave me saved me from despair and self-destruction, and enabled me to become helpful, so that no other assistance is now necessary." Such a confession fills a void which administering to a luxury never can; and all the satisfaction originated in first helping a little child over the crossing.

### STOP AND LOOK AROUND!

LIFE is full of passing pleasures
   That are never seen or heard,
Little things that go unheeded—
   Blooming flower and song of bird;
Overhead, a sky of beauty;
   Underneath, a changing ground;
And we'd be the better for it
   If we'd stop and look around!

Oh, there's much of toil and worry
   In the duties we must meet;
But we've time to see the beauty
   That lies underneath our feet.
We can tune our ears to listen
   To a joyous burst of sound,
And we know that God intended
   We should stop and look around!

Drop the care a while, and listen
   When the sparrow sings his best;
Turn aside, and watch the building
   Of some little wayside nest;
See the wild flower ope its petals,
   Gather moss from stump and mound;
And you'll be the better for it
   If you stop and look around!

# THE FENCE STORY

A MAN who prided himself on his morality, and expected to be saved by it, was constantly saying, "I am doing pretty well on the whole. I sometimes get mad and swear, but then I am strictly honest. I work on Sabbath when I am particularly busy, but I give a good deal to the poor, and I never was drunk in my life." This man hired a canny Scotchman to build a fence around his lot. He gave him very particular directions. In the evening, when the Scotchman came in from his work, the man said, "Well, Jock, is the fence built, and is it tight and strong?" "I canna say that it is all tight and strong," replied Jock, "but it is a good average fence, anyhow. If some parts are a little weak, others are extra strong. I do n't know but I may have left a gap here and there, a yard wide, or so; but then I made up for it by doubling the number of rails on each side of the gap. I dare say that the cattle will find it a very good fence, on the whole, and will like it; though I canna just say that it's perfect in every part." "What!" cried the man, not see-

310

ing the point. "Do you tell me that you have built a fence around my lot with weak places in it, and gaps in it? Why, you might as well have built no fence at all. If there is one opening, or a place where an opening can be made, the cattle will be sure to find it, and will go through. Don't you know, man, that a fence must be perfect, or it is worthless?"

"I used to think so," said the dry Scotchman, "but I hear you talk so much about averaging matters with the Lord it seems to me we might try it with the cattle. If an average fence won't do for them, I am afraid an average character won't do for you in the day of judgment. When I was on shipboard, and a storm was driving us on the rocks, the captain cried: 'Let go the anchor!' but the mate shouted back: 'There is a broken link in the cable.' Did the captain say when he heard that: 'No matter, it's only one link. The rest of the chain is good. Ninety-nine of the hundred links are strong. Its average is high. It only lacks one per cent. of being perfect. Surely the anchor ought to respect so excellent a chain, and not break away from it?' No, indeed, he shouted, 'Get another chain!'

"He knew that a chain with one broken link was no chain at all. That he might as well throw the anchor overboard without any cable, as with a defective one. So with the anchor of our souls. If there is the least flaw in the cable, it is not safe to trust it. We had better throw it away and try to get a new one that we know is perfect."

# Put Yourself in My Place.

I CANNOT wait any longer. I must have my money, and if you cannot pay it I must foreclose the mortgage and sell the place," said Mr. Merton.

"In that case," said Mr. Bishop, "it will of course be sold at a great sacrifice, and after the struggles I have made, my family will again be homeless. It is hard. I only wish you had to earn your money as I do mine; you might then know something of the hard life of a poor man. If you could only in imagination, put yourself in my place, I think you would have a little mercy on me."

"It is useless talking; I extended this one year, and I can do so no longer," replied Mr. Merton, as he turned to his desk and continued writing.

The poor man rose from his seat, and walked sadly out of Mr. Merton's office. His last hope was gone. He had just recovered from a long illness which had swallowed up the means with which he had intended to make the last payment on his house. True, Mr. Merton had waited one year when he failed to meet the demand owing to illness in his family, and he had felt very much obliged to him for so doing. This year he had been laid up for seven months, during which time he could earn nothing, and all his savings were then needed for the support of his family. Again he failed, and now he would again be homeless, and have to begin the world anew. Had heaven forsaken him, and given him over to the tender mercies of the wicked?

After he had left the office, Mr. Merton could not drive away from his thoughts the remarks to which the poor man gave utterance, "I wish you had to earn your money as I do mine."

In the midst of a row of figures, "Put yourself in my place" intruded.

Once after it had crossed his mind he laid down his pen, saying, "Well, I think I should find it rather hard. I have a mind to drop in there this afternoon and see how it fares with his family; that man has aroused my curiosity."

About five o'clock he put on a gray wig and some old cast-off clothes and walked to the door. Mrs. Bishop, a pale, weary-looking woman opened it. The poor old man requested permission to enter and rest a while, saying he was very tired with his long journey, for he had walked many miles that day.

Mrs. Bishop cordially invited him in, and gave him the best seat the room afforded; she then began to make preparations for tea.

The old gentleman watched her attentively. He saw there was no elasticity in her steps, no hope in her movements, and pity for her began to steal into his heart. When her husband entered, her features relaxed into a smile, and she forced a cheerfulness into her manner. The traveler noted it all, and he was forced to admire this woman who could assume a cheerfulness she did not feel, for her husband's sake. After the table was prepared (there was nothing on it but bread and butter and tea), they invited the stranger to eat with them, saying, "We have not much to offer you, but a cup of tea will refresh you after your long journey."

He accepted their hospitality, and, as they discussed the frugal meal, led them without seeming to do so, to talk of their affairs.

"I bought this piece of land," said Mr. Bishop, "at a low price, and instead of waiting, as I ought to have done, until I saved the money to build, I thought I would borrow a few hundred dollars. The interest on the money would not be near so much as the rent I was paying, and I would save something by it. I did not think there would be any difficulty in paying back the money; but the first year my wife and one of the children were ill, and the expense left me without means to pay the debt. Mr. Merton agreed to wait another year if I would pay the interest, which I did. This year I was for seven months unable to work at my trade and earn anything, and, of course, when pay-day comes around—and that will be very soon—I shall be unable to meet the demand."

"But," said the stranger, "will not Mr. Merton wait another year, if you make all the circumstances known to him?"

"No, sir," replied Mr. Bishop; "I saw him this morning, and he said he must have the money and should be obliged to foreclose."

"He must be very hard-hearted," remarked the traveler.

"Not necessarily so," replied Mr. Bishop. "The fact is, these rich men know nothing of the struggles of the poor. They are men, just like the rest of mankind, and I am sure if they had but the faintest idea of what the poor have to pass through, their hearts and purses would open. You know it has passed into a proverb, 'When a poor man needs help he should apply to the poor.' The reason is obvious. Only the poor know the curse of poverty. They know how heavily it falls, crushing the heart of man, and (to use my favorite expression) they can at once put themselves in the unfortunate one's place and appreciate difficulties, and are therefore ready to render assistance as far as they are able. If Mr. Merton had the least idea what I and my family had to pass through, I think he would be willing to wait several years for his money rather than distress us."

With what emotion the stranger listened may be imagined. A new world was being opened to him. He was passing through an experience that had never been his before. Shortly after the conclusion of the meal he arose to take his leave, thanking Mr. and Mrs. Bishop for their kind hospitality. They invited him to stay all night, telling him he was welcome to what they had.

He thanked them, and said, "I will trespass on your kindness no longer. I think I can reach the next village before dark, and be so much further on my journey."

Mr. Merton did not sleep much that night; he lay awake thinking. He had received a new revelation. The poor had always been associated in his mind with stupidity and ignorance, and the first poor family he had visited he had found far in advance, in intelligent sympathy and real politeness, of the exquisite and fashionable butterflies of the day.

The next day a boy called at the cottage, and left a package in a large blue envelope, addressed to Mr. Bishop.

Mrs. Bishop was very much alarmed when she took it, for large blue envelopes were associated in her mind with law and lawyers, and she thought that it boded no good. She put it away until her husband came home from his work, when she handed it to him.

He opened it in silence, read its contents, and said, fervently, "Thank Heaven!"

"What is it, John?" inquired his anxious wife.

"Good news, wife," replied John; "such news as I never hoped for or even dreamed of."

"What is it? What is it? Tell me quickly! I want to hear, if it is anything good."

"Mr. Merton has canceled the mortgage; released me from the debt, both interest and principal; and says any time I need further assistance, if I will let him know, I shall have it."

"I am so glad! It puts new life into me," said the now happy wife. "But what can have come over Mr. Merton?"

"I do not know. It seems strange after the way he talked to me yesterday morning. I will go right over to Mr. Merton's, and tell him how happy he has made us."

He found Mr. Merton in, and expressed his gratitude in glowing terms.

"What could have induced you" he asked "to show us so much kindness?"

"I followed your suggestion," replied Mr. Merton, "and put myself in your place. I expect that it will surprise you very much to learn that the strange traveler to whom you showed so much kindness yesterday was I."

"Indeed!" exclaimed Mr. Bishop, "can that be true? How did you disguise yourself so well?"

"I was not so much disguised, after all; but you could not very readily associate Mr. Merton, the lawyer, with a poor wayfaring man."

"Well, it is a good joke," said Mr. Bishop; "good in more senses than one. It has terminated very pleasantly for me."

"I was surprised," said Mr. Merton, "at the broad and liberal views you expressed of men and their actions generally. I su posed I had greatly the advantage over you in means and education; yet how cramped and narrow-minded have been my views beside yours! That wife of yours is an estimable woman, and that boy of yours will be an honor to any man. I tell you, Bishop," said the lawyer, becoming animated, "you are rich—rich beyond what money could make; you have treasures that gold will not buy. I tell you, you owe me no thanks. Somehow I seem to have lived years since yesterday morning. What I have learned at your house is worth more than you owe me, and I am your debtor yet. Hereafter I shall take as my motto, 'Put yourself in his place,' and try to regulate my actions by it."

> We cannot measure the need
>   Of even the tiniest flower,
> Nor check the flow of the golden sands
>   That run through a single hour.
> But the morning dews must fall,
>   And the sun and summer rain

Must do their part and perform it all,
  Over and over again.

The path that has once been trod
  Is never so rough to the feet;
And the lesson we once have learned
  Is never so hard to repeat.
Though sorrowful tears may fail,
  And the heart to its depths be driven
With storm and tempest; we need them all
  To render us meet for heaven.


## FORGIVE AND FORGET.

Forgive and forget, it is better
  To fling all ill feeling aside
Than allow the deep, cankering fetter
  Of revenge in your breast to abide;
For your step o'er life's path will be lighter,
  When the load from your bosom is cast,
And the glorious sky will seem brighter,
  When the cloud of displeasure has passed.

Though your spirit swell high with emotion
  To give back injustice again,
Sink the thought in oblivion's ocean,
  For remembrance increases the pain.
O, why should we linger in sorrow,
  When its shadow is passing away,—
Or seek to encounter to-morrow,
  The blast that o'erswept us to-day?

Our life's stream is a varying river,
  And though it may placidly glide
When the sunbeams of joy o'er it quiver,
  It must foam when the storm meets its tide.
Then stir not its current to madness,
  For its wrath thou wilt ever regret;
Though the morning beams break on thy sadness,
  Ere the sunset, forgive and forget.

*—Robert Gray.*

# THE INFIDEL CAPTAIN

THE ship *St. Thomas*, Captain, Robert Williams, was bound from New York to Liverpool, in the month of June. Favored by a fresh westerly wind, she soon cleared the land, and on the first Sunday out was going along finely with all drawing sail set. The chief mate, Mr. Wm. Briggs, after the crew had breakfasted, and the watch had been set, asked the captain if he had any objections to calling the men aft to prayers.

"No objection whatever, Mr. Briggs, provided you do the preaching and praying yourself; for you know well enough that I have but little faith in such exercises."

Captain Williams was between forty and fifty years of age, a plain, blunt seaman, who was more ambitious of being considered an enterprising shipmaster than a Christian. His mate was not quite thirty, and was indebted to him for his promotion from before the mast to second mate, and then to that of chief mate; they had sailed together many years, and each had boundless confidence in the other.

Appreciating the motives of his mate, he always permitted him to have prayers on board when the state of the weather was favorable, although he took no interest in religious matters himself.

Mr. Briggs ordered the watch to arrange some seats on the quarter-deck, while he went forward himself and invited the watch below to come aft, and listen to the reading of the Scriptures, and such other religious exercises as the occasion might suggest, remarking at the same time, that it was not his desire to force any man against his will. Without a murmur the watch below, as well as that on deck, repaired to the quarter-deck, and were soon seated around the capstan. The captain took charge of the deck himself, that is, looked out for the proper steerage of the ship, and relieved the second mate, whose watch it was, to join the men at prayers. These arrangements completed, the chief mate placed a Bible on the capstan, read a chapter from the New Testament, made some remarks upon it, and then prayed; after which he read a sermon, and closed with prayer. The whole exercise occupied about an hour, and seemed to produce a good effect upon the men, who, during the rest of the day in their intercourse with one another, talked about religion.

That afternoon, when it was the mate's watch on deck, Captain Williams entered into conversation with him as follows :—

"I say, Briggs, what does all your preaching and praying amount to in the long run? I have managed to get along very well thus far without either, and if I were to die to-day, I could safely say that I never injured any man knowingly, and have always endeavored to do my duty to my family and to all. What more can a man do, even if he has all the religion in the world?"

"Captain Williams," replied the mate, "this world, sir, is not our home; we are here only for a few short years, and then we go to the place for which we have prepared ourselves."

"Place!" interrupted the captain, "place—what do you or I or any one else know about any other place than this world? Place, indeed! you do not suppose that I am silly enough to believe the Bible, with its strange fish-stories, and unaccountable yarns about miracles, etc.?"

"Yet," replied the mate, "you believe Bowditch's Navigator, and rely upon its statements."

"Of course I do, because I have tested their correctness by actual experience."

"And for the same reason I believe the Bible, and so will you, sir, when you come to Christ and learn of him the truth."

"I have heard that statement before, Briggs. But how would you propose for me to come to Christ?"

"By retiring to your stateroom alone, sir, and throwing yourself upon your knees, and imploring him with your whole soul to enlighten you. Continue this process every moment you can spare from the ship's duty, and I will be answerable that you will not pray long in vain, if you pray sincerely.

"But you must first convince me, Briggs, that the Bible is true before I make a fool of myself in my stateroom."

"My dear captain," replied the mate, "I cannot con-

21

vince you, that is the work of the Holy Spirit; but I can, and often do pray for you. Yet let us recur to Bowditch's Navigator again, and see if we cannot make out a case from it in favor of the Bible. Both of us believe the Navigator, yet neither of us knows thoroughly the principles by which all its numerous tables have been calculated, many of which we use every day without question. If we make a bad landfall, or, at the end of a day discover that we have made a different course from that which we projected, we do not attribute the errors to Bowditch, but to our own miscalculation. It is just so with the humble inquirer after truth; the Bible is his Navigator; he believes it the fountain of living truth, endeavors to shape the course of his life by it; and when he errs, he looks for the error in himself, not in the Bible."

"Still, Briggs," said the captain, "I do n't believe the Bible. The fact is, I have never looked into it since I was a boy."

"The greater your loss, captain; but I have no doubt your mother believed it, and has often spoken to you about God, and Christ, and taught you to pray when you were a child. If you will take the trouble to visit Jim Wood's gin-palace, in Playhouse Square, when we reach Liverpool, and enter into conversation with the people there about the Bible, they will laugh at you, and sneeringly tell you it is a humbug; in short, repeat your own arguments; but if you will leave there and obtain admission into the best society, you will find that every person present will speak with reverence of the Bible. Now I know you love good company here, and that you dislike the low, vulgar conversation of the profane; therefore, I should like to see you make some effort to prepare yourself for the society of the redeemed in heaven."

"What you have said about my mother, Briggs, is true as the needle to the pole, God bless her; I can't help saying so, for she was good to me; and if there is a heaven she is sure of it."

"And, of course, captain, you would like to join her there, when you have run down your reckoning here. You have either to join her, or such fellows as those who frequent places like Jim Wood's. Which like you the best—gamblers, drunkards, and thieves, or your mother? This is the simple question which you must decide for yourself."

Here the ship's duty interrupted the conversation, but that night Captain Williams thought much of the teachings of his mother, her earnest prayers to God in his behalf, and the flimsy arguments with which he had so long deluded himself about the Bible; and the more he thought the more uneasy he became. He felt that he was a sinner in the sight of God, unworthy of the many favors he enjoyed, and during the whole of that passage, whenever an opportunity offered he engaged in earnest conversation with his mate. He was alarmed at the prospect of being forever separated from his mother, for he loved her dearly; and this feeling soon gave birth to others of a more spiritual nature, and finally he was led to exclaim, "What shall I do to be saved?"

# EVERY HEART HAS ITS OWN SORROW

VERY heart has its own sorrow." There was a sad smile upon the lips that said it, and the eyes of the speaker were full of unshed tears, as if the heart rebelled a little, while a sigh stole up and was breathed out wearily. She sat in the full glow of the firelight, a patient, gentle woman, and on a low cushion at her feet was a young girl with her face hidden in her hands and sobbing passionately.

"Don't think so much about it, Maggie; it is all for the best. It seems strange and dark now, but the time will come when you will see that it was all right." All the time she smoothed softly the golden curls that fell over the flushed forehead—the head was lifted at length, and a fair face looked up, stained and swollen with weeping.

"I can't see how you can say this, Miss Levick. The time will never come when I shall see that it was all right."

The young face was hidden again, and tears dropped like rain through the small, white fingers. By and by they

324

ceased flowing and the head was laid with a long, tired sob upon the lap where it had rested before. The hours went by in silence, while the firelight shone clear and steady in the room, sometimes bathing the watchers in its radiance, then flickering and going out like the hopes that they had cherished.

Maggie Harlan had cause to weep. Six years before her mother died, just as the sensitive, high-spirited child was learning to feel her need of a tender counselor, whose love was even greater than the many faults that tried it sorely. Her eldest brother graduated, and with impaired health went to Cuba for the winter. He never returned, so Maggie had only her father to cling to. Mr. Harlan almost idolized her, but he was an invalid, and felt that his child needed some influence besides his own in molding aright a character that already showed strong points, that might be shaped for good or evil.

Bidding farewell to the old home they removed to a quiet country village, where there was a long-established female seminary, and here Maggie had been to school, advised, aided, and benefited by Mrs. Champlan, the head of the school, and also the mother of daughters, causing her to take a warmer interest perhaps in the motherless girl, who not only proved an amiable pupil, but a brilliant scholar.

Mrs. Champlan employed numerous teachers, and it is with one we find Maggie. Miss Levick had been there only six months. She was not one of those brilliant characters that dazzle at first acquaintance; but she possessed a quiet, unobtrusive loveliness that won surely upon the affections of those who knew her. She had learned many lessons in the school of life; adversity and sorrow had been her teachers, and if they had made darkness in her heart, it was in this she had learned patience, and lip and eye told by their chastened beauty of a peace, storms could not disturb.

Maggie Harlan knew nothing of her history; she had come a stranger to Dalton. Well educated, a skilful musician, and speaking the languages with fluency, Mrs. Champlan was glad to employ her; and to Maggie especially had she proved a most devoted friend.

Mr. Harlan's health had been slowly but surely failing since the death of his wife, but his friends were so accustomed to his pale face and wasted figure that they little realized how near his feet were to the dark river. Hopeful and cheerful, he seldom spoke of bodily infirmities.

Three months ago he left home partly to attend to business in a distant city, and partly from the hope that travel might be of service to him. He only reached the place of his destination, was seized with severe hemorrhage, and died in a few hours. Only strangers were with him, strangers ministered to his last wants, and strangers sent back to his home the news of the desolation that had come to it.

It was a terrible blow to Maggie; all the more terrible for falling so suddenly. She moved about in a kind of stupor for several days, till the funeral was over, and she was left alone with no other friend than Miss Levick.

It was uncertain with regard to Mr. Harlan's property. He had always passed for a man of wealth, lived handsomely, and enjoyed all that money could bring. But

Maggie remembered that he had often spoken anxiously with regard to the future, and it was with some misgivings that she awaited the investigation of his affairs. It proved as she feared. There was very little property beyond what would pay outstanding debts, and a very heavy mortgage was held upon the place where they lived. It was arranged that Maggie should go to Mrs. Champlan, graduate with the close of the present term, and then become a teacher.

This is the last night in the dear old home; all day has Maggie borne up bravely—now utterly overcome.

"It is a hard lesson to learn, darling, but some hearts have learned it, and when the agony was passed have blessed God for so teaching them. Sorrow sooner or later comes to all, and it works in the heart of each patience or despair. It all depends upon the way and manner in which they receive it."

"Perhaps you have the power to choose," said Maggie, "but I have not. It is not so much for you to be patient; it is your nature, and then you can't have so great cause for grief."

How Miss Levick's heart went backward at the words of this weeping child, while she repeated to herself many a precious promise.

Hour after hour they sat there; the sun had gone down, and the purple twilight shrouded the outer world; while Maggie's thoughts were busy with memories of the beautiful past, that was gone from her forever—shrinking from the future that looked so blank and cheerless, and keen agony as the present sorrow rose up in all its intensity—a radiant cup of joy dashed from her lips just as she was beginning to taste its sweetness, and her heart was full of murmuring and despair.

Miss Levick's words irritated instead of soothed her, and she could not help feeling there was not so much sympathy as she had a right to expect.

The teacher felt all this, and her tears dropped silently as she thought over Maggie's words.

"You have not so great cause for grief." There was a lesson in her past life that her heart prompted her to unvail for the instruction of the young mourner, and though she shrank from the task she determined it should be done.

"Maggie," she began in a low voice, "I have no home, Maggie. There are times when my path looks dreary to me. Once loving hands clasped mine, but one by one they have all lost their hold upon me and crumbled away into dust, while I am left to walk alone. I do not murmur at this, though there have been times when my heart has said, 'The Almighty hath dealt very bitterly with me.' And if you will listen I will tell you how a heart more impulsive and passionate than yours was brought to rest quietly in the hands of One who doeth all things well.

"I was born in New England, and amid its wild, picturesque scenery I grew to love nature most devoutly—not calm, serene, quiet; I gloried in the war of elements, the play of the winds, the lightning, the thunder. When very young it was one of my pastimes to be out in the rain-storms; there was something in this akin to my own passionate nature. I did not like anything tame and restrained. My mother was a warm-hearted, loving woman, but so given to the world, so immersed in the whirl of society that she could not spend much time with her children. She saw that we were well fed, well dressed, well behaved, and her duty was done. I remember so well how prettily she looked—the dainty cap and collar, and when I used to put my arms about her neck and tell her how pretty she was, she would put me aside for fear I should spoil her toilet.

"My father was a proud-spirited man, who dearly loved my wild, uncontrolled ways; there was no danger of mussing him, and rare sport we used to have during his hours of leisure. I loved my father fondly, and people said that I had more influence over him than any other human being. Wealthy, and possessed of a social disposition, our house was a rendezvous for all. An Englishman by birth, my father was accustomed to seeing his sideboard well filled, and by degrees he grew to frequent it too often.

"When I was about twelve years old my mother died, and after four years spent in school I returned to find a great change in my father. He would at times be gloomy and morose for days together, keeping the whole house in a state of fear and discomfort by his sudden caprice and unreasonable exactions. This would pass away and he would appear as usual. These attacks grew to be more frequent, and at last came to be his habitual frame, and his frequent absence from home, which at first was a great sorrow to me, came to be looked for as a great relief.

"Months passed on, and at last I woke up to know what others had known for a long time, that my father was drinking deeply and losing constantly at play. O, Maggie,

I can never tell you the terrible suffering through which I passed. I left society and shut myself up at home, determined, if it was possible, to save him. I had influence with him : but how could I appeal to him—how let him know that I knew the places he frequented and the company he kept !

"Then change came. I grew indignant that he should bring all this misery upon me—the poverty and disgrace that I felt sure must follow such a course. Then in a moment of tenderness I would plead and expostulate with him, begging him with tears to leave his habits of dissipation for my sake, for his own sake, for the sake of my dead mother ; while he would talk and weep, telling me that he could not break away; there was something continually drawing him to the gaming-house—he knew it was ruining him, but he must go, while the bitter, burning tears would roll over his face. Little by little every available article of property was disposed of and poverty stared us in the face.

"At length my father's constitution failed under the wear of constant excitement, and he was forced to leave his customary resort and confine himself to the house, and not unfrequently to his bed. Remorse preyed upon him, and his sufferings at times were terrible. With all this I was not impatient, neither did I leave him, for it was a part of my being, the love I had for him; and though at times a flood of bitterness possessed my soul—wretched, helpless, tortured with distress of mind and body, I sought to comfort and console him.

"He lingered for two years a pitiable wreck of what he

had once been, and died, I trust, repentant, leaving me alone and utterly destitute.

"I had relatives in Baltimore, said to be wealthy, and for a few weeks I trusted in their kindness; but there was no notice of my letters for a long time, and then one came couched so blandly, sympathizing with me in my loss, hoping I was well, but saying not a word of the future, or manifesting the least care or concern for what might become of me. Bitter were the tears, but it roused me. I determined to rely upon myself. My father had been a thorough scholar, and I was educated according to his system. There was nothing superficial, and the extent of my reading, both in English and the classics, was far more than the course usually prescribed for ladies. I also inherited a talent for music which had been carefully cultivated, so that I was well able to teach any branch that might be desired. Through the kindness of our family physician I obtained a situation in a seminary at some distance from my home, as music teacher. My deep mourning, together with my extreme youth, procured sympathy and kindness from many; but I rejected all the overtures and led a life of perfect isolation, as much alone as if in a wilderness. I aimed to be kind and courteous in my demeanor to all, but no one was admitted in the least degree into my confidence, and every emotion was carefully concealed from observation. Satisfied with my books and my music, learning language after language, not that I liked study so passionately, but it made me forget, I felt that I never could be again what I had been. My chief solace, when not studying, was at the instrument; and here with my pupils did I spend hour after hour, reveling not alone in the written music, but improvising according to my will. These pieces pleased me best, for here I could pour out my anguished feelings, the mournful, withering wail of my despair.

"How long this might have lasted I can not say; but my heavenly Father, against whom my heart, without knowing it, rebelled so grievously, was pleased to deal mercifully with me, and sent me in my withering, deadening grief a great and precious gift. You have often asked me about this miniature, Maggie," and she unclasped a bracelet from her arm. It was richly chased, and contained the likeness of a noble-looking man in the prime of manhood.

"It was my husband, my noble, generous husband," and she pressed her lips to the dumb semblance.

"Harris Levick was an inmate of the same boarding-house with me, but for a long time we were as perfect strangers. He pitied me at first; and not repulsed by the manner in which his advances were met, he persevered until my heart gave way, and I learned first to regard him as a friend, a brother, and after that to love him with all the devotion of one whose love flowed in but one channel to one object. Once more I entered society because he wished it, and again sunshine rested in my heart and on my life.

"Months passed; we were married, and I left my labors at the seminary to preside over a home simplè in all its furnishing, for Harris was not wealthy, but oh, what a paradise it was to me! We had books, flowers, and

music.  We had young hearts full of love for each other
and hope for the future, and for one short year I forgot all
the bitterness of the past; and when love's signet ring was
clasped with one sweet pearl I felt that God was good to
me, and thought I was grateful for his blessings.  Four
years with rare delight swept over me, and when God
touched my treasures I found that my heart was as proud
and as bitter as ever.

"Harris was a lawyer, with fine talent and a steadily increasing practice.  For a young man he was said to excel,
and all looked forward to a brilliant future for him.  How
many times we talked over the home we should possess in
a few years, planning its surroundings and its adornments
with almost satisfaction, hardly thinking that change might
mar the programme; and still would Harris often close
this dreaming by, 'If God wills,' and seated by his side
with no wish for anything beyond his love, I too could re-
spond, 'If God wills.'  Yes, it was easy to say, 'Thy will
be done,' when that will brought me only what I craved.

"We had been married four years.  Willie, my precious baby, was three years old, the joy of our home, the
dearest, most affectionate little heart.  There was a particular case on the docket.  My husband had need of all
his skill and ability, besides it was necessary that he should
meet personally with several connected with it, and on
whom much depended.  This rendered a journey to Chicago necessary.  How I remember the morning he left
me; bright and beautiful as it was, I could not help the
tears that would come.  True, it was comparatively a short
journey, still I could not keep down the sobs.

"'I shall be gone only a week, darling, it will soon pass. Cheer up, here is Willie, bright as a sunbeam, and I will write if possible every day.'

"Try as I would, I could not restrain myself.

"'Why, Allie, had I thought you would have felt so bad I would not have gone.'

"'It is very foolish I know, Harris, but it seems to me that I shall never see you again,' and I wept convulsively.

"'God bless and keep my treasures,' said Harris.

"I kissed him passionately again and again, and then saw the door close after him.

"It was two days before I heard from my husband; he was well, business prospering, would be home in the time specified, and I was sorry that I had been so foolish; the days were pleasant, and he needed change; he might have made a pleasant excursion of it if I had not been so babyish; and I told Willie of all my weakness, and I promised I would never give way again. I knew my husband was never so happy as when at home; he was ambitious in his profession, a stirring business man; it would be necessary for him to go away often, and his leaving should never be clouded again. Thus I resolved. Willie, putting his dimpled arms about my neck would say to me, 'Good, pretty ma, don't cry any more when pa goes away.'

"The week was nearly passed, Harris would close his business and leave in the morning. How my heart thrilled as at night I dressed myself carefully, and put the little suit his father liked best on Willie! Then, seating myself and taking my baby on my lap, I rocked him and told him stories to while the time away till I heard the tramp of the iron horse.

"Nine o'clock rung out from the little French clock on the mantel. A moment and the rumbling of the cars was heard, while the whistle screeched out its warning, and Willie bounded from my arms, 'Pa come, pa come!'

"'Not yet, darling,' and I whiled him back to wait patiently. It was far past his usual bedtime, but his eyes were never brighter. This was an unusual occasion, and he could sleep later in the morning. An hour passed, it seemed to me an age; again and again I went to the door to listen. By and by there was a carriage at the gate, and footsteps coming up the graveled walk.

"'There is more than one; my husband must have brought company, that is what has kept him so long at the depot.' And I took Willie by the hand and opened the door. Four gentlemen stood on the steps, but my husband was not among them. I staggered back, and should have fallen but for the kindly care of one.

"'Tell me all; I can bear it; my husband is dead.'

"I did not need the words, I knew it. But when they told me of the accident, the terrible collision, the fearful death of so many, and my husband among the number, I felt the good slipping away from me. My grief was too bitter, my eyes were dry, and my brain like bursting. Why should God take one and not the other? And I clasped my child to my heart; and if I ever prayed earnestly it was that we might both go.

"'We thought it would be a comfort to you to see your husband; the body will soon be here.'

"And the humane man began making preparations to receive it. All the while I sat mechanically clasping my child tightly and passionately, asking to be taken out of a life so wretched as mine would be without his presence.

"The door opened, and a litter borne by four men was placed in the middle of the room. Gently they arranged everything, and with the delicacy of those who know what sorrow is, left me alone with my dead.

"There lay my husband dressed just as when he left Chicago—his face calm and serene, while the blood still oozed from a wound in the temple, and his breast was mangled and bleeding; still I could not make it real, while Willie begged so hard for 'pa to wake up.' Poor child! he could not realize his misery; he did not know what it was to be fatherless.

"Days passed. They put my dead from me. How was I to live without him? Alas! had I read the lesson rightly I should perhaps have been spared another. Hardly three months had passed when scarlet fever broke out in the village, and Willie sickened and died.

"My cup was full; the waves of bitterness rolled over me; I was ready to curse God who had dealt so severely with me; and no words can describe the darkness, like the shadow of death, that settled over my soul. I neither wept nor prayed. I thought of God only as an enemy whose hand was relentlessly against me, and every power of my body and mind seemed locked up by a stony despair. I followed my baby to the grave, but it was as one who neither saw nor heard. I went back to my lonely home and brooded silently over my hard fate.

"The autumn days hung their beauty all around me, but I had no eye to see, no ear to catch the joyfulness

HE IS NOT HERE; HE IS RISEN.

floating around me. Christmas came, a bright, beautiful winter morning, and I stood by the window watching passers-by. There were no friends, no Christmas cheer for me. Why was my fate so pitiless? As I stood by the window, my heart making bitter responses to every peal of the bell, our clergyman passed, a kind, benevolent-hearted man; he bowed kindly, and then entered.

" ' Are you not going out this morning, Mrs. Levick?'

" ' No sir. I have nothing to rejoice over, unless it be that every drop in my cup has turned to bitterness.'

" He did not answer me at once, but taking both my hands, and looking earnestly in o my face said, ' Almost every house was smitten; we lost two of our darlings.'

" He passed on to the church, and presently I heard the swelling notes of the organ, and the voice of the people. Every note came directly to my ear, for the door was being opened and closed continually.

" ' Ah!' thought I, ' they can sing, they can observe Christmas; they have lost only children, I have lost all.'

" When the service was over I watched to see the people go back to their homes. My heart smote me not a little as I saw that not less than one-half the congregation wore the badge of bereavement. There was a widow with her fatherless children; feeble age tottered on missing the strong arm of manhood on which it had been accustomed to lean; little children, motherless, walked with demure steps by their father's side; and there a lonely couple thinking of the little ones that used to follow them with dancing steps.

" ' What a wretch  suffering world it is!' and I

22

bowed my head upon my hands and wept, the first tears I had shed since they took my baby from my arms. Just then baby's old nurse came in—the dear old motherly heart —the sight of my grief touched her.

"'He knoweth what is best; each heart has its own sorrow,' and she held me in her arms just as she used to hold Willie. Then she talked to me a long time of God's goodness and love; that he knew and pitied our anguish; that this life was not all, there was a future, and that it would not be long till we should stand on the farther shore.

"Somehow her simple words went directly to my heart; and although I wept till I was nearly exhausted it did me good, and that night I slept like a child.

"I awoke next morning with a strange feeling of weakness in every limb, and a sense of bewilderment and confusion that I tried in vain to shake off. Past events, even my recent bereavement, would rise up for an instant before me, and then float away into dim distance. I was prostrate with high fever, through which I was tenderly watched by Mrs. Bryan, aided by friends whose approach I did not now repel.

"After long delirium and unconsciousness I awoke at last to reason, and for several days bore reluctantly with what I fancied was Mrs. Bryan's needless caution in keeping the room so dark. At length I could bear it no longer, I wanted to see the sunlight once more, and insisted that the window should be opened. Poor Mrs. Bryan put me off till to-morrow, then the curtains were rolled up, and the blinds thrown open; I knew it, for I felt the pure air on my cheek. But, alas! I could dimly see the sun shining through the rose tree, and the white spire of the village church; all was dim and faint as before.

"It was not that my room was darkened; the light had gone out of my eyes, I was almost blind; I should never see the sunshine nor the flowers again; all my life I must be a helpless, dependent creature, a burden to myself and to others.

"I remembered then my ingratitude, the hardness of my heart, because he had taken my idols, and I felt the Lord had justly smitten me. Day after day I could see less of the flickering sunlight, and at length it was gone to me entirely.

"Oh how beautiful now seemed to me the broad green earth! How I longed to look upon the sweet flowers! Once I would not look at them because they reminded me of those his hands had so often gathered for me. Now I longed but to look at them, while the song of the birds filled me with pleasant music. For hours did I sit and listen to the robins as they crooned out their love songs in the old elm tree, when suddenly a thought struck me: 'These winged creatures warble and bask in the sunlight, answering the purpose of their existence, while I, a rational creature, am gloomy and sad of heart, and full of complainings. I am of more consequence in His sight than a bird.' These reflections brought tears, and I found myself offering up a prayer that I too might become as happy in the purpose of my life. This prayer was the earnest wish of my heart, and it was not long till I found the Saviour, and, leaning upon him, felt happier in my blindness than when I walked alone with my wicked heart.

"My chastening was severe, but the Lord raised up friends in my necessity.   After three months of total blindness, the result of long-continued nervous excitement, my sight was gradually restored.   In the meantime I had made the acquaintance of a family from the South, who pressed me so kindly to return with them to their own home that I could not refuse.

"This home was in the suburbs of New Orleans, where the mild air and sweet perfume of orange groves did much toward establishing health.   Alas, that blight, war and desolation should sweep over such a home!   How I felt I hardly know, nor in what way I found myself in camp and hospital.   The lengthened watch that knew no variation in the long wards, the terrible suffering of the brave men who had periled their all for the Union, and I ministering to their wants, aiding them to bear suffering patiently, binding up their wounds, above all, pointing them to Him whose precious love had brought him to do more for them than they had done for others—sad as it was, it was no doubt the very thing for me; I forgot my own griefs, personal sorrow was unthought of.   I felt thankful for the benefits I had received, leaned more and more upon his protecting care, and looked forward, not blindly and with mute despair, but with hope of a joyful reunion on the other shore.   For me I can say, 'It is good that I have been afflicted.'   I feel a firm confidence in the goodness and mercy that will not leave me nor forsake me."

The hands of the clock were slowly creeping past the midnight hour; the leaping flames were gone; in their place were only embers glowing redly under the white ashes, even as hope will live and glow in a strong heat under all the smoldering ashes of disappointment.

Maggie rose from her seat and folded her arms about her teacher's neck.

"I pray God to teach me the sweet lesson you have learned. I am so sorry that I said 'you had not so much cause for grief as I.' But why do they call you Miss Levick?"

"Your question is very natural. It was simply a mistake on the part of Mrs. Champlan, and I had not energy enough at the time to correct it. After that I felt it was just as well, I should escape questioning."

They went forth in a few hours, each to her appointed lot, and the angels looked down upon them both.

## ALONE.

"ALONE with God!" the keynote this
　　Of every holy life,
The secret power of fragrant growth,
　　And victory over strife.

"Alone with God!" in private prayer
　　And quietness we feel
That he draws near our waiting souls,
　　And doth himself reveal.

"Alone with God!" earth's laurels fade,
　　Ambition tempts not there;
The world and self are judged aright,
　　And no false colors wear.

"Alone with God!" true knowledge gained,
　　While sitting at his feet;
We learn life's greatest lessons there,
　　Which make for service meet.

# Evening Prayer.

O
UR Father."

The mother's voice was low and tender, and solemn.

"Our Father."

On two sweet voices the tones were borne upward.

It was the innocence of reverent children that gave them utterance.

"Who art in heaven."

"Who art in heaven," repeated the children, one with her eyes bent meekly down, and the other looking upward, as if she would penetrate the heavens into which her heart was aspiring.

"Hallowed be thy name."

Lower fell the voice of the little ones. In a gentle murmur they said,—

"Hallowed be thy name."

"Thy kingdom come."

And the burden of the prayer was still taken by the children—

"Thy will be done on earth as it is in heaven," filled the chamber.

And the mother continued—

"Give us this day our daily bread."

"Our daily bread," lingered a moment on the air, as the mother's voice was hushed into silence.

342

"And forgive us our debts as we also forgive our debtors."

"And lead us not into temptation, but deliver us from evil."

"For thine is the kingdom, and the power, and the glory, forever."

"Amen."

All these holy words were said piously and fervently by the little ones, as they knelt with clasped hands beside their mother. Then as their thoughts, uplifted on the wings of prayer to their heavenly Father, came back again and rested on their earthly parents, a warmer love came gushing from their hearts.

Pure kisses—tender kisses—the fond "good-night." What a sweet agitation pervaded all their feelings. Then two dear heads were placed side by side on the snowy pillows, the mother's last good-night kiss given, and the shadowy curtains drawn.

What a pulseless stillness reigns without the chamber. Inwardly, the parents' ears are bent. They have given those innocent ones into the keeping of God's angels, and they can almost hear the rustle of their garments as they gather around their sleeping babes. A sigh, deep and tremulous, breaks on the air. Quickly the mother turns to the father of her children, with a look of earnest inquiry upon her countenance. And he answers thus her silent questions:—

"Far back through many years have my thoughts been wandering. At my mother's knee thus said I nightly my childhood's evening prayer. It was that best and holiest of all prayers, ' Our Father,' that she taught me. Childhood and my mother passed away. I went forth as a man into the world, strong, confident, and self-seeking. Once I came into great temptation. Had I fallen in that temptation, I should have fallen never to rise again. I was about yielding. All the barriers I could oppose to it in the in-rushing flood, seemed just ready to give way, when, as I sat in my room one evening, there came from an adjoining chamber, now first occupied for many weeks, the murmur of low voices. I listened. At first no articulate sound was heard, and yet something in the tones stirred my heart with new and strong emotions. At length there came to my ears, in the earnest, loving voice of a woman, the words,—

"'Deliver us from evil.'

"For an instant, it seemed to me as if that voice were that of my mother. Back with a sudden bound, through all the intervening years, went my thoughts, and a child again I was kneeling at my mother's knee. Humbly and reverently I said over the words of the holy prayer she had taught me, heart and eye uplifted to heaven. The hour and power of darkness had passed. I was no longer standing in slippery places, with a flood of water ready to sweep me to destruction ; but my feet were on a rock. My pious mother's care had saved her son. In the holy words she had taught me in childhood was a living power to resist evil through all my after life. Ah! that unknown mother, as she taught her child to repeat this evening prayer, how little dreamed she that the holy words were to reach a stranger's ears, and save him through the memory of his own childhood and his own mother. And yet it was so. What a power there is in God's word, as it flows into and rests in the minds of innocent childhood."

Tears were in the eyes of the wife and mother, as she lifted her face and gazed with a subdued tenderness, upon the countenance of her husband. Her heart was too full for utterance. A little while she thus gazed, and then with a trembling joy, laid her hand upon his bosom. Angels were in the chamber where their dear ones slept, and they felt their holy presence.

HALLOWED, ay, hallowed! not alone in prayer,
    But in our daily thoughts and daily speech;
At altar and at hearth-stone—everywhere
    That temple-priests or home-apostles preach.
Oh, not by words alone, but by our deeds,
    And by our faith, and hope, and spirit's flame,
And by the nature of our private creeds,
    We hallow best, and glorify *thy* Name.
Nature doth hallow it. In every star,
    And every flower, and leaf, and leaping wave,
She praises Thee, who, from Thy realm afar,
    Such stores of beauty to this fair earth gave.
But these alone should not Thy love proclaim—
    Our hearts, our souls respond—"*All hallowed be Thy Name.*"

# THE HAPPY NEW YEAR

**H**APPY New Year, papa!" The sitting-room doors were thrown open, and a sweet little girl came bounding in. Her cheeks were all aglow. Smiles played around her cherry lips, and her eyes were dancing with sunny light.

"Happy New Year, my sweet one!" responded Mr. Edgar, as he clasped the child fondly to his heart. "May all your New Years be happy," he added, in a low voice, and with a prayer in his heart.

Little Ellen laid her head in confiding love against her father's breast, and he bent down his manly cheek until it rested on the soft masses of her golden hair. To her it was a happy New Year's morning, and the words that fell from her lips were heart-echoes. But it was not so with Mr. Edgar. The cares of this world, and the deceitfulness of riches, had, like evil weeds, found a rank growth in his heart, while good seeds of truth, which in earlier life had sent forth their fresh, green blades, that lifted themselves

346

in the bright, invigorating sunshine, gave now but feeble promise for the harvest-time.

No; Mr. Edgar was not happy. There was a pressure on his feelings; an unsatisfied reaching out into the future; a vague consciousness of approaching evil. Very tenderly he loved his little one; and as she lay nestling against him, he could not help thinking of the time when he was a child, and when the New Years were happy ones. Ellen loved no place so well as her father's arms. When they were folded tightly around her, she had nothing more to desire; so she lay very still and silent, while the thoughts of her father wandered away from the loving child on his bosom to his own unsatisfied state of mind.

"For years," he said within himself, "I have been in earnest pursuit of the means of happiness, yet happiness itself seems every year to be still farther in the distance. There is something wrong. I cannot be in the true path. My days are busy and restless, my nights burdened with schemes that rarely do more than cheat my glowing fancy. What is the meaning of this?"

And Mr. Edgar fell into a deep reverie, from which he was aroused by the voice of his wife, as she laid her hand upon his shoulder.

"A happy New Year, and many joyful returns!" she said, in loving tones, as she pressed her lips to his forehead.

He did not answer. The tenderly spoken good wishes of his wife fell very gratefully, like refreshing dew, upon his heart; but he was distinctly conscious of not being happy.

So far as worldly condition was concerned, Mr. Edgar

had no cause of mental depression. His business was prosperous under a careful management, and every year he saw himself better off by a few thousand dollars. Always, however, it must be told, the number fell short of his expectations.

"There is something wrong." Mr. Edgar's thoughts were all running in one direction. A startling truth seemed suddenly to be revealed to him, and he felt inclined to look at it in all possible aspects. "Why am I not happy?" That was urging the question home; but the answer was not given.

After breakfast, Mr. Edgar left home and went to his store. As he passed along the street, he saw at a window the face of a most lovely child. Her beauty, that had in it something of heavenly innocence, impressed him so deeply that he turned to gain a second look, and in doing so his eyes saw on the door of the dwelling the name of Abraham James. There was an instant revulsion of feeling; and for the first time that morning Mr. Edgar remembered one of the causes of his uncomfortable state of mind. Abraham James was an unfortunate debtor who had failed to meet his obligations, among which were two notes of five hundred dollars each, given to Mr. Edgar. These had been placed by the latter in the hands of his lawyer, with directions to sue them out, and obtain the most that could be realized. Only the day before—the last day of the year—he had learned that there were two judgments that would take precedence of his, and sweep off a share of the debtor's property. The fact had chafed him considerably, causing him to indulge in harsh language toward his debtor. This language was not just, as he knew in his heart. But the loss of his money fretted him, and filled him with unkind feelings toward the individual who had occasioned the loss.

No wonder that Mr. Edgar was unhappy. As he continued on his way, the angry impulse that quickened the blood in his veins subsided, and through the mist that obscured his mental vision, he saw the bright face of a child, the child of his unfortunate debtor. His own precious one was no lovelier, no purer; nor had her lips uttered on that morning in sweeter tones, the words, "A happy New Year, papa!"

How the thought thrilled him.

With his face bowed, and his eyes upon the ground, Mr. Edgar walked on. He could not sweep aside the image of that child at the window, nor keep back his thoughts from entering the dwelling where her presence might be the only sunbeam that gave light in its gloomy chambers.

When Mr. Edgar arrived at his store, his feelings toward Mr. James were very different from what they were on the day previous. All anger, all resentment, were gone, and kindness had taken their place. What if Mr. James did owe him a thousand dollars? What if he should lose the whole amount of this indebtedness? Was the condition of the former so much better than his own, that he would care to change places with him? The very idea caused a shudder to run along his nerves.

"Poor man!" he said to himself, pityingly. "What a terrible thing to be thus involved in debt, thus crippled, thus driven to the wall. It would kill me! Men are very cruel to one another, and I am cruel with the rest. What are a thousand dollars to me, or a thousand dollars to my well-to-do neighbor, compared with the ruin of a helpless fellow-man? James asked time. In two years he was sure he could recover himself, and make all good. But, with a heartlessness that causes my cheek to burn as I think of it, I answered, 'The first loss is always the best loss. I will get what I can, and let the balance go.' The look he then gave me has troubled my conscience ever since. No wonder it is not a happy New Year."

Scarcely had Mr. Edgar passed the dwelling of his unfortunate debtor, when the latter, who had been walking the floor of his parlor in a troubled state of mind, came to the window and stood by his child, who was as dear to him as a child could be to the heart of a father. "Happy New Year, papa!" It was the third time since morning dawned that he had received this greeting from the same sweet lips. Mr. James tried to give back the same glad greeting, but the words seemed to choke him, and failed in the utterance. As the two stood by the window, the wife and mother came up, and leaning against her husband, looked forth with a sad heart. Oh, no! it was not a happy New Year's morning to them. Long before the dawn of another year, they must go forth from their pleasant home; and both their hearts shrunk back in fear from the dark beyond.

"Good morning, dear," said Mr. James, soon afterward, as, with hat and coat and muffler on, he stood ready to go forth to meet the business trials of the day. His voice was depressed, and his countenance sad.

The business assigned to that day was a painful one for

Mr. James.  The only creditor who had commenced a suit was Mr. Edgar, he having declined entering into any arrangement with the other creditors, coldly saying that, in his opinion, "the first loss was always the best loss," and that extensions were, in most cases, equivalent to the abandonment of a claim.  He was willing to take what the law would give him.  Pursuant to this view, a suit had been brought, and the debtor, to anticipate the result, confessed judgment to two of his largest creditors, who honorably bound themselves to see that a *pro rata* division was made of all his effects.

The business of this New Year's Day was to draw up as complete a statement as possible of his affairs, and Mr. James went about the work with a heavy heart.  He had been engaged in this way for over an hour, when one of his clerks came to the desk where he was writing, and handed him a letter, which a lad had just brought in.  He broke the seal with a nervous foreboding of trouble; for, of late, these letters by the hands of private messengers had been frequent, and rarely of an agreeable character.  From the envelope, as he commenced withdrawing the letter, there dropped upon the desk a narrow piece of paper, folded like a bill.  He took it up with almost reluctant fingers, and slowly pressed back the ends so as to read its face and comprehend its import.  Twice his eyes went over the brief lines, before he was clear as to their meaning.  They were as follows :—

"Received, January 1, 18—, of Abraham James, One Thousand Dollars, in full of all demands.

"HIRAM EDGAR."

Hurriedly, now, did Mr. James unfold the letter that accompanied this receipt.   Its language moved him deeply. *"Abraham James, Esq.,*

"DEAR SIR : I was not in a right state of mind when I gave directions to have a suit brought against you.   I have seen clearer since, and wish to act from a better principle. My own affairs are prosperous.   During the year which has just closed, my profits have been better than in any year since I started business.   Your affairs, on the contrary, are unprosperous.   Heavy losses, instead of fair profits, are the result of a year's tireless efforts, and you find yourself near the bottom of the wheel, while I am sweeping upward.   As I think of this, and of my unfeeling conduct toward you in your misfortunes, I am mortified as well as pained.   There is an element in my character which ought not to be there.   I am self-convicted of cruelty. Accept, my dear sir, in the enclosed receipt, the best reparation in my power to make.   In giving up this claim, I do not abandon an item that goes to complete the sum of my happiness.   Not a single comfort will be abridged.   It will not shrink the dimensions of my house, nor withdraw from me or my family any portion of food or raiment.   Accept, then, the New Year's gift I offer, and believe that I have a purer delight in giving than you in receiving.   My best wishes are with you for the future, and if, in anything, I can aid you in your arrangements with creditors, do not fail to command my service.

"Most truly yours,

"HIRAM  EDGAR."

For the space of nearly five minutes Mr. James sat very

still, the letter of Mr. Edgar before him. Then he folded it up, with the receipt inside, and placed it in his pocket. Then he put away the inventories he had been examining, and tore up several pieces of paper, on which were sundry calculations. And then he put on his warm overcoat and buttoned it to the chin.

"Edward," said Mr. James, as he walked down the store, "I shall not return this afternoon. It is New Year's Day, and you can close up at two o'clock."

It cost Mr. Edgar a struggle to write the receipt in full. A thousand dollars was a large sum of money to give away by a single stroke of the pen. Love of gain and selfishness pleaded strongly for the last farthing; but the better reason and better feelings of the man prevailed, and the good deed was done. How light his heart felt, how suddenly the clouds were lifted from his sky, and the strange pressure from his feelings! It was to him a new experience.

On the evening that closed the day, the first evening of the New Year, Mr. Edgar sat with his wife and children in his elegant home, happier by far than he was in the morning, and almost wondering at the change in his state of mind. Little Ellen was in his arms, and as he looked upon her cherub face, he thought of a face as beautiful, seen by him in the morning, at the window of his unfortunate debtor. The face of an angel it had proved to him; for it prompted the good deed from which had sprung a double blessing. While he sat thus, he heard the door-bell ring. In a few minutes the waiter handed in a letter. He broke the seal, and read :—

"MY DEAR SIR: This morning my dear little Aggy, the

23

light of our home, greeted me with a joyous 'Happy New Year.' I took her in my arms and kissed her, keeping my face close to hers, that she might not see the sadness of mine. Ah, sir! the day broke in gloom. The words of my child found no echo in my heart. I could have wept over her, if the strength of manhood had not risen above the weakness of nature. But all is changed now. A few minutes ago the 'Happy New Year' was flowing to me from the sweet lips of my child, and the words went thrilling in gladness to my heart. May the day close as happily for you and yours, as it is closing for me and mine. God bless you!

"ABRAHAM JAMES."

Mr. Edgar read this letter twice, and then handed it, without a word, to his wife.

The story, to which she listened eagerly, was briefly told. When Mr. Edgar had finished, his wife arose, and, with tears of love and sympathy in her eyes, crossed over to where he was sitting, and throwing her arms around his neck, said, "My good, my generous husband! I feel very proud of you this night. That was a noble deed; and I thank you for it in the name of our common humanity."

Never had words from the lips of his wife sounded so pleasant to the ears of Mr. Edgar. Never had he known so happy a New Year's Day as the one which had just closed. And though it saw him poorer than he believed himself in the morning, by nearly a thousand dollars, he was richer in feeling—richer in the heart's unwasting possessions—than he had ever been in his life.

GOD BE MERCIFUL TO ME A SINNER.

# THE SCRIPTURE QUILT

IN one of the boxes sent to us by the Sanitary Commission," writes a Christian worker in a southern army hospital, "was a patch-work quilt of unusual softness and lightness. When we opened it, we found a note pinned to it. It read as follows:—

"'I have made this Scripture quilt for one of the hospital beds, for I thought that while it would be a comfort to the poor body, it might speak a word of good to the precious soul; the words are so beautiful and blessed, and full of balm and healing! May it be blessed to the dear boys in the army, among whom I have a son.'

"It was made of square blocks of calico and white cotton intermingled, and on every white block was written a verse from the Bible or a couplet from one of our best hymns. On the central block, in letters so large as to catch the careless eye, was that faithful saying, in which is our hope and strength—'Christ Jesus came into the world to save sinners.' And below it the prayer of all prayers,

'God be merciful to me a sinner.' The head border, which would be nearest to the sick man's eye, and oftenest read, had the sweetest texts of promise, and love, and comfort. Among them I read, 'God so loved the world, that he gave his only-begotten Son, that whosoever believeth in him should not perish.' 'Come unto me, all ye that labor and are heavy-laden, and I will give you rest.' 'Ho, every one that thirsteth, come ye to the waters!' 'I sought the Lord, and he heard me, and delivered me from all my fears.' 'Oh,' we said, 'Oh that all our beds had such quilts! God will surely speak through these texts to the sick and wounded men! They will read them when they will read nothing else. Who knows how much good they will do?'

"It was not long before a man sick with pneumonia was brought in, and we put our new quilt on his bed. He noticed nothing at first, he was too sick; but when he grew better, I saw him intent on the texts. 'Handy to have 'em here!' he said, pointing to them as I stood near him. 'You know how to value them, then,' I said. 'I do,' he answered, with heartiness. After that I saw many studying the quilt —almost all who lay beneath it. One poor fellow, who had tossed in pain and feverishness for several days, caught sight of the words, 'And I will give you rest.' He beckoned to me, and said, 'Rest! where can I get it? Rest for body and mind, both! I am half mad—sick, as you see, but sicker—as no one can see. Tell me how to get rest!' 'Did you never hear of the way?—never hear of Jesus?' 'Tell me again.' I told him the story of the cross. 'Died for my sins?' he asked. 'Yes, yours. He saw you in your sins and pitied you, loved you, died to save you from

sin and give you rest; to make you happy.'   'I have never
been happy—never.  I have been too wicked.  And he
*really* died for me?  I never felt it before.  It never seemed
to me a real thing.'   'I hope you will come to feel it the
most real thing.  Have you seen the lines—

> "'None but Jesus, none but Jesus,
>   Can do helpless sinners good'?

"'It's true.  I know it is none but Jesus!  I've tried
everything else.'

> "'I'll go to Jesus, though my sins
>   Have like a mountain risen,'

I repeated.  'I can't go.  I feel that I can't do anything.
I am here a very wretched man; and that is all.'  'Just
leave yourself to God, then,—

> "'Here, Lord, I give myself away,
>   'Tis all that I can do.'

That's all you have to do.'  'Is that verse here?'  I
showed it to him on the quilt.  'I'll keep it before me.
Oh for rest! a little rest!' he groaned again.  Not long
after he found it,—found peace in believing, and left his
hospital bed, happier than he had ever been before.

"An Irishman lay under the Scripture quilt.  One day
when nearly well, he was looking at it.  'Is that radin?'
he asked, putting his finger on the text.  'Yes.'  'Sure,
and what does it say?'  I read, 'And God shall wipe away
all tears from their eyes, and there shall be no more death,
neither sorrow, nor crying, neither shall there be any more
pain.'  'Ye might rade that,' he said, pointing to another
text.  'I love them that love me, and they that seek me
early shall find me.'  'It is the Lord who says this,' I

added after the text. 'Sure, it's good to a lonesome pareson to hear what you rade.' 'So it is. There is no book like the Bible in dark and trying hours.'

" At last came the boy who had the best right to the comfort of our Scripture quilt,—the son, of whom the good woman who made it spoke in the note attached. It was a strange circumstance that he should have come to lie beneath it, but so it was. He had lain there nearly senseless for more than a week, when I saw him kiss the patch-work. I thought he might be wandering, or if not, had found a text of hope or consolation that seemed to suit his need, and marked with my eye the place he had kissed, to see what it was. It was no text, but a calico block, the pattern a little crimson leaf on a dark ground. He kept looking at it, with tears in his eyes, and I was almost sure his mind was wandering. Nay, he was never more in his right mind, and his thoughts were at home with his mother. A bit of the gown he had so often seen her wear had carried him back to her. He kissed it again. I approached him. He looked up, and smiled through his tears.

" 'Do you know where this quilt came from?' he asked. 'Some good woman sent it to us through the Sanitary Commission.' 'You don't know her name, nor where it came from?' 'No, but I saved a note that was pinned to the quilt.' 'Would you be willing to let me see it some time when it is convenient?' 'Oh, yes. I'll get it now.' I got it for him; his hand trembled, and his lips grew white as he opened it and saw the writing. 'Please read it to me quite slowly,' he said, returning it. I read it. 'It is from my mother; shall you keep it?' 'Yes,' I answered, 'I value it very much, and also the quilt.' He put his hands over his eyes. I thought he wished to be alone, and left him. As I stood by his bed the next day, I was wondering if he had not seen his mother's texts, as well as the bit of her gown. He had, and pointed one out to me. It was, 'Father, I have sinned against heaven and in thy sight, and am no more worthy to be called thy son.' 'I am no more worthy,' he whispered. I put my finger on the next white block, and read aloud, 'When he was yet a great way off, his father saw him, and had compassion, and ran and fell on his neck, and kissed him.' As I looked up, I saw there were tears upon his cheeks, and his lips were tremulous. He covered his eyes, and I left him. A few days after, when he had grown much stronger, he held up to me the text I had shown him. 'I was a great way off,' he said, 'but He has met me and had compassion on me.' 'You feel the Saviour's love?' 'It fills me with peace. What love! What a Saviour!' 'Shall I not write to your mother and tell her that her son, who was dead, is alive again; was lost, and is found?' 'Will it not be too much trouble?' 'Oh, no, a pleasure instead.' I wrote the blessed tidings, making the mother's heart rejoice. And now our Scripture quilt was even dearer and more sacred than before."

> HOWEVER dark the skies may appear,
> And however souls may blunder,
> I tell you it all will work out clear,
> For good lies over and under.
> —*Ella Wheeler Wilcox.*

# SPEAK TO STRANGERS

**W**HO was that quiet-appearing girl that came into church quite late, last Sabbath?" I asked a friend of mine who was an active member in the church which I had recently joined.

"Did she wear a striped shawl and a dark dress?" inquired my friend. "If so, it was Annie Linton, a girl who is a seamstress in Brown's shop."

"I did not notice her clothes in particular," I answered, "but her face attracted me; I should know it among a thousand faces. How could you pass by a stranger so indifferently, Mrs. Greyson? I expected that you would ask her to remain to Sabbath-school, and go into your Bible-class, but you did not once look at her."

"I did not once think of it, and if I had, probably she would not have accepted the invitation, as she is a stranger in town, and undoubtedly will not remain here long," my friend replied quickly, in the way of defense.

I said nothing more, for Mrs. G. was really an excellent

360

Christian woman, with this one fault,—carelessness,—which sometimes caused her to make grave mistakes.

But I could not help thinking about the stranger girl. Her large dark eyes and finely formed face revealed more than ordinary intelligence, and in some way I gained the impression that she was deeply impressed with religious conviction, if not a Christian already. It seemed to me that she left the church very reluctantly, and was half waiting an invitation to the Bible-class.

The next Sabbath she came again and occupied the same seat,—just in front of my own. She bowed her head very reverently during prayer, and once during the sermon I saw her lip quiver with emotion, and a tear came into her eye. The services closed, and the stranger lingered as before. My friend, good Mrs. G., again forgot to speak to the girl. She passed out of the church slowly, and did not come again. I thought she must have left town, as I had not seen her for several days; but one Sabbath, as I attended another church, I saw her again. She seemed a little more at ease, I thought, and there was a quiet smile on her face. After the services were concluded, I saw many a pleasant smile given to the stranger girl, and I understood the secret of the changed look upon her face. I made some inquiries, and learned that she had joined this church, and was earnest and active in all its work. I also learned that she had made a profession of religion just before coming to our village, and had an unusually clear experience. How much the indifference of our own people had to do with her finding a home in another church, I know not.

Several years have passed since this occurred, but I
have never forgotten it.   Many a stranger's hand I have
clasped as I thought of Annie Linton s sweet face.   I was
young in Christian experience then, and that lesson was a
profitable one to me.

Speak to the stranger, Christian friend, with the assurance that no evil will grow out of it.   It is better sometimes to step over the rules of etiquette than to chill  some
warm stream of God's new-given love by coldness and indifference.

### LOVING WORDS.

LOVING words are rays of sunshine,
  Falling on the path of life,
Driving out the gloom and shadow
  Born of weariness and strife.

Often we forget our troubles
  When a friendly voice is heard,
They are banished by the magic
  Of a kind and helpful word.

Keep not back a word of kindness
  When the chance to speak it comes;
Though it seems to you a trifle,
  Many a heart that grief benumbs

Will grow strong and brave to bear it,
  And the world will brighter grow,
Just because the word was spoken;
  Try it—you will find it so.

# THE MAJOR'S CIGAR

**A**FTER a separation of ten years I met my old friend, Major ——, at a railway station. If he had not spoken first I should not have recognized my Virginia comrade of '64. It was not merely the disguise of a silken hat and shaven cheek, but —as I told him after we had chatted a little about each other's ups and downs since the war—I was sure this was the first time I ever saw him away from the table without a cigar in his mouth.

"Haven't smoked for five years," was his reply. "I'm down on tobacco as thoroughly as you ever were."

"Good! Tell me all about it."

We locked arms, and walked leisurely up and down the platform. Dropping the dialogue, this was, in substance, his story :—

"It wasn't a sudden conversion. I never was quite so easy in my mind over it as I pretended to be. I intended to taper off when I got home from the army. And I did, smoked less in three weeks than I used to in one. But one summer I went off on some business for our company, which kept me up in the mountains, among the charcoal-burners, three days longer than I expected. I got out of cigars, and could n't obtain any for love or money. In forty-eight hours I was more uncomfortable and unstrung than I ever was before in all my life. I actually borrowed an old Irishman's filthy clay pipe, and tried to smoke it. I thought of that miserable summer we spent crawling about the trenches in Virginia, and I wished I was there again, with a cigar in my mouth. Then I began to realize what a shameful bondage I was in to a mere self-indulgence. I, a man who secretly prided himself on his self-control, nerve, and manliness,—who never flinched at hard fare or rough weather,—a downright slave to a bad habit ; unnerved and actually unfit for business for lack of a cigar. It made me angry at myself ; I despised myself for my pusillanimity.

"Going into the matter a little further, I found that the money I had spent for cigars in a dozen years would have paid for my house and furnished it. I had smoked away more money than I had laid out for our library, our periodicals, and our intellectual culture generally. Cigars had cost me nearly twice as much as I had given to church work, missions, and charity. My conscience rose up at the record. I knew I could not plead any equivalent for the outlay ; it had not fed me ; it had not strengthened me ; it had simply drugged me. Every cigar had made the next cigar a little more necessary to my comfort. To use the mildest word, it had been a *useless* expenditure.

"My detention in the mountains was calculated to open my eyes to my domestic shortcomings, and I saw, as I never saw before, how selfishly unsocial tobacco had made me at home. I smoked before I was married, and my wife never entered any protest against my cigars afterward. But our first baby was a nervous child, and the doctor told me it would not do for it to breathe tobacco smoke. So I got in the way of shutting myself up in the library of evenings, and after meals, to enjoy my cigars. As I look at it now, nothing is more absurd than to call smoking a social habit. It's a poor pretense of sociability, where a man is simply intent on his own enjoyment. My wife owns now, that my tobacco-tainted breath and tobacco-saturated clothing were always more or less a trial to her. The satisfaction it has given her to be rid of a tobacco atmosphere, and the thought of my contemptibly selfish indifference to her comfort all those years, have humbled me, I tell you. And I wouldn't exchange my own daily satisfaction nowadays in being a *cleaner* man—inside and outside—for the delight that anybody gets out of his cigars.

"I didn't need to go outside of my own doors to find reasons enough for giving up the habit; but I think I found still stronger ones, after all, when I went away from home. The more I thought about the harm tobacco does in the community at large, the more sure I felt that it was time for me to stop giving it the moral support of my example. I know I smoked too much, and that my nervous system is the worse for it; and I think the people who are likely to be hurt the most by it are just the ones who are most likely to smoke excessively. And then, I've noticed that the medical men who stand up for tobacco, are always men who use it, and are liable to the suspicion of straining a point in justification of their own self-indulgence.

"On one point, though, I believe the authorities agree. No one denies that it is a damaging indulgence for boys. It means a good deal when smoking is forbidden to the pupils in the polytechnic schools in Paris, and the military schools in Germany, purely on hygienic grounds. The governments of these smoking nations are not likely to be notional on that matter. But the use of tobacco by our American boys and men is excessive and alarming. We ought to save our rising generation for better work than they can do if tobacco saps the strength of their growing years, and makes the descent easier, as no doubt it often does, to worse vices. I don't know how to forgive myself for the temptation I set before my Sabbath-school class of bright boys, year after year, by my smoking habits.

"It isn't in the family, either, that the selfishness of the habit is most apparent. I don't believe, other things being equal, there is any other class of men who show such a disregard in public for other people's comfort as tobacco users do. A man would be considered a rowdy or a boor who should wilfully spatter mud on the clothing of a lady as she passed him on the sidewalk. But a lady to whom tobacco fumes are more offensive than mud, can hardly walk the streets in these days, but that men who call themselves gentlemen—and who *are* gentlemen in most other respects—blow their cigar smoke into her face at almost every step. Smokers drive non-smokers out of the gentlemen's cabins on the ferry-boats, and the gentlemen's waiting-rooms in railway stations, monopolizing these rooms as coolly as if only *they* had any rights in them. I can't explain such phenomena except on the theory that tobacco befogs the moral sense, and makes men specially selfish."

The Major's train came in just then, and as he took my hand to say good-by, its smoking-car drew his parting shot: "See there! Did you ever reflect how the tobacco habit levies its taxes on everybody? The railway company furnishes an extra seat to every smoker, which, in the nature of the case, must be paid for by an extra charge on the tickets of all the passengers. What a stir it would raise, if the legislature should attempt to furnish luxuries to any special class, at public cost, in this way. How we'd vote them down! I vote against *this* thing by throwing away my cigar!"

## WHAT TO MIND.

*Mind your tongue!* Don't let it speak
  An angry, an unkind,
A cruel, or a wicked word;
  Don't let it, boys—now, mind!

*Mind eyes and ears!* Don't ever look
  At wicked books or boys.
From wicked pictures turn away—
  All sinful acts despise.

*And mind your lips!* Tobacco stains;
  Strong drink, too, keep away;
And let no bad words pass your lips—
  Mind everything you say.

*Mind hands and feet!* Don't let them do
  A single wicked thing;
Don't steal or strike, don't kick or fight,
  Don't walk in paths of sin.

# THE LITTLE SISTERS

"YOU were not here yesterday," said the gentle teacher of the little village school, as she placed her hand kindly on the curly head of one of her pupils. It was recess time, but the little girl addressed had not gone to frolic away the ten minutes, not even left her seat, but sat absorbed in what seemed a fruitless attempt to make herself mistress of an example in long division.

Her face and neck crimsoned at the remark of her teacher, but looking up, she seemed somewhat reassured by the kind glance that met her, and answered, "No, ma'am, I was not, but sister Nellie was."

"I remember there was a little girl who called herself Nellie Gray, came in yesterday, but I did not know she was your sister. But why did you not come? You seem to like to study very much."

"It was not because I didn't want to," was the earnest answer, and then she paused and the deep flush again

368

tinged her fair brow ; "but," she continued after a moment
of painful embarrassment, "mother cannot spare both of us
conveniently, and so we are going to take turns. I'm going to school one day, and sister the next, and to-night I'm
to teach Nellie all I have learned to-day, and to-morrow
night she will teach me all that she learns while here. It's
the only way we can think of getting along, and we want to
study very much, so as to sometime keep school ourselves,
and take care of mother, because she has to work very hard
to take care of us."

With genuine delicacy Miss M—— forbore to question
the child further, but sat down beside her, and in a moment
explained the rule over which she was puzzling her young
brain, so that the hard example was easily finished.

"You had better go out and take the air a few moments, you have studied very hard to-day," said the teacher,
as the little girl put aside the slate.

"I had rather not—I might tear my dress—I will stand
by the window and watch the rest."

There was such a peculiar tone in the voice of her pupil
as she said, "I might tear my dress," that the teacher was
led instinctively to notice it. It was nothing but a nine-
penny print of a deep hue, but it was neatly made and had
never been washed. And while looking at it, she remembered that during the whole previous fortnight Mary Gray
had attended school regularly, she had never seen her wear
but that one dress. "She is a thoughtful little girl," said
she to herself, "and does not want to make her mother any
trouble. I wish I had more such scholars."

The next morning Mary was absent, but her sister oc-

24

cupied her seat. There was something so interesting in the two little sisters, the one eleven, and the other eighteen months younger, agreeing to attend school by turns, that Miss M—— could not forbear observing them very closely. They were pretty faced children, of delicate forms, the elder with dark eyes and chestnut curls, the other with orbs like the sky of June, her white neck veiled by a wealth of golden ringlets. She observed in both, the same close attention to their studies, and as Mary tarried within during the play time, so did Nellie· and upon speaking to her as she had to her sister, she received the same answer, " I might tear my dress."

The reply caused Miss M—— to notice the garb of her sister. She saw at once that it was of the same piece as Mary's, and upon scrutinizing it very closely, she became certain that it was the same dress. It did not fit quite so nicely on Nellie, and was too long for her, and she was evidently ill at ease when she noticed her teacher looking at the bright pink flowers that were so thickly set on the white ground.

The discovery was one that could not but interest a heart so benevolent as that which pulsated in the bosom of that village school-teacher. She ascertained the residence of their mother, and though sorely shortened herself by a narrow purse, that same night, having found at the only store in the place a few yards of the same material, purchased a dress for little Nellie, and made arrangements with the merchant to send it to her in such a way that the donor could not be detected.

Very bright and happy looked Mary Gray on Friday

morning, as she entered the school at an early hour. She waited only to place her books in neat order in her desk, ere she approached the teacher, and whispering in a voice that laughed in spite of her efforts to make it low and deferential—"After this week sister Nellie is coming to school every day, and oh, I am so glad!"

"That is very good news," replied the teacher kindly. "Nellie is fond of her books, I see, and I am happy to know that she can have an opportunity to study them every day." Then she continued, a little good-natured mischief encircling her eyes and dimpling her sweet lips—"But can your mother spare you both conveniently?"

"Oh, yes, ma'am, yes, ma'am, she can now. Something happened that she didn't expect, and she is as glad to have us come as we are to do so." She hesitated a moment, but her young heart was filled to the brim with joy, and when a child is happy it is as natural to tell the cause as it is for a bird to warble when the sun shines. So out of the fullness of her heart she spoke and told her teacher this little story.

She and her sister were the only children of a very poor widow, whose health was so delicate that it was almost impossible to support herself and daughters. She was obliged to keep them out of school all winter, as they had no suitable clothes to wear, but she told them that if they could earn enough by doing odd chores for the neighbors to buy each of them a new dress, they might go in the spring. Very earnestly had the little girls improved their stray chances, and very carefully hoarded the copper coins which usually repaid them. They had nearly saved enough to buy a dress, when Nellie was taken sick, and as the mother had no money beforehand, her own treasure had to be expended.

"Oh, I did feel so bad when school opened and Nellie could not go, because she had no dress," said Mary. "I told mother I would n't go either, but she said I had better, for I could teach sister some, and it would be better than no schooling. I stood it for a fortnight, but Nellie's little face seemed all the time looking at me on the way to school, and I could n't be happy a bit, so I finally thought of a way by which we could both go, and I told mother I would come one day, and the next I would lend Nellie my dress and she might come, and that's the way we have done this week. But last night, do n't you think, somebody sent sister a dress just like mine, and now she can come too. Oh, if I only knew who it was, I would get down on my knees and thank them, and so would Nellie. But we do n't know, and so we've done all we could for them—we've prayed for them—and oh, Miss M——, we are all so glad now. Aint you too?"

"Indeed I am," was the emphatic answer. And when on the following Monday, little Nellie, in the new pink dress, entered the schoolroom, her face radiant as a rose in sunshine, and approaching the teacher's table, exclaimed, in tones as musical as those of a freed fountain, "I am coming to school every day, and oh, I am so glad!" The teacher felt as she had never done before, that it is more blessed to give than to receive. No millionaire, when he saw his name in public prints, lauded for his thousand-dollar charities, was ever so happy as the poor school-teacher who wore her gloves half a summer longer than she ought, and thereby saved enough to buy that little fatherless girl a calico dress.

## OUR RECORD.

WE built us grand, gorgeous towers
   Out toward the western sea,
And said in a dream of the summer hours,
   Thus fair should our record be.

We would strike the bravest chords
   That ever rebuked the wrong;
And through them should tremble all loving words
   That would make the weary strong.

There entered not into our thought
   The dangers the way led through,
We saw but the gifts of the good we sought,
   And the good we would strive to do.

Here trace we a hurried line,
   There blush or a blotted leaf;
And tears, vain tears, on the eyelids shine,
   That the record is so brief.

# THE WIDOW'S CHRISTMAS

**M**RS. MULFORD was a woman who doted on ruins. Nothing in the present was as beautiful as she had enjoyed in the past; and it seemed utterly impossible for her to imagine that there was anything in the future that could compensate her for the trials she had endured.

In her girlhood Mrs. Mulford had been surrounded with the luxuries of life; and after her marriage her surroundings were but a trifle less magnificent. In such an air of luxury and ease, her children were being reared when suddenly a great change came.

Mr. Mulford was a rash speculator, and on that memorable "Black Friday," the idol he had worshiped, the god of gold, proved itself to be nothing but clay, and was as dust in his hands. He could not rally from the shock; pride, ambition, courage, were all annihilated; and Mrs. Mulford, to whom beggary seemed worse than death, could only mingle her tears with his in speechless agony.

Arthur, the eldest child, a boy of fourteen, endeavored to comfort his grief-stricken parents.

"I will work for you, father.  I can easily get a place in a store."

"My boy! my boy!" said the poor man, clasping his son affectionately in his arms; "stay by your mother, and the girls, they will need you, dear boy!"  And he imprinted a kiss on the glowing cheek, that had in it a father's blessing and farewell.

The next morning Mrs. Mulford was a widow, and her children fatherless.  A trifle the creditors allowed her was all she had to depend upon, the money she had inherited from her father having been swept away by the financial tornado.

She had taken a little place in the country, and with Arthur's help, and Bridget's,—who had followed the fortunes of her mistress—had succeeded in making things look quite cozy and attractive.

"Sure, ma'am," said Bridget, in her homely attempts to comfort her mistress, who dragged herself about like a sable ghost, "if ye'd only smile once in a while ye'd be surprised at the comfort ye'd get!"

"Ah, Bridget," Mrs. Mulford replied, with a long-drawn sigh, "my smiling days are over.  I try to be patient, but I cannot be cheerful."

"Ah, but, it's the cheerful patience that brings the sunshine; and ye really shouldn't grieve the children so."

"Do they mind it, Bridget?"

"Sure, an' they do!  Master Arthur, bless the boy! says it's just like a tomb where ye are; and Miss Minnie and Maud have their little hearts nearly torn out of them ; and they are such wee, little birdies ! "

But Mrs. Mulford could not be easily beguiled from her sorrow, especially as she was obliged to have recourse to her needle to eke out the limited allowance, and every stitch she took was but an additional reminder of the depth to which she was reduced.

To such a disposition the needle is but a weapon of de- spair, bringing neither comfort nor hope, nor in any way lightening the burdens of life. The recurrence of an anni- versary was, to Mrs. Mulford's mind like the unveiling of a monument to the departed, and was usually spent in solitude and tears.

She had managed to exist through the Thanksgiving season, and Bridget had done her best to make the occasion worthy to be remembered—by the children at least ; and if it hadn't been for that kitchen goddess, I don't see how the house could have held together.

She had always some comical story to tell the children, something to excite their wonder or admiration, and every few days would surprise them with some fresh molasses candy or cunning little cakes baked in curious patty pans.

Minnie and Maud rather enjoyed their poverty, as it al- lowed them more freedom and exemption from little rules that society enjoined. It was such fun to roll in the snow, and draw each other on the sled, without any caution in re- gard to ruffles and frills that used to be such a torment to them, and such a restraint on their buoyant natures.

Christmas was drawing near, and its approach filled Mrs. Mulford with uncontrollable despondency. It had been a

ANNOUNCEMENT TO SHEPHERDS.

gay season in her young days, and her own children knew
it as the season of especial rejoicings and unlimited toys and
candies.   Now it was all so changed!   Even a moderate
expenditure was not to be thought of, when it was so difficult to procure even the necessaries of life, and she really
wished the day was over, for she dreaded its arrival.   The
furniture never looked so dingy and faded, nor the curtains
so coarse, nor her surroundings so pitiful, as when she
looked around and thought that Christmas was coming.

Neither did the past ever seem so beautiful and glowing
as when she cast a retrospective glance in that direction at
this memorable season   But in the kitchen all was anima-
tion and excitement ; as different an atmosphere as if there
were ever so many degrees of latitude between them ; Mrs.
Mulford occupying the frigid, and Bridget the torrid zone.
Every afternoon and early in the morning, Minnie and
Maud were down in a corner of the kitchen very busy over
some mystery, in which Bridget was as much interested as
they were themselves.

Arthur bustled about from one room to another, always
the active, cheery, hopeful boy, who kept everybody informed of what was going on in the outside world ; and he,
too, evidently had some weighty secret pressing against the
buttons of his jacket.   Christmas eve came, and the children began to think it never would be dark enough for
them to get ready for Santa Claus.

"What are you going to do, Minnie?" inquired Mrs.
Mulford, as Minnie brought in the stockings to hang by
the fire.

"Get ready for Santa Claus, mamma," was the reply.
"You know that to-morrow is Christmas!"

" But Santa Claus do n't come to poor people, my child,"
and the tears filled her eyes at the recollection of the
generous gifts of former years.

"Oh, yes he does, mamma," said Minnie, who was eleven
years old, and two years the senior of her sister; "yes he
does! He knows where we live." And she continued
pinning the stockings upon the line she had stretched across
the mantel.

"I wish I could have afforded a tree!" sighed the
mother, watching her daughter's movements with considerable curiosity.

" We do n't want a tree, do we, Maud? A stocking is
ever so much nicer. It looks so funny all stuffed out, and
then you do n't know what's in it, and you have to shake it
out, and hunt way in the toe! Then you can put such tiny
things in, to make everybody laugh."

Then she pinned on the names which Arthur had
printed very nicely on slips of paper, and stood off a little
distance to admire her handiwork.

Bridget was called in from the kitchen to see if it was
all right, and Arthur was induced to leave his work just for
a minute to note the effect of the display.

"Here now!" he exclaimed, "I told you to hang up the
clothes bag for me. You do n't suppose that little thing
will hold all my treasures, do you? Is the chimney clear?"
And he pretended to search anxiously for anything that
might prevent the descent of good old Santa Claus, whose
coming had never before been anticipated with such un-
qualified delight.

Mrs. Mulford was in the midst of a troubled dream,

when shouts of "Merry Christmas! Merry Christmas!"
rang through the house, and awakened her to the reality of
the day she so long had dreaded.

She knew how dreadfully disappointed the children
would be, it is so hard for them to understand the exigencies
of life, and wished she might keep her room all day and
have Bridget bring up her meals.

"If ye please, ma'am," said the worthy maid-of-all-work,
not stopping to knock at the door, "if ye please, ma'am,
ye'd better come down-stairs; the children are nigh about
crazy waiting for ye;" and the sunshine of her face illuminated the long room after she had retreated down the
stairway.

"They can't feel very bad," said Mrs. Mulford, as she
slowly turned from her room. "It seems to me I never
heard them laugh so heartily. Oh, to be a child again!"
And she sighed heavily.

As she entered the sitting-room, what a sight met her
eyes! There were wreaths of green over her portrait and
papa's; a narrow border running round the mantel; and
festoons falling in every direction.

"Come, mother," said Arthur, "you first; Bridget can
hardly wait, and our breakfast won't be worth eating."

"Oh, no," said the mother, " Maud should have the
first chance; and the impatient child eagerly availed herself
of the privilege.

It was astonishing what an amount of goodies rolled out
of that stocking, and after they were laid aside there were
one or two parcels to be opened. There was a nice pair of
warm gloves, just what she wanted to use in drawing the

sled, or making snow-balls; a new doll, and a book full of pictures. Minnie's stocking was quite as bountifully stocked, and every new surprise seemed to enkindle their mirth and enthusiasm.

Arthur had filled his own stockings with all sorts of odds and ends, on purpose to increase the fun and hilarity, and pretended to be surprised that Santa Claus patronized second-hand shops. Bridget sat down with the children to unload her collection of treasures, and even Mrs. Mulford was forced to laugh heartily at her comical remarks, especially when she drew out a potato, which was labeled, "The last of the Murphys!" "May they always be first in the field!" said Bridget.

When Mrs. Mulford was finally induced to examine the contents of her own stocking, the children, with Bridget, who was only an older child, gathered around, and watched anxiously the proceedings.

There were a pair of nice brackets hanging outside, which Arthur had cut with a penknife; and as she took up each article that had been wrought by loving little fingers, the worsted pulse-warmers, the pretty mats and tidies, she felt that it was indeed possible for love to build upon the old ruins a beautiful palace for the heart to dwell in.

"Forgive me, my dear children!" she exclaimed, embracing them each in turn. "Bridget, my good girl, we will begin the world anew. I have been a weak woman."

"Sorry a bit of it!" said Bridget, wiping away her tears with the corner of her apron. "It's a heavy cross ye had, but we're all going to help carry it."

"And, mother," broke in Arthur, "I've got a situation in a grocery store."

" Arthur ! "

" Yes. It is n't much, but I'll learn the business; and then, you know, I can take care of you."

What a Christmas breakfast they had! It was n't so much what was on the table, although Bridget had made delicious waffles, and everything was super-excellent, but it was the guest that sat at the board with them that made it a feast to be remembered. While they were at the table, talking over plans in which the mother manifested un-doubted interest, there was a sudden, sharp knock at the door that startled all the inmates of the house.

"A new calamity!" sighed Mrs. Mulford, falling back into the old attitude.

" It must be Santa Claus himself!" exclaimed Bridget, putting her head through the kitchen door. Arthur ad-mitted the gentleman, so swarthed in an immense scarf about the neck and chin as to leave one in doubt as to whether he were friend or foe.

" Well, well!" said the stranger, divesting himself of his wraps, and stamping the snow from his boots in the little hall; " Such a tramp as I have had! Where's Carrie?"

" Carrie?" inquired Arthur, fearing he had admitted a lunatic.

" Yes, Carrie. My niece, Carrie Wharton. Are you her boy?"

"I don't know, sir."

" No more do I. She was Carrie Wharton, married Ned Mulford, and a long tramp I've had to find her."

" Have you any bad news?" inquired Arthur, laying a detaining hand on the stranger's arm; " because, if you have, I'd rather you would n't mention it to-day. My name is Arthur Mulford, and we've had such a happy Christmas."

"No fear, my boy, bless your tender heart! Why, I've come from Santa Claus myself, and am chock full of sunshine that turns into gold." Saying which, he entered the room where Mrs. Mulford and her children were sitting, and Bridget hurrying to clear off the breakfast things.

"Carrie!" said the stranger in eager tones, advancing toward Mrs. Mulford, who seemed to have heard a voice from the far-away past. She was in her own home again, a careless child; father and mother were living, death had never crossed her threshold, and all was joy and happiness. A bewildered moment, and then a flash of recognition.

"Uncle Nathan!"

"Yes, dear child! Would I could have got to you sooner;" and he held the weary head close to his generous heart, and smoothed the worn brow.

"I felt I was growing old, and had a hankering after a home to die in, and always the face of my little niece, Carrie, seemed to give me the heartiest welcome."

"Then you did n't die," said Arthur, looking on the scene as if it were a part of a fairy story.

"Of course I did n't. Came near it, a dozen times, but always escaped. Could n't see why I was spared and better folks taken, but it's all clear now. Why, I had as hard work finding out anything about Ned Mulford, or Ned Mulford's widow, as if I'd been trying to find Captain Kidd."

"It's because of our poverty," sighed the widow.

"Yes, I suppose so. It's the way of the world! But who cares? We'll begin the world anew."

Mrs. Mulford stared at hearing her own words repeated, and Bridget, who kept an ear on the proceedings, stood for a moment in open-mouthed amazement, much as if she feared that there was to be another great convulsion of nature.

"Yes," continued Uncle Nathan, "yes, that's what brought me back.   Money don't make a home, I know that well enough, for I've seen it tried.   Arthur, what are your plans?"

"I was going into Mr. Chase's grocery the first of January."

"Do you want to?   Any taste for hams, herrings, tape, and shoe-strings?"

"No, sir," replied Arthur, laughing at the combination, "but I'd like to help mother.   I promised father to see after her."

"You've done your duty.   But my opinion is you'd rather go to college than into a grocery."

"Oh, sir!" and the flush on the boy's face was not to be misunderstood.

"College it is, then.   Carrie, you are to be my house-keeper; these are my little girls;" clasping the children in a hearty embrace, "and see if we don't turn out a happier family than any Barnum ever exhibited."

The Christmas dinner was a marvel of cookery, and Uncle Nathan enlivened the meal with accounts of his adventures.

"And this was the Christmas I had dreaded!" said Mrs. Mulford, as she retired to her room.

The children had reluctantly gone to bed, fearing that

this good "Santa Claus," as they persisted in calling Uncle Nathan, would disappear in the night, and leave them as suddenly as he came.

Arthur dreamed of his books and college, and woke up half a dozen times in the night to assure himself that the great man sleeping so soundly beside him was not simply the magician of the "Arabian Nights."

Mrs. Mulford's pride was truly humbled by this manifestation of God's goodness, and long and earnestly she prayed that henceforth, whatever trials might come upon her, she might bear the burden with cheerful patience, trusting in God to lead her through the shadows into the sunshine of a more perfect day. And in after life no memory was more precious to her than that of a Christmas morning when the children taught her a lesson of unselfishness and duty.

Come into our homes, oh ye Christmas angels! Brush away the cobwebs that regret and selfishness have strewn around, and put in their stead the wreaths and vines that are fragrant with the immortality of love! No home so poor that will not be the brighter for your coming! No heart that is not enriched by your presence, oh ever blessed Christmas guests!

> "THERE are as many lovely things,
>   As many pleasant tones,
> For those who dwell by cottage hearths
>   As those who sit on thrones."

# WITH A WILL, JOE

IT was a summer afternoon; the wheelbarrow stood before Mrs. Robin's door; the street was empty of all traffic, for the heat was intense. I sauntered languidly along on the shady side opposite the widow's house, and noticed her boy bringing out some linen in baskets to put on the wheelbarrow. I was surprised at the size of the baskets he was lugging along the passage and lifting on to the wheelbarrow, and paused to look at him. He pulled, and dragged, and then resting a moment began again, and in the silence of the street, I heard him saying something to himself. I half crossed the road. He was too busy to notice me, and then, in a pause of his toil, I heard him gasp out, "With a will, Joe." He was encouraging himself to a further effort with these words. At last, bringing the large basket to the curbstone, he ran in and got a piece of smooth wood as a lever; resting one end of the basket on the wheelbarrow, he heaved up the other end, and saying a little louder than before, "With a will, Joe," the basket was mounted on to the wheelbarrow.

As he rested, and looked proudly at his successful effort, he saw me, and his round, red face, covered with perspiration, became scarlet for a moment, as I said, "That's a brave boy." The mother's voice sounded in the passage, "I'm coming, Joe," and out she came as the child, pointing to the basket, said, "I've managed it, mother." It was a pretty sight, the looks of the widow and her willing boy. Though no further word was spoken, the sense of satisfaction on each face was very plain, and I have no doubt in each heart there was a throb of pleasure that words have no language for.

I went on my way, but the saying, "With a will, Joe," went with me. How much there was in that simple phrase, "With a will!" How different is our work according as we do it with or against our will. This little fellow might have cried or murmured, or left his mother to do the work, and been dissatisfied with himself, and a source of discontent to his mother, but he had spurred himself on to toil and duty, with his words, powerful in their simplicity— "With a will, Joe."

Often since have I recalled the scene and the saying. When some young lady complains to me, "I have no time to give to doing good. I've visits to make, and shopping to do, and embroidery to finish, how can I help the poor when I'm so pressed for time?" I am apt to say mentally, "How different it would be with her, if she had ever said to herself, 'With a will.'"

Yes, with a will we can do almost anything that ought

to be done; and without a will we can do nothing as it should be done. To all of us, whatever our station, there come difficulties and trials. If we yield to them we are beaten down and conquered. But if we, ourselves, conquer the temptation to do wrong, calling the strength of God to aid us in our struggle with the enemy, we shall grow stronger and more valiant with every battle, and less liable to again fall into temptation. Our wisdom and our duty are to rouse ourselves,—to speak to our own hearts as the child did in his simple words, "With a will, Joe." When there is any wrong thing that we want to do, our will then is strong enough. The *Evil One* comes with his temptation, and helps us to our ruin, with his strength.

The times when we flag are when we want to do right. "When I would do good, evil is present with me," was the testimony of the apostle of the Gentiles, and it is the experience of all, unless they go to Him who can make our wills obedient to his will. Our prayer should be, "Create in me a clean heart, O God, and renew a right spirit [will] within me."

### DO WITH YOUR MIGHT.

WHATSOE'ER you find to do,
   Do it, boys, with all your might!
Never be a *little* true,
   Or a *little* in the right.
      Trifles even
      Lead to heaven,
Trifles make the life of man;
      So in all things,
      Great or small things,
Be as thorough as you can .

# AFFECTING SCENE IN A SALOON

ONE afternoon in the month of June, 1870, a lady in deep mourning, followed by a little child, entered one of the fashionable saloons in the city of N——. The writer happened to be passing at the time, and prompted by curiosity, followed her in to see what would ensue. Stepping up to the bar, and addressing the proprietor, she said :—

"Sir, can you assist me? I have no home, no friends, and am not able to work."

He glanced at her and then at the child, with a mingled look of curiosity and pity. Evidently he was much surprised to see a woman in such a place, begging, but, without asking any questions, gave her some change, and turning to those present, he said :—

"Gentlemen, here is a lady in distress. Can't some of you help her a little?"

They cheerfully acceded to the request, and soon a purse of two dollars was made up and put into her hand.

"Madam," said the gentleman who gave her the money,

388

"why do you come to a saloon? It isn't a proper place for a lady, and why are you driven to such a step?"

"Sir," said the lady, "I know it isn't a proper place for a lady to be in, and you ask me why I am driven to such a step. I will tell you, in one short word," pointing to a bottle behind the counter labelled "whisky,"—"that is what brought me here—whisky. I was once happy, and surrounded with all the luxuries wealth could produce, with a fond, indulgent husband. But in an evil hour he was tempted, and not possessing the will to resist the temptation, fell, and in one short year my dream of happiness was over, my home was forever desolate, and the kind husband, and the wealth that some called mine, lost—lost, never to return; and all by the accursed wine cup. You see before you only the wreck of my former self, homeless and friendless, with nothing left me in this world but this little child;" and weeping bitterly, she affectionately caressed the golden curls that shaded a face of exquisite loveliness. Regaining her composure, and turning to the proprietor of the saloon, she continued:—

"Sir, the reason why I occasionally enter a place like this is to implore those who deal in this deadly poison to desist, to stop a business that spreads desolation, ruin, poverty, and starvation. Think one moment of your own loved ones, and then imagine them in the situation I am in. I appeal to your better nature, I appeal to your heart, for I know you possess a kind one, to retire from a business so ruinous to your patrons.

"Do you know the money you take across the bar is the same as taking the bread out of the mouths of the famishing? That it strips the clothing from their backs, deprives them of all the comforts of this life, and throws unhappiness, misery, crime, and desolation into their once happy homes? O! sir, I implore, beseech, and pray you to retire from a business you blush to own you are engaged in before your fellow men, and enter one that will not only be profitable to yourself, but to your fellow-creatures also. You will excuse me if I have spoken too plainly, but I could not help it when I thought of the misery, the unhappiness, and the suffering it has caused me."

"Madam, I am not offended," he answered, in a voice husky with emotion, "but I thank you from the bottom of my heart for what you have said."

"Mamma," said the little girl—who, meantime, had been spoken to by some of the gentlemen present—taking hold of her mother's hand, "these gentlemen want me to sing 'Little Bessie' for them.  Shall I do so?"

They all joined in the request, and placing her in the chair, she sung, in a sweet, childish voice, the following beautiful song:—

"Out in the gloomy night, sadly I roam;
I have no mother dear, no pleasant home;
No one cares for me, no one would cry
Even if poor little Bessie should die.
Weary and tired I've been wandering all day,
Asking for work, but I'm too small, they say;
On the damp ground I must now lay my head;
Father's a drunkard, and mother is dead.

"We were so happy till father drank rum,
Then all our sorrow and trouble begun;
Mother grew pale, and wept every day;
Baby and I were too hungry to play.

Slowly they faded, till one summer night
Found their dead faces all silent and white;
Then with big tears slowly dropping, I said,
'Father's a drunkard, and mother is dead.'

"Oh! if the temperance men could only find
Poor, wretched father, and talk very kind;
If they would stop him from drinking, then
I should be very happy again.
Is it too late, temperance men? Please try,
Or poor little Bessie must soon starve and die.
All the day long I've been begging for bread;
Father's a drunkard, and mother is dead."

The game of billiards was left unfinished, the cards thrown aside, and the unemptied glass remained on the counter; all had pressed near, some with pity-beaming eyes, entranced with the musical voice and beauty of the child, who seemed better fitted to be with angels above than in such a place.

The scene I shall never forget to my dying day, and the sweet cadence of her musical voice still rings in my ears, and from her lips sunk deep into the hearts of those gathered around her.

With her golden hair falling carelessly around her shoulders, and looking so trustingly and confidingly upon the gentlemen around her, the beautiful eyes illuminated with a light that seemed not of this earth, she formed a picture of purity and innocence worthy the genius of a poet or painter.

At the close of the song many were weeping; men who had not shed a tear for years wept like children. One young man who had resisted with scorn the pleadings of a loving mother, and entreaties of friends to strive and lead a better life, to desist from a course that was wasting his fortune and ruining his health, now approached the child, and taking both hands in his, while tears streamed down his cheeks, exclaimed, in deep emotion :—

"God bless you, my little angel. You have saved me from ruin and disgrace, from poverty and a drunkard's grave. If there are angels on earth, you are one! God bless you! God bless you!" and putting a note into the hand of the mother, said :—

"Please accept this trifle as a token of my regard and esteem, for your little girl has done me a kindness I can never repay; and remember, whenèver you are in want, you will find me a true friend;" at the same time giving her his name and address.

Taking her child by the hand she turned to go, but, pausing at the door, said :—

"God bless you, gentlemen! Accept the heartfelt thanks of a poor, friendless woman for the kindness and courtesy you have shown her." Before any one could reply she was gone.

A silence of several minutes ensued, which was broken by the proprietor, who exclaimed :—

"Gentlemen, that lady was right, and I have sold my last glass of whisky; if any one of you want any more you will have to go elsewhere."

"And I have drunk my last glass of whisky," said a young man who had long been given up as sunk too low ever to reform, and as utterly beyond the reach of those who had a deep interest in his welfare.

# NELLIE ALTON'S MOTHER

"MAMMA, O mamma!" cried an eager young voice; and Nellie Alton, a plump, rosy school-girl of twelve summers, rushed into her mother's room, and, flinging her text-books on the sofa, seated herself on an ottoman at her mother's feet. Mrs. Alton looked up from her sewing with a quiet smile, and said, as she pushed back the tangled curls from Nellie's uplifted forehead,—

"What is the matter with my daughter? Has anything serious occurred at the institute?"

"O mamma," said Nellie, half reproachfully, "you can't have forgotten that it is just a week to-day since I received that invitation to Minnie Shelburne's party. You said at the time, that you didn't know whether I might accept, and I think I've been very patient not to tease you about it. Almost all the girls are going. Mrs. Doane has bought the loveliest silk for Carrie and Jessie; and Mrs. Hilton has three women sewing on Emma's dress. Here

I am not knowing whether I can go.   Cousin Sue said she thought my 'mother a woman of great deliberation.'"

"In years to come you will rejoice over the truth of that remark, my darling."

"But, mamma, please decide now, won't you?"

"I have decided, my dear.   Last night your father and I had a long talk about the matter, and we agreed—"

"To let me go?" cried eager Nellie.

"No, dear.   Anxious for your truest good, we were sorry we should have to disappoint you.   But we cannot grant you a harmful pleasure."   Nellie bit her lip, while her eyes filled with tears.

"May I ask your reasons, mamma?"

"Yes, dear; and I feel that my sensible little daughter cannot but be satisfied with them.   All the advantages you are now having tend to make you, at some future time, a useful woman in society.   To obtain their full benefit, your mind must remain undiverted from your studies, and you must be kept free from everything that will detract from your health and strength.   Parties will excite you, deprive you of sleep, fill your mind with foolish fancies, retard you in your school work, and make you thin, pale, and irritable. We should sadly miss our bright, blooming Nellie.   Do you wonder we refuse to let you attend the party?"

"But just once cannot hurt me," pleaded Nellie.

"The one party, my child, will be followed by a score of them.   If you go to Miss Shelburne's, the other girls will wonder why you cannot attend theirs, and ill feeling will arise.   We will talk no more about it now.   Sometime you will thank me for my course.   Are you satisfied?"

" I'll try to be, mamma," said Nellie; but there were a few suspicious drops on her eyelashes.

The night of the party arrived. Nellie had had a very trying week at school, for the girls thought of nothing else besides their fine preparations. She bore it bravely, and after tea sat resolutely down to her lessons, which were unusually difficult. Half-past eight found her closing her books with the air of a conqueror, while she exclaimed,—

"Now, mamma, they're all done, every one. May I run over and see Cousin Sue off?"

Consent was given, and Nellie entered her uncle's vestibule just as Sue was descending the stairs, in a cloud of lace and pink silk. She felt a little choking in her throat, but said, quietly, "Sue, you look lovely; but to-morrow's French exercise is terribly hard."

"And Miss Propriety Stay-at-home has prepared for it, I infer. Aren't you sorry you can't go?" said Sue, settling her flounces with a satisfied air.

"Mother knows best," said Nellie, decidedly; then she went home. While her sixth hour of sleep, sweet and restful, was passing by, poor, tired, cross Sue returned home, and wearily climbed the stairs to her room.

Next day Nellie came home, saying, "I am at the head of all my classes. Some of the girls were late, others had headaches, all of them were disagreeable, and none of them had half prepared their lessons. Professor Marshly was very angry, but he thanked me for my good example to others. You dearest mother! I'll trust you as long as I live." And grateful Nellie sealed the compact with a kiss.

Years afterward, two ladies were seated in a pleasant

room engaged in conversation. One of them reclined on a sofa, and her sallow features and restless, dissatisfied manner marked her an invalid. The face of the other was bright with health and vivacity. Her sunny smile and cheery voice showed her a stranger to sickness and pain.

"Nellie, my dear," sighed the former, "you can have no idea of the dreadful condition of my nervous system. I spend the greater part of the day on the sofa. The children are a perfect worriment, everything about the house goes wrong, Ralph looks so discontented. I cannot enjoy society at all. In fact, the doctor says I had too much dissipation when young, and ruined my constitution with the parties and late suppers. I would give my fortune for your good health and cheerful spirits."

"Cousin Sue, I remember when you used to drive off to parties, and think scornfully of my quiet home evenings."

"I remember, Nellie. Do hand me the hartshorn and another cushion, and please lower that shade a little. There, thank you. Now will you inform me to what you owe your healthy, happy life?"

At this moment the door opened, and a silver-haired, sweet-faced lady entered. Nellie rose to meet her, and twining one arm about the lady's waist, "Cousin Sue," she said, "my perfect health, my calm, happy mind, the good I am enabled to do for God and humanity, the comfort I succeed in giving to my husband and children, the knowledge I have of my heavenly Father, and the love I bear him, I owe to the judicious care, the wise counsel, and the tender love and prayers of my mother."

# Look to Your Thoughts.

**M**ANY suppose that if they can guard themselves against improper words and wicked deeds, they cannot be very guilty on account of thoughts which may revolve in their minds, however corrupt they may be. They look upon their thoughts as things which spring up in the heart by some laws of association which they cannot understand, or which, if understood, they cannot control. As they have not summoned, so neither, in their view, can they dismiss them ; but must surrender themselves to their influence for a period, longer or shorter, until some circumstance occurs which gives a new direction to the current of thinking. When they confess their sins, there are oftentimes words and deeds which they admit to be greviously in conflict with the demands of the divine Word. But it rarely happens that any unhallowed imaginations in which they have indulged awaken emotions of genuine sorrow. Now the thoughts are the guests we entertain—the company we receive into the innermost privacy of our bosoms. And just as a man is censurable who voluntarily and habitually consorts with corrupting company, so is he to be condemned who deliberately entertains depraved thoughts.

Let every one, and especially every young man, remember that *God holds us responsible for our thoughts.* Man can take cognizance only of the outward appearance. His observation must be limited to those words and actions which can be perceived by the senses. But the scrutiny of Omniscience extends further, penetrating the evil which hides our inner selves from the view of others ; it explores the most private recesses of the spirit, and perfectly understands that portion of our character which others cannot scan. Man can only call us good or evil, as our words and actions authorize. But He whose glance enters the heart and surveys the emotions which are there cherished, condemns, as wicked, every unhallowed thought ; and will as surely take these into the account in determining our final retribution as he will consider in that reckoning our outward acts. "Guard well your thoughts." "Your thoughts are heard in heaven," says a distinguished poet. Never was there a more scriptural sentiment.

But perhaps there may be those to whom this may look like a harsh procedure. If it were true, as some suppose, that we could not control our thoughts—that they rushed uninvited upon our attention, that they detained that attention for a time, longer or shorter, just as they pleased, and that they departed as unceremoniously as they entered our mind—then I grant that it would be hard to make us responsible for such visitors. If we had no power over our own mental operations, it would seem as unjust to punish us for our delinquencies in these particulars as to censure us for the depravity of a resident of Asia or Africa. But can you defend such a position as this? Have you no power to determine what themes *shall* and what shall *not* employ your meditations? Are you the mere slave for your thoughts, compelled to follow as they, by some caprice, may direct? No intelligent mind in which the will is ruler is prepared to admit that it has been subjected to such vassalage.

The truth is, and I appeal to your own consciences in support of the declaration, that you are endowed with the power of thinking upon just such subjects as you may prefer. You can, at pleasure, direct your attention to any topic, agreeable or disagreeable, lawful or unlawful, connected with the past, present, or future; you can revolve it in your mind for a longer or shorter period, and then you can dismiss it entirely from your consideration. If this were not true; if your thoughts were not under the control of the will, you would be incompetent to manage your business; you would be disqualified for every pursuit of life involving the exercise of reason. You would in truth be insane.

Now it is because God has given us the power over our own thinking that it assumes a moral complexion in his sight. The man who resigns himself to unholy reveries, or who entertains in his own heart purposes which, if acted out, would render him liable to the censure of his fellow men, and to condemnation from God, is as certainly guilty, though it may not be to the same extent, as though he had been openly corrupt and abandoned. "Out of the heart," says the Saviour, "proceed evil thoughts." Here observe that our Lord plainly teaches that our thoughts may be evil or sinful, and therefore may expose him who harbors them to punishment. And lest any one should be disposed to look upon evil thoughts as an offense too trivial to awaken any concern, mark the company in which this sin is found.

Learn from those offenses with which it is classed something of the enormity to which it may rise. "Out of the heart proceedeth evil thoughts, murders, adulteries, fornications, thefts, false witness, blasphemies."

One of the most important counsels in the entire volume of Revelation, is the direction of the wise man: "Keep thy heart with all diligence." This is the fountain whence issue the streams which are to fertilize and gladden, or to pollute and destroy. No one was ever wicked in speech or action who was not first wicked in heart. The deeds of atrocity which shock us in execution were first performed in heart—in thought. Had this been "kept," had the early idea been restrained, the result so fearful in development might have been averted. Young men, look to the springs of action, as you would avoid acts which involve you in ruin and disgrace. Keep the heart as you would secure a conduit, which, with God's blessing, will make you honorable, lawful, and happy now, and all that you desire hereafter. *Look to your thoughts.*

"BUILD a little fence of trust around to-day;
Fill the space with loving thought, and therein stay;
Look not from its sheltering bars upon to-morrow,
God will help thee bear what comes, of joy or sorrow."

# Other Reprints now Available

MAY BE ORDERED FROM YOUR LOCAL BOOK STORE

## STORIES WORTH REREADING

73 stories originally compiled in 1913 to provide children and youth with stories that inspire, instruct, and entertain. Gathered from nearly 20 different publishers including Fleming H. Revell, D. L. Moody, Mennonite, Etc. A treasure house for pastors, teachers, and others who tell childrens stories.320 pages, 5-1/2 x 8-1/2, $7.95 1-881545-01-6

## SABBATH READINGS for the HOME CIRCLE

Nearly 60 stories and 30 poems gathered during the 1870's. Originally compiled to provide families with suitable sabbath reading. Stories gathered from church papers; Methodist, Lutheran, Presbyterian, etc. Well illustrated. 400 pages, 5-1/2 x 8-1/2, $9.50 1-881545-02-4

## CHOICE STORIES for CHILDREN

Over 40 stories gathered from several sources to provide children with the best character building literature. Excellent reading for the family that cares. Well illustrated. 136 pages, 6 x 8-1/4, Four color cover, $6.95 1-878726-08-0

## THE KING'S DAUGHTER And Other Stories For Girls

Over 40 stories and 100 illustrations from the turn of the century. Every story contains an important lesson. Excellent reading for the family circle and of special interest for girls. 224 pages, 4-1/2 x 7, Four color cover, $4.95 ISBN 1-878726-04-8

## TIGER AND TOM And Other Stories For Boys

Nearly 40 stories and 100 illustrations compiled as a companion to The King's Daughter. Excellent for boys. These books are character building at its best. They are a treasure to have. 224 pages,4-1/2 x 7, Four color cover, $4.95 ISBN 1-878726-06-4

## LITTLE JOURNEYS INTO STORYLAND

Over 40 well illustrated stories that live and lift. Several short biographical sketches of prominent Blacks.235 pages,5-1/2x8-1/2,Four color cover,$6.95 ISBN 1-881545-06-7

## WITHIN THE PALACE GATES

Author Anna Siviter

"Anna Siviter, by weaving the rich tapestry of the ancient Persian court as a backdrop for the story of Artaxerxes's noble cupbearer, allows us to grasp the deep significance of Nehemiah's devotion to God, to Jerusalem and to his people...." June Strong Originally published in 1901.320 pages, 5-1/2x8-1/2, Four color cover, $7.95 ISBN 1-881545-11-3

## CHRIST OUR SAVIOUR (Gift Edition)

Author. E. G. White

First published in 1896 for the sake of children and youth. Written especially that children might know Jesus as a personal friend and saviour. Well illustrated.184 pages, 6 x 8-1/4, Four color cover, $5.95 ISBN 1-878726-07-2

## BEST STORIES FROM THE BEST BOOK (Gift Edition)

Author: J. E. White

The best in Bible stories and lessons for the family. "These things.....were written for our admoniation" Cor.10:11.This book is prefaced with an easy reader section for young children with many four color illustrations. 200 pages, 6 x 8-1/4 Four color cover, $6.95 ISBN 1-878726-03-x (Also in German Edition)

## CHILD'S POEMS

Nearly 40 poetic stories complied in 1878 as a companion to Sabbath Readings and the Golden Grain Series. The same instructive values are taught. 128 pages, 4-1/4 x 6 $3.95 ISBN 1-878726-19-6

## CHRIST'S OBJECT LESSONS

Author: E. G. White

Author uncovers new and deeper levels of meaning in more than 25 parables and metaphors. Eye-opening concepts and the new resevoirs of inspiration in every chapter.

432 pages, 5-1/2 x 8-1/2, Four color cover, $8.50 ISBN 1-878726-16-1.

## EDUCATION

Author: E. G. White

It is rare, indeed, for a book devoted to the subject of education to be read so widely or to endure so well the tests of changing times as has the book Education.

You will find every chapter rich with biblical principles and insights. **Raymond Moore** quotes on back cover: "I regard the book, "Education", as the greatest spirtual book on the subject this side of the Bible. I have experimented with it's ideas and find them faultless". 324 pages, 5-1/2 x 8-1/2, Four color cover, $7.95, ISBN 1-878726-17-X